AMERICAN POLICE DILEMMA

To the Daughter of a Cop!!
Hope you enjoy reading
about another Cop's experiences
Best
[illegible]

AMERICAN POLICE DILEMMA

✦

PROTECTORS OR ENFORCERS?

Johannes F. Spreen
with Diane Holloway, Ph.D.

iUniverse, Inc.
New York Lincoln Shanghai

AMERICAN POLICE DILEMMA
PROTECTORS OR ENFORCERS?

iUniverse, Inc.

For information address:
iUniverse, Inc.
2021 Pine Lake Road, Suite 100
Lincoln, NE 68512
www.iuniverse.com

ISBN: 0-595-26982-6

Printed in the United States of America

I dedicate this book to my daughter, Elizabeth Diane Spreen, and her mother, my dear wife Elinor, whom I lost to multiple sclerosis, for their support and pride in me through the years. I also dedicate it to my now good wife, Sallie, for her love, support and encouragement in this effort. She has made my life very worthwhile.

I also dedicate this to our grandchildren that I inherited; five at our marriage and now eight altogether: Stefanie, Jay, and Jessica; Jacob, Jacquelyn and Heidi; Brad and Pamela, with the hope that some of these words will be of help and assistance in their lives and careers.

This book is intended to help people live a fuller life. To prevent life from being boring, one must plan a life of new adventures, new worlds, and new ideas. In that way, each day will be gloriously different and will be greeted with eager expectations.

The world is a dangerous and fascinating place. To plan perpetually for safety is as ridiculous as dodging lightning in a thunderstorm. We have, in fact, only one real concern in life: to live, live dangerously since we must, but at any rate to use all the time that fate allows us.

Contents

Part II Detroit Police Commissioner

Part III Newspaper Columns

Part IV Oakland County Sheriff

Part V Opinions

Preface

Since 1941 I served in the New York City Police Department, as Commissioner of the Detroit Police Department and as elected Sheriff of Oakland County, Michigan.

I ended all this in 1985 but still I keep abreast of the law enforcement (policing) field as a concerned citizen. After a lifetime in law enforcement, I've seen and learned a lot and formed many opinions about the decline of police work in America and what can be done about it. I believe what was important then is still important now, perhaps even more so. I feel that my study, practice and beliefs in professional policing have anticipated much of what policing faces now.

At my age of 83, I do have definite opinions and I am not afraid to state them and never have been. I will present the truth as I know and feel it for the benefit of police professionalism and my fellow citizens of America.

I have written columns, first for the *Detroit News* in 1970-1972 and more recently for the *Times Herald*, Port Huron, Michigan. Rather than using a formal style of writing, I decided to express my opinions in informal letter style in this book.

Although I'm writing these letters to my only child, my daughter Betty, others may find them enlightening and valuable. If so, I am pleased.

Foreword

"I was accorded the priceless gift of serving with Commissioner Spreen as a New York City Police Department officer, sergeant, lieutenant and captain. As we studied together for higher rank, I was most impressed with his ability to speak and write in a manner that produced understanding and other beneficial results. These attributes are certain to bring forth a book which, in the light of Commissioner Spreen's broad experiences, will enrich the lives of readers who are part of, or in support of, the field of criminal justice."

William J. McCullough, Colonel, U.S. Army; President, Loose-leaf Law Publications, author of *Minuteman/Activist* and *Hold Your Audience.*

"Johannes Spreen was a police officer extraordinary; a man who helped restructure and develop New York City Police Academy training leading to a college program, a "West Point" for police officers—now John Jay College for Criminal Justice. Johannes Spreen is a man of enthusiasm, indeed a prophet; always ahead of his time and a friend for over 60 years.

Rudolph P. Blaum, Retired Captain, New York City Police Department, served in the operation and development of the New York Police Service College Program, now John Jay College. He is Former President of the American Education Association in Center Moriches, New York.

"Johannes Spreen is a model for growing older, a teacher in 'How to Age Positively.' He keeps his mind active, body moving and spirit soaring. He was awarded St. Clair County's 'Outstanding Senior Citizen' of 1999. A man of 83 who still teaches Body Recall, Memory Improvement, Conversational German, all gratis. He and his wife, Sallie, have been involved in

senior entertainment doing comedy skits he writes for our annual fund-raising shows 'Off Our Rockers.' Johannes is a real treasure for St. Clair County."

Laura L. Newsome, Executive Director of the St. Clair County Council on Aging, Inc.

"Johannes Spreen has extraordinary credentials and a range of knowledge that will achieve great results."

Dr. Isaiah "Ike" McKinnon, Former Detroit Chief of Police, and Professor, University of Detroit, Mercy.

"This book should be mandated for all concerned police and public alike. Commissioner Spreen is a visionary and perfect role model for police and their leaders."

Dr. Diane Holloway, retired psychologist and author who helped the Dallas Police Department develop their first Police Assessment Center and later served the city as their first "Drug Czar."

Acknowledgments

I thank my daughter, Betty, and with loving memory, her mother, my wife Elinor, for their love, support and strong belief in me.

Special thanks to my good wife Sallie Ann Spreen for her love, support and encouragement throughout the years I have known her.

So much thanks to Diane Holloway for finding me, working with me and putting this book together. Both Sallie and I are indebted to you, Diane. We realize that without your tremendous help and expertise, this book would have never been.

And to my good friend and tennis buddy Bob Kozlow, who after a luncheon and listening to me suggested the title of this book. Thanks, Bob.

My thanks to Bob Cheney for his brilliant work in proofreading and reviewing this book before publication.

Also thanks to all the people and police I have met and worked with along life's road, both the good and the bad. One can learn from both.

Introduction

I saw the flames. I saw stores looted. I saw buildings collapsing. I saw citizens shot. I saw police shot. I saw the Michigan National Guard take over the city. I saw U.S. Army paratroopers sent in to save the city.

I was watching television from my easy chair in my home in Lynbrook, New York.

I saw the killing of a great city: Detroit.

Then why the hell did I ever consider taking over the job of the Top Cop, Detroit Police Commissioner 11 months later? I had heard a few other police officials had turned Mayor Cavanagh down.

Why then did I fly to Detroit and shake Mayor Cavanagh's hand on June 21, 1968 (the longest day of the year, and the start of summer), and be sworn in as the Commissioner?

Should I have had my head examined?

When I told my friends and neighbors in New York I was taking the job as Police Commissioner of Detroit they were all aghast. Almost with one voice, with shock and amazement they uttered "Not Detroit."

The day of the swearing in was July 22, 1968 (I had to establish residency in Detroit for 30 days). This was one day short of the anniversary of the riot the year before.

The Detroit Free Press and the Detroit News were on strike. But all the radio and television people were there. The large Police Commissioner's office was over-crowded. The Mayor and other city officials were there.

They asked many questions such as "Why did I take the job?" and "What were my goals?"

Why did I take the job? I saw it as important, a challenge, an opportunity. Yes, perhaps an inexorable obligation to put my years of study and practice into effect for the greater good of professional law enforcement.

Many questions the media asked seemed geared to apprehension about the future, particular the next day, July 23rd.

After awhile one reporter, Joe Weaver of CBS television, asked, "Commissioner, what is the first thing you will do?"

My quick retort was, "When you guys get out of here, I'm going to sit down and prepare a detail (arrangements, manpower, equipment, etc.) for the World Series."

It broke up the conference. Apparently the feeling was, this new Commissioner exudes an air of confidence and take chargeness.

This was July 22, the middle of the baseball season. We did win the World Series in that year, 1968.

PART I

Career As a New York City Cop

o o o o o o o o o o o o o o o o o o o o o o o o o o o o o

"Of all the tasks of government, the most basic is to protect its citizens against violence."

—Secretary of state John Foster Dulles, April 22, 1957

How I Become a Cop

Dear Betty,

I'm getting up in age now and I worry that I may die without explaining myself and my life to you. I would hate for you to have to rely on what others say about me. Others will have plenty to say because I was in the news a lot, so I want you to hear it from me.

I'll tell you about how I became a cop for the New York Police Department, my tenure as a professor, how I became police commissioner of Detroit, how I became Sheriff of Oakland County, and why they put me in jail. Along the way, I'll tell you what I really think about what is wrong with law enforcement and I know much of this will differ with what you've heard. Brace yourself!

I guess the best way to do this is to start at the beginning. My career as a policeman began pretty much by accident rather than intent or long-standing wish. I was 19 years old, two years out of high school, still groping for a genuine sense of vocation, and struggling against the limited job opportunity environment that still prevailed as an aftermath of the Great Depression of the 1930s.

I applied for and took the civil service examinations for admission to the New York Police and Fire Departments. I passed both exams but the Police Department was the first to reply, and that was it.

There was nothing in my personal background to steer me inexorably and inevitably into police work. I started out life in the United States as a "displaced person," before the expression had ever been coined. I was born in Germany, September 28, 1919, in a village outside of the city of Bremen. I have only the dimmest recollection of my birthplace.

My clearest early remembrance is of the ocean liner, the *S.S. Seydlitz*, which carried me and my mother and sister to New York City in 1923, following my father and brother who had preceded us. I remember some man who thought he was helping me to have a more exciting trip by holding me on top of the railing as if he were going to throw me overboard. I not only didn't enjoy it, I cried as only a frightened four year-old can cry. For years afterward, I was afraid of the water, any water, whether swimming or boating.

We settled in Brooklyn, and the first home I can remember was a fourth-floor "railroad flat" with windows in the front and rear only, and sidewalls flush against the adjoining tenements. It was at 147 Cooper Street, near the borough boundary between Brooklyn and Queens.

The first thing I had to do was learn the language. When I started in the first grade at age six, I still had an accent. Even seven years after the Armistice, it was still a bad time to be a kid with a German accent in Brooklyn. I took a lot of beatings and what they would call harassment today, until I learned to run fast, and finally to speak with a Brooklyn instead of a Bremen accent.

My father was a cigar-maker when the depression started in 1929. Most people switched to cheaper smokes. Like most other families, we endured the hard times as best we could.

We moved across the borough boundary into the Ridgewood section of Queens in the year Franklin D. Roosevelt became president. I entered Richmond Hill High School. I went out for the high school baseball team, and competed briefly for the shortstop position against another teenager named Phil Rizzuto. He not only turned out to be the pride of the Richmond Hill High baseball team, he went on to become the pride of the New York Yankees. We called him "Scooter Rizzuto."

With that kind of competition, I soon shifted to pitching, where my height (I was then close to my maximum six feet five inches) may have intimidated batters more than my roundhouse curve. I took the usual "general" curriculum, and graduated in 1937, prepared for college scholastically, but not economically.

When I took the written civil service examination, police candidates also had to pass a series of physical performance tests as well as a medical examination. I ran and hurdled and jumped and chinned and swung on ladder bars, and discovered I'd not only passed the physical, but also achieved the highest score in the performance tests. I had my first taste of personal publicity when the *New York Daily News* and the now-defunct tabloid newspaper, the *New York Daily Mirror*, ran my picture in a centerfold, in action, as part of its coverage of the new crop of police rookies. Even though I had no college credit, I placed 183rd out of 33,000 applicants on the examination in 1939.

Two childhood accidents just missed disqualifying me. Once I was struck by a car and received a concussion and a barely perceptible impairment of hearing in one ear. On another occasion I was hammering a nail, when it suddenly flew up and the point struck me in the eye, leaving a scratch scar on the cornea. When I first took the police physical, I was straining with my left eye, until the examiner finally told me to "just take it easy." I relaxed and passed.

The first class of 300 was sworn in and appointed June 5, 1940 at the New York World's Fair. But not me! I would not be 21 until September 28th. Feeling that they would start a new class after that class graduation, there was no concern.

Then Edna, my first wife, and I were at Madison Square Garden for the 1940s Graduate Show called "Around the Clock with New York's Finest."

Mayor Fiorello LaGuardia was there and spoke. My heart fell into my shoes when he declared that there would be no more appointments to the police force for five years because of the draft, the Selective Service Act.

The only reason the next class of 300 was appointed on June 9, 1941 (me included) was because of the "Mad Dog" killings, as the media termed them. I'll describe that in my next letter. People were shocked and outraged. We on the Police Department eligible list created a group effort to gain political and community support for more police to be appointed and so the next class entered June 9, 1941. There was another class of 160 in September of 1941. My friend, Bill McCullough, was in that class. Then there were no more classes until the end of World War II.

Well, that's enough about my beginnings for now.

Love, Dad

"Mad Dogs"

Dear Betty,

I wrote you before that I would not have been hired in 1941 but for the "Mad Dogs" and the efforts of the eligible list of police applicants who supported more police officers in the city. I want to tell you exactly what happened, which is an eye-opener about the "Insanity Defense."

On January 14, 1941, Anthony, 35, and William, 28, Esposito, held up a payroll carrier for a linen company at the corner of Fifth Avenue and 34th Street. You remember the movie *Miracle on 34th Street* with Edmund Gwenn playing Santa Claus. I took you to see it.

The Esposito brothers shot and killed the linen company manager without warning as he rode on the elevator in his building. When the brothers ran out of the building, they were confronted by Patrolman Edward (Eddie) Maher. Maher chased them down Fifth Avenue and a gunfight made hundreds of pedestrians run for cover. Maher shot William in the leg. As he approached him face down, Esposito rolled over and killed Maher with a gun he had in his waistband. Others were wounded in the chase but the brothers were captured after pedestrians and a cab driver brought them down.

The Esposito brothers reached trial in May 1941 and used the insanity plea for their defense. They didn't want to die. They tried to convince the court that they were crazy by banging their heads on their defense table to the point of bleeding. They howled like wolves and ate papers and anything that was on their table. When the jury was present, they barked like dogs, cried, drooled, and walked into the courtroom like apes.

The press called them "Mad Dogs." At the end of the trial, Judge John Fesci said that laws should be enacted to keep such people out of the courtroom. On May 1, 1941, a jury took one minute to find them both guilty of murder in the first degree. They were sentenced to die in the electric chair at Sing Sing.

Six days later, policemen in a commuter train took them to Sing Sing. When they arrived, a local police car picked up the police and the brothers to take them to prison reception. Anthony grabbed the wheel of the police car and tried to crash it. A fight broke out between the brothers and the policemen. Anthony bit the hand of the driver and William tried to get the detective's gun. Police hit the boys with blackjacks and they were dragged from the car screaming and cussing.

William continued to fight and was beaten until he passed out. Both were carried into Sing Sing. On Death Row, they continued their efforts to appear insane. They talked gibberish, moaned, howled, and refused to eat food. The Governor had the situation investigated and found that the Espositos had come from Italy, most family members including the brothers had already been in prison, and they were taught to hate the police. The Governor did not grant clemency.

The Esposito brothers continued to act crazy, lost weight, and were carried to the electric chair unconscious, below 80 pounds, and near death. They were executed for their violent crimes despite trying to hide behind the insanity plea.

Dear, you have to remember that in those days, criminals were often executed with little delay. Those boys probably thought they would outsmart everyone by pretending to be crazy. They didn't fool anyone but they surely made their own last days miserable. The attention focused on them was constant and that is why we on the list to join the NYPD pressed for more officers, and therefore got ourselves hired.

It was terrible that it took a crime scene and a chase to get more help to protect innocent citizens.

Love, Dad

I Got Hired

Dear Betty,

June 9, 1941, was a special day in New York City. The 206 newest members of the recruit class took their places and heard words of praise from Mayor Fiorello La Guardia at the City Hall Plaza. In addition, promotions were announced. I want you to have a feeling for what kind of man the Mayor was. You may recall that he was the Mayor portrayed in the musical *Most Happy Fella* on Broadway. I always liked his comment after he made a bad personnel appointment, "When I make a mistake, it's a beaut!"

Police Commissioner Lewis Valentine reminded the audience that promotion in the Department depended "wholly and solely upon your own qualifications and your ability to perform honest, efficient and effective service."

Mayor LaGuardia in the course of his remarks called attention to the additional responsibilities that confront the Department by reason of the proclamation of the President of the United States declaring a state of unlimited emergency to exist, after which he read the proclamation appointing Valentine to be Police Defense Coordinator for the City of New York.

The Mayor also said that 175 retired policeman had volunteered for duty in the event of an emergency or an attack by a foreign enemy.

Mayor LaGuardia said, "I want to warn you; I am old in this game. I have been in public office 37 years. I know a faker. I can smell one ten blocks away and I recognize one when I read a line he writes or hear a word he says....I was given a confidential report by an organization that made a thorough, secret, scientific investigation of the Police Department with all its multiple duties. And it shows a state of efficiency and a degree of law enforcement so high and so perfect, although in a city of seven and a half million people, reflecting conditions that would do credit to a small community of 5,000 people in a rural district....

"We have to sleep at night, or whenever we have off time between tours for the purpose of sleep. So never do anything that would disturb that sleep...Stick with your old friends. I know what it means. When I moved over here to this office I could have made many new friends but my wife and I don't associate with anyone we did not associate with before I became Mayor. Stick to that! You know many people who will think that you have suddenly become a great fellow just because you now have a shield. Live within your means. Don't try to live up to the Joneses...

"Let me add another warning: You and I don't shape the foreign policies of our government. The American people have delegated that authority and power to their officials, and as members of the Police Department you will refrain from taking any active sides in any controversy concerning the foreign relations of the United States...as police officers you are not free to take any active part in politics. We stress that again and again. We mean what we say."

You probably realize now that there was nobody quite like LaGuardia.

Love,

Dad

The Day I Became a Cop

Dear Betty,

Another special day in my life was September 4, 1941, when we had commencement exercises for my new recruit class. It was a very rainy night and the audience was entirely drenched but still very enthusiastic. You will have another chance to see what kind of wisdom Mayor LaGuardia imparted, plus some other interesting references.

There were 206 of us who had just graduated from the Police Academy. There were some promotions and a special ceremony for the six women and first Negro to enter the ranks of the department.

LaGuardia said, "You must not be discouraged by any weakling or slimy character who seeks to undermine the morale of the people; of anyone who is so congenitally weak and dreadful that he seeks to appease with any system or individual with which we do not agree. There are bound to be weaklings in a population of 130 million people, but they do not count."

Commissioner Lewis Valentine explained to the audience that Father Knickerbocker was a generous and kindly employer. "He gives you security of tenure, full pay (except for the first three days) while on sick report, three weeks vacation, promotion on merit and fitness, economic security and a liberal and generous pension system."

The occasion marked the introduction of Lieutenant Samuel Battle, the first Negro to enter the ranks of the Department, as successor to the late Lou Gehrig as a member of the New York City Parole Commission. The Mayor said, "He is appointed for one reason and one reason only, and that is because he is qualified to do the job."

Then he addressed us. "You have chosen this as your life's work. It is a profession and it includes many other branches of highly scientific work. It requires a great deal of care and attention. It demands interest and courage. If you feel sheepish at any time, quit. As the Police Commissioner said, do not bring discredit upon this great Department, and if any time you feel that you cannot look into the muzzle of a gun, take up another profession, because you are assuming risks in the profession which you have chosen."

Betty, there was a breakdown of what people did before they went to the police academy. You may be interested in these results. Among the 200 men, the average age was 25, height 5'10", weight 168 pounds, 194 attended high school, 121 had attended college and 89 had degrees, and the job held by the most men (42) was clerical work. Of the six women, three were teachers, the average age was 27, height 5'4", weight 136 pounds, 3 were married, 3 were single, and all had attended college and had degrees.

I wonder how that compares with people these days. We always called our force "New York's Finest" and I believe it was.

Love, Dad

Fiorello and Me

Dear Betty,

I noticed an article in the Phoenix newspaper that said over a century ago, the military band from Whipple Barracks, Arizona Territory, went into camp east of Phoenix along with a battalion of the 11th U.S. Infantry. On February 18, 1896, the musicians were under the direction of Achilles LaGuardia, who was the father of Fiorello, three times mayor of New York City.

That reminded me of when I was a young police officer. The annual baseball game between the New York Fire Department and the New York Police Department was in progress at the Polo Grounds, home of the New York Giants then.

I was a rookie cop, assigned the uniform for duty that day. Traditionally the Mayor was escorted to show impartiality, from the first base side of the Polo Grounds to the third base side during the middle of the game. I was delighted to escort Mayor LaGuardia to the other side of the field. But when the Mayor saw me, he took a look and asked for another officer.

I was told later that he looked at my height of 6'5" and said, "No way." He was only about five feet tall and probably didn't want to look that much shorter than another man. That was the long and short of it for me!

The next year I was pitching for the New York Police team in the Polo Grounds and the Mayor was watching me. Here's how that came about.

After I was appointed to the New York Police Department, I spent three months at the Police Academy at 7 Hubert Street in Brooklyn for academic training at Randall's Island, and an Armory in the Bronx for physical training. The next year I went to the baseball game in New Hyde Park between the New York Police and James Barton's Night Hawks, a team in the Baseball Alliance. James Barton, by the way, was the star of the play "Tobacco Road" on Broadway.

Someone told the manager that I was there and was a good pitcher. I was in civvies. The manager, Steve Whalen, took a player, Bip Foley, to go with me to the locker room so I could put on his uniform. I was real surprised.

Now, Betty, I went in to pitch and did well. The police team was far behind. Then I came up to bat with the bases loaded. That night I was real lucky and impressed the police team by hitting a triple to the wall (almost a home run.) Boy, was I in favor with Steve Whalen and that police team.

A little later, I was the relief pitcher at the Polo Grounds at the Fireman-Police ball game. Now Mayor LaGuardia was watching me.

I played with the New York Police ball team the rest of 1942. At the beginning of the baseball season in 1943, I entered the U.S. Army Air Corps. No baseball while a cadet. Later as an instructor at Victorville Army Air Corps, I did some great pitching for our team including a no-hit ballgame against the Las Vegas Horned Toads in Las Vegas.

By the way, LaGuardia would become famous for another funny line of his. He was speaking to the U.N. Relief Administration at the end of World War II. He reminded them, "Ticker tape ain't spaghetti!"

Love, Dad

How I Got Into the War

Dear Betty,

As you know, Pearl Harbor occurred on Sunday, December 7, 1941. I was in the kitchen with my wife Edna that Sunday morning and heard the shocking news. We both realized that our lives would be changed.

I had entered the New York City Police Department on June 9, 1941, and had spent three months in the Police Academy for physical and mental training. However, now a new and grave concern for Americans was the start of the war with Japan after FDR's "day of infamy" speech to the nation.

I had been assigned to the 110th precinct, Elmhurst, Queens. Edna and I had moved from the small basement apartment near the 104th precinct and rented a nice upstairs apartment in a nice house in Elmhurst. We loved it there, things were good, and we had a nice neighbor named Peter Palumbo. But now, war clouds loomed over us. Edna continued to work in New York and I continued to work the 110th precinct.

Things were bad for our country. I was an American citizen, through my parents. (Thank you Mutter und Vater.) I still spoke German at home with them. (Again, thank you.)

Prior to entering the Police Department, I had gotten my own citizenship paper (called Derivative Citizenship.) Interestingly, I had to send to Germany for my birth certificate. It came back with a Swastika stamp. (I wish I still had it.)

During the rest of 1941 and 1942, I stayed with the Police Department and then enlisted in the Army Air Corps Cadet program on April

30, 1943. Upon my induction, a United States Army sergeant tried to dissuade me from enlisting in the Air Corps because of my eyes.

I was sent to Atlantic City, the beautiful resort area of hotels, and I'm sure that I never would have gotten there otherwise on my meager police pay.

The first stop was at the Traymore Hotel, then the hotel with the Big Elephant in front called The Dennis. I had a week at the Claridge. I had gotten septicemia from an abrasion on my hand on the training field. There was dirt and stuff, in addition to kids throwing up, sweating, and stinking in the heat. It almost stopped my military career.

I met friends from all over but didn't ship out when they did. After I was passed over for the second time, having said goodbye to friends I met, I asked why. Was it because I was born in Germany? I got no answer except that it was an "Intelligence" decision. I was told to go back to the Dennis Hotel and wait for someone to contact me. After a few days, someone did. I was informed that because I had a high score and was a police officer, they assigned me to military government for duty in Germany after we won.

I guess I wanted to impress Edna. One of our friends who had entered the Air Corps earlier had come home on a furlough. He looked sharp as a new pilot and lieutenant. Edna and her mother were impressed. So I wanted to join the Air Corps. I asked if I might be able to go to Officers' Candidate School. I remember the uniform and wings Lou Bigelow had on. He informed me that after training, I would be a staff sergeant. I declined. I wanted the Air Corps. So I finally shipped out with a new group and new friends.

You make friends easily in wartime. We all had a common cause. Wasn't there a phrase that "You make friends fast in a foxhole?" Of course, if one could make the Air Corps, one could stay out of that "fox hole."

Shortly after that, I was on a train for Vermont. We were supposed to spend five months at Norwich University College Training Detachment in Vermont. The college level courses included beginning flight training on Piper Cubs. Our math instructor, a good teacher in a sharp looking uniform, impressed me. That's where the idea first came to mind that what I'd do after the war was to become a teacher of mathematics. I was good in math and won the math prize from public school, a beautiful wristwatch made by Isaac Jewelry store in Ridgewood, New York.

I did not receive the normal five months at college. Eleven cadets had washed out at Norwich so eleven of us were scheduled to fill the group for Classification. One of my friends, who became a friend for life, was Lyle Smith from Detroit. I never realized that I would go to Detroit much later.

Although I had no college and would not until after 35 years of age, I must have been pretty smart. Out of 500 men that had arrived at the University, only 11 of us were sent on to Nashville, Tennessee for classification as to be a pilot, navigator, bombardier, or failure.

We were put in temporary quarters along with hundreds of other candidates and went through testing, psychological evaluations, and other criteria to determine which we would be. Day by day names were posted. Some cadets were terribly dismayed to find out they were "washed out." We all sweated out those daily postings.

I was accepted and started out to be a bombardier and was later made an instructor. Later I found out I had qualified for the other positions but at 6'4" I could not fit in a fighter jet. (I had scrunched down and was measured at 6'4".) I would have liked to be a pilot or navigator. Either could later lead to a job with an airline. But bombardier? Possibly a job as a bartender with a long, highly polished mahogany bar who could send beer steins unerringly to the right spot and customer.

I remember a psychologist asked me if I could bomb the city where I was born in Germany. Guess my answer was all right. I said I did not know any of my relations there, that my loved ones came here, and I would if necessary. But sir, I respectfully request assignment to the

Pacific Theater of war. Now why did they call that a "theater?" It was certainly no fun for anyone!

I also learned that through the Army Air Corps, I scored a 149 on the Intelligence Test, which was very high. Officers Candidate School in the Army required 110 or higher. The Air Corps requires 115, I believe. I only met one other man who had a higher score, George Hadlock. I learned that 149 would easily get me into MENSA where you have to be in the top 2 percent of the population in intelligence. I scored in the 96th percentile, but needed to score in the 98th for MENSA.

(I took a MENSA test a few years ago in Arizona but didn't buy reading glasses and suddenly had to go to the bathroom so I just missed out qualifying, probably. I have tried to get my Army records with the 149 score but I was told that they were destroyed in a fire in St. Louis.) I guess this reminds me of that old quotation, "It is hard to fail, but it is worse never to have tried to succeed."

We bombed the hell out of Germany. But when I went to Germany in 1970, all my records were at the church where I was baptized and in the City Hall. In fact, I had sent to Germany for my birth certificate in 1939 when I applied for the police. I got it back from Germany with a Hitler swastika stamp, as I mentioned earlier. But I got new copies when I went to Germany in 1970 and 1980 so I guess our bombing during WWII was not as good as I thought it was.

Actually, we did not bomb haphazardly. We did not hit small villages. We bombed submarine pens, major factories, steel mills, etc.

Love, Dad

What I Did in the War

Dear Betty,

I took a long troop train ride from Nashville, Tennessee across the United States to Los Angeles once I was classified. I had never been to California before. It was so warm and sunny. I loved my time there. Then I went on to Santa Ana for Pre-Flight Training and I believe more testing and psychological evaluations.

Our instructors were tough. Beds had to be made according to army specifications, square corners, tight sheets, so a quarter would bounce. My friend, Lyle Smith, had the top bunk and I had the bottom. We had to scrub the floors and scour the showers, even skimming them with razor blades.

Lyle and I finally got a weekend off. I remember eating in a great restaurant in LA. Having been a cop in New York, I told Lyle the cops knew the good restaurants. Asking an L.A. cop and stating I was one we were directed to a restaurant called Lawry's. It had a great roast beef and I believe that's how the chain got started.

Then some of us shipped to Victorville Army Air Force Base for Bombardier training. The climate was unusual for a New Yorker. We were in the Mojave Desert. In the mornings we fell into formation with overcoats on. By lunch time, shirtsleeves, and back to overcoats in the evenings.

The planes we used for training were AT-11s. My instructor was a New Yorker, Raymond Boslet. Knowing I had been a cop, he always kidded me about stealing apples from the fruit stands.

The training was tough. Some washed out. But I really enjoyed it.

Then finally on May 20, 1944, we graduated. I had an officers' uniform, bombardier's wings, and looked sharp.

I was surprised to learn I would remain at Victorville as an Instructor. I think Ray Boslet had something to do with that.

I went home on a short furlough. That was when I took my first wife, Edna, to dinner and pulled out the gold cigarette case filled with cigarettes, even though I disliked her smoking and other things. But I still wanted to keep our marriage together. Unfortunately, or maybe fortunately, we did not stay together.

I spent almost a year in Victorville as an instructor. I had three narrow brushes with death.

First there was a night bombing run with our pilot Bert Optiz. Suddenly I noticed the lights on the wings of the plane ahead were reversed. We dove just in time. The other plane was flying the bombing route in reverse!

Second, there was a real near air collision, so close as to tear the doors off our plane. On bombing patterns, even if a target (like a shack) light was out, planes were still required to fly the heading called for. Suddenly, our plane was jolted in the air. A plane on our right cut too soon and whizzed just in front of us, ripping our door off. We were all shook up! We all thought about each night flight. The pilot of the other plane was so shaken up that he refused to fly for a while.

Third, while an instructor at Victorville, I pitched on the Victorville Army Base Baseball team. We were heading to Las Vegas to play the Las Vegas Horned Toads. Our plane was in close formation with another plane. Two other planes were ahead of us. A captain on another plane radioed us to cut out flying so close.

It seems that the year before, four planes went to Las Vegas flying too close in formation. The wingtips hit and one plane crashed killing the others aboard. There were two brothers, both captains, and one was on one of the planes. The other did not know for a while if his brother had been killed. It turned out that they were both okay. But that's why we were ordered to desist from such close flying.

By the way, that weekend I pitched a no-hit game against the Las Vegas Horned Toads. On another trip, I pitched a shutout 4-0 against the El Toro Marine Base. Pretty good, eh?

Another highlight at Victorville was the New Year's Eve 1944 at the Officers' club. One of the captains was married to Priscilla Lane. Her sister, Rosemary Lane, also was there. Priscilla had a great shape and was dressed in a very fetching cat's costume. I don't know if you ever had occasion to see movies with the Lane sisters but they had some great films such as *Four Daughters, Arsenic and Old Lace, Saboteur, Meanest Man in the World,* and others.

The Lane sisters first sang with the Fred Waring band and then entered show business where Priscilla (Pat) became better known than Rosemary. On May 22, 1942 she married Air Force Lt. Joseph Howard. The following year she gave up her show business career to follow Joe around during his military stint and often appeared in camp shows.

Tennessee Ernie Ford and cowboy actor Tim Holt were also at Victorville. Son of actor Jack Holt, Tim starred with his father and Humphrey Bogart in *The Treasure of Sierra Madre.* He attended the Culver Military Academy before his show business career and left the movies in 1942 to serve as a bombardier. He was wounded the last day of World War II in Tokyo and was awarded the Purple Heart and the Distinguished Flying Cross. He was able, however, to return to the movies and starred in numerous cowboy films, some with sidekick Richard Martin whose nickname was Chito. They even had a series of comic books named the Tim Holt comics. Besides his westerns, he was in *Hitler's Children, The Magnificent Ambersons,* and other films.

Later one of our bombardier students became a movie star himself, Paul Picerni. Paul was born in Queens, New York, and was commissioned as a 2nd Lieutenant Bombardier at Victorville Air Force Base. He flew 25 combat missions (in the China, Burma, India theater of war) and received the Air medal with three Oak Leaf Clusters and the Distinguished Flying Cross.

After the military, Paul went to college as a drama major and besides his movies, became the Los Angeles Rams NFL half-time master of ceremonies, a job he performed for 30 years. Some of his rather forgettable movies were *Mara Maru, Desert Song, Operation Pacific, The House of Wax* and others. He probably became best known for playing Elliot Ness' sidekick in a television series called *The Untouchables* starring Robert Stack. I understand he is known as the "Benefit King" because he has emceed so many banquets and benefits through the years.

One day, some of us were shipped to Langley Field for radar training. We sat around, got two furloughs and went home to New York without ever getting the radar training.

After that, we were sent to Lincoln, Nebraska for B29 training. I met my crew: Pilot Chris Alevazos, Co-Pilot Bill Palmer, Engineer Larry Fowler, Radio Operator John Ruggero, Navigator Hayden Bradford plus five other enlisted men but their names escape me now. We trained as a team. For a time, we were at Smokey Hill Air Corps Base. Edna and I had a small apartment in someone's home at that time. Then I went to Harvard, Nebraska.

One of my proudest moments came when the results of all B29 team bombing practice runs, captured by pictures, showed me having the lowest CE (circular error) of anyone for the bulls-eye (the shack).

Captain Charles Navarro, a brother of Mexican silent screen star Ramon Navarro, (Ramon was the original star in *Ben Hur* later played by Charlton Heston) was our Group Captain. His cousin was Mexican silent screen actress Delores Del Rio.

Charles had on the wall Bulls-Eye (shack) targets with green strings attached to each B29 crew. There were five concentric circles for the center (the shack). Our crew string was the shortest (29 feet from the target) whereas some other crews were even outside the 500 feet circle. My crew was very proud of me. And that stayed up for quite a while.

Then the time came for our bomb group to fly to Okinawa. One squadron had already gone. My footlocker, with some booze in it and my baseball glove, was already over there. We got our new B29 plane and test flew it the first day. Next day we got our mosquito netting and other equipment for Okinawa. In two more days, we would head for a California base from which we took off for Okinawa.

Then the atom bomb was dropped on August 6, 1945. But that's another story. You see, our colonel had talked to us before August 6 and mentioned that we would go down in history. I kiddingly nudged my navigator, Hayden Bradford, and said, "I hope we don't go down in flames."

Then we knew what he was talking about. Just the week before August 6th we were all in readiness. Then the bomb! Later we learned that if the Enola Gay piloted by Paul Tibbetts had not dropped the bomb for whatever reason, we might have had to. I felt relieved that my crew, I was lead Bombardier, did not have to face that moment.
Love, Dad

My First Wife

Dear Betty,

You know I was married four times. Your mother, Elinor, passed away, a victim of multiple sclerosis. Edna and Mona I divorced. Sallie, I am very happily married to.

Let me tell you a little more about all the wives I've loved before. I did love them; otherwise I would not have married them.

Betty, you know that at one time I smoked, and quite heavily. Let me tell you what started me, something I regret to this day.

As you know, I was married before I married your mother. Her name was Edna DeFliese. She was at Richmond Hill High School with me but I never dated her.

One day, after graduation, I was working at the Eberhard Faber Pencil Company, 37 Greenpoint Avenue, Brooklyn. Taking the subway to work one morning I saw the figure of a woman (a nice figure) wearing a large picture hat.

I think I have a thing for picture hats. (Your mother was wearing one the night I met her.)

When the figure turned around I saw it was Edna DeFliese. We talked and made a date. That's how it started.

We were married in February 1940. Interestingly, my father and mother had to sign consent for me to get married. Edna didn't. We were both under 21. But New York law was unique. The man could not marry without parental consent if he was under 21. Not so for the woman. Curious?

It would have been better if my parents had not signed that consent.

Edna and I had a happy marriage in the beginning. I worked at Eberhard Faber as a mail clerk until I quit one day. The office manager, Gus New, wanted me to take on a more important job but at no increase in salary. Eberhard Faber was sort of a slave shop. I started in 1937 at $13 a week. Each year I got a dollar a week raise...$14, then $15. They required a lot of overtime. All one got was one dollar called "supper money," nothing else.

When Gus New refused to pay commensurate with the new job he wanted me to do, and said, "I know you are going on the Police Department," I quit.

It seems that Paul, the porter, had shown pictures of me on the centerfold of the *New York Daily News* and also the *New York Daily Mirror* (now defunct) that showed me competing on the first day of a New York Police Agility Test. Both the newspapers had pictures of me (then known as Hans, a short form of Johannes.) Mother always called me Hans. I changed the use of Hans to Johannes before I entered the New York City Police Department.

Their picture of me running a mile, ladder walking, hurdling, and wall climbing were shown by Paul to everyone at Eberhard Faber. I was very proud. But Gus New was not nice.

I then went to work for the Muirson Label Company in Brooklyn until I entered the Police Department. My boss there, Rudy Matthews, was a real nice guy. He also wanted me to take on a much bigger job, at more pay. But I told him I would be going to the Police Department and asked if I could work in the factory. There I could get overtime. He agreed.

Edna and I rented an apartment in Elmhurst in Queens when I worked at the 110th Precinct.

Then one Sunday morning, December 7, 1941, the radio announced that Japan had bombed Pearl Harbor.

Some time just before I went into the service as an aviation cadet, we were living at Edna's parents' home in Glendale, still in Queens, New York.

I needed some stamps to mail letters. Edna said there were some in her pocket book. She made a bad mistake. In her bag, I saw a pack of cigarettes. At that time I was utterly against smoking. I felt that it was an ugly habit and very unhealthy.

We had a terrible argument about it, because she had told me she definitely was not smoking. A lie!

A few days later, I entered the U.S. Army Air Corps as a cadet. I was sent to Atlantic City. By this time, I had been a policeman two years. Edna did come down to visit me and I thought all was okay again.

However, she was very put out regarding insurance from the Army if I was killed. I guess maybe because she had lied about smoking I had either put my mother in as beneficiary or had split the insurance between Edna and my mother. I don't quite remember. One thing led to another.

I had been sent to Norwich University for cadet training. It was the oldest military academy next to West Point. While there, I received a letter from Edna that her father had died. If it had been a telegram, I would have been able to come home in time for the funeral and maybe things could have been patched up. As you can imagine, she was very upset that I did not come home for his funeral, but her letter arrived after the funeral.

After the University, we were sent to Nashville for classification, and thence to Santa Ana, California for Pre-Flight School, and then to Victorville, California.

For the next year, I received very little mail from Edna. I sent mail but much of it went unanswered. I felt very sad and thought again and again of things I could have done differently. That's why I started that "Little Black Book" of notes and points to help make me a better person.

I was made a lieutenant on May 20, 1944, and received a furlough to go home to New York. I knew I would return as a Bombardier Instructor to Victorville Army Air Corps Base where I had trained.

When I arrived in New York, I took Edna out to dinner, resplendent in my new lieutenant's uniform and wings. At dinner, I pulled out a gold cigarette case, filled with cigarettes and offered her one. She was surprised.

I never smoked all the time I was in the service. But I felt if she wanted to smoke, all right. I wanted to keep our marriage together. Again, this was a bad decision. It led to my smoking later, where I returned to the police department in 1946 smoking up to three packs a day for 20 years until the summer of 1966, when I quit cold turkey. That was also the year I retired from the New York City Police Department.

Edna stayed with me in Victorville. The A-bomb came on August 6, 1945.

After the war, I thought we could make a marriage but I discovered a few things. Suffice it to say that I divorced her in 1946 on the grounds of adultery.

Well, that was all behind me by the time I met your mother.

Love, Dad

Guarding Raided Premises

Dear Betty,

I think you might find this interesting. Many things happen to police officers. Some funny, some tragic, some weird.

When I was a young rookie cop attached to the 110th Precinct, I was given an assignment to guard a "raided premises." Basically when an arrest is made for certain illegal activity, a police officer was assigned inside the premises so that particular activity would not continue.

I was assigned to premises like a storefront where arrests had been made of prostitutes. At that time we worked six days on and 32 hours off. I was assigned here on the late shift (midnight to 8 a.m.) for six days.

But the prostitute, a pretty black woman (called "colored" then) lived and slept there. I was uncomfortable to say the least. First, she was quite bold and said, "You're a pretty handsome cop" and invited me to join her in her bed. She kept that up for a few nights.

But worst was the part that I was afraid to sit anywhere. Cockroaches abounded and were all over the place. I did not want to bring them home on my uniform.

For the next few nights, I sat in a steel chair in the middle of the room. I had brought in sheets of white wrapping paper and placed the white paper all around that steel chair. I stayed all night, sitting in that chair, watching for those roaches to come on that white paper and stomping them.

I was thankful I never got that assignment again.

Love, Dad

Death Was So Close

Dear Betty,

You might want to know that being a New York City policeman was not only dangerous for police but also dangerous for those we pursued. Let me tell you about an incident that haunts me to this day.

In the old days, to save time, certain basic messages were transmitted by police dispatchers at headquarters to radio cars by means of a numbered code. Code signals eliminated long explanations. However, the police cars carried a receiver only. If the men wanted to talk back to headquarters or clarify messages, one of the officers had to go to a telephone or call box.

Initially just three situations were coded. Signal 30 meant "felony in progress by armed men." Then the dispatcher gave the locations. Signal 31 meant "felony in which a car was involved." Signal 32 meant "investigate" and the problem might be anything from a nosebleed to a disaster. There are many more code signals in use now, but 50 years ago, there were just three.

I was assigned to a radio car with a partner in Queens. We were on the 4 p.m. to midnight shift and it was about 10 p.m. We had parked near a candy store while my partner went inside for a malted and sandwich. I stayed behind the wheel, with the motor running and the radio receiver on. The street was a main bus route on the way to LaGuardia Airport.

Messages kept coming over the radio. Suddenly I heard my car number called, just as a large bus passed by, diesel engine roaring.

I heard the dispatcher say, "Signal thirty...." Then came the roar of the bus, and as it faded I heard the dispatcher. "...Polk Theater, two men fleeing." The theater was just a few blocks away. I had no time to locate a call box and recheck the message. I called my partner.

We were quickly on the scene and saw two male figures running from Polk Theater down a side street. We swerved after them and they ducked up a side drive between two houses. I slammed on the brakes, and we jumped out and ran up the dark driveway with revolvers drawn. We came to a row of garages.

My partner darted to the left around one garage, so I started to go around the same garage to the right. I saw what looked like a shadowy figure trying to squeeze in behind a tall clothes pole that was too narrow for complete concealment.

I was still running forward when I heard two shots to my left. It was chilling. Was it my partner? Had he been shot?

I was within two steps of the pole, with my gun pointed, and my finger near the trigger, when the shadowy figure started to move. The only thing that kept me from shooting was that we were so close together. One more lunge brought us in contact and I grabbed the fugitive and overpowered him.

It was no armed felon. It was a frightened teenage boy. Within a few seconds I heard my partner's voice. He came back to me shaking his head. He had fired two warning shots but the other shadowy figure had escaped by climbing onto a garage roof and skipping down the other side out of sight.

We found out it was another teenage boy. The pair had been window peeping up and down alleys.

When we reported in, we found that someone had called about prowlers near the Polk Theater. The complete message, which had been drowned out by the passing bus, was a Signal 32, a simple instruction to investigate.

Every circumstance had conspired to put me within an arm's length of shooting a defenseless boy, foolish but not a criminal.

In all my 25 years in New York City as an active police officer, that was the closest I came to firing at another human being.

I believe that's the experience of more police officers, despite the shooting stories that make the headlines.

But a police officer only has to have one experience like that to remind him of the awesome power he holds in his hand, and with only a split second to decide whether to use it.

That power is a terrible burden for mortal man. It really belongs Up There.

Love, Dad

The Truth About Crime Prevention

Dear Betty,

When I was a youngster growing up in Brooklyn, my first recollection of a policeman was a big red-faced man in a long blue coat who stood at the street corner directing traffic where I had to cross to go to school. He looked stern but kindly. We kids looked up to him. Unfortunately, the police were portrayed in Keystone Kops and movies as the butt of humor and unbelievably dumb.

When I grew old enough to take an interest in newspapers, I discovered bootleggers and gangsters were portrayed as dead heroes. Later the G-men came along to restore some of the good guy image to law enforcement.

When I got into policing after World War II, the image (the word in this usage hadn't been invented yet) of a policeman was as a crime solver, the expert at detection. As for the guy who walked the streets trying to keep things "cool" so no crime would occur, he was not glamorous.

As we move toward higher goals of professionalism, it seems that we become more estranged from the general public. We have appeared to be moving away from rather than toward more constructive service, especially for the community groups and neighborhoods that are afflicted with the more serious crime problems.

What does the victim care, after the fact, that society has been avenged and the law enforced because the criminal has been arrested and punished? The true yardstick of effective policing is the absence of crime.

Protection of the fundamental rights of all citizens is the essential police role. Yet as police tasks have multiplied and organization has grown more complex, a gradually declining number of police officers actually perform the protective role. Most large departments have specialists in traffic, youth, vice and criminal investigation. The patrol division has been screened out of many of its more stimulating and personally rewarding service functions. Preventive policing is less exciting than a car chase, smashing a vicious dope ring, or cracking a difficult murder case.

However, the better the patrol force does its job, the less need there is for wild chases, shots in the night and arduous investigations. Unfortunately the glamour, reputation and financial rewards of the specialists make that the goal of the best police officers in the ranks.

Exotic new equipment alone is not the answer. The answer to more effective crime prevention is a combination of the right equipment and the right person. He need not be highly educated but needs to be a good cop, alert, dedicated, trained, motivated to take charge of his own beat and make it his own piece of turf. If he is fully accepted and respected by the people in his beat, he can spot trouble before it happens and be there to prevent it. Such a person deserves to be ranked at the top of a profession whose goal for nearly 180 years has been to measure its effectiveness by the elimination of crime.

You can see why I always enjoyed commending the basic "beat" cop.
Love, Dad

How I Met Your Mother

Dear Betty,

You now know something about my first wife, Edna. Let me tell you about how I met your mother. It was 1947 in the summer. It was the time of the American Legion Convention in New York City.

I was a member of New York Police Post 1103. Our headquarters for the convention was a New York City Hotel.

That fateful day was my duty as C.Q. (Charge of Quarters) all afternoon that Friday. It was my obligation to greet and entertain visiting police Legionnaires from other parts of the country. Of course, this often necessitated me having an occasional drink with these visitors.

After quite a few drinks that day, having done my stint, I was going home when someone said, "Would you like to meet Jim Fallon's daughter?"

Feeling pretty good then, I said "Sure!"

Elinor, your mother to be, was standing across the ballroom floor with her back to me. She had on a brown dress and a large brown picture hat. When she turned around, I liked what I saw.

It brought my mind to that song from *South Pacific,* "Some Enchanted Evening You Will Meet a Stranger."

Elinor was the daughter of a fellow police officer and a member of our 1103 Police Post.

(I have to admit that I must have a yen for ladies wearing large picture hats. Remember Edna, my first wife, was wearing a large, yellow picture hat the day I saw her on the subway platform.)

That chance meeting across a crowded room was on a Friday. The next night I already had made a date with the lady I was currently going with, Phyllis Avery. I told Elinor about Phyllis when I made a date with her for Sunday.

Phyllis was a lovely girl, very shapely and an accomplished ballet dancer. She was very photogenic and graceful. I understood she had modeled for Canada Dry Ginger Ale. I did bring Phyllis to the Saturday Queens Police Post 1103 Legionnaires party at the hotel. In fact, I introduced Phyllis to Elinor, just saying she was the daughter of Jim Fallon, a friend of mine.

Elinor told me later they hit it off. Phyllis told her how much she liked me, and that she was going to stop smoking because I didn't like it. (Of course later I got pretty hooked on smoking myself.)

Elinor told me later that she felt pretty smug knowing that she had a date with me the next night, Sunday.

Well, Elinor and I kept dating. Phyllis realized I had fallen for someone else. She became very upset. I liked Phyllis very much; we had fun together at Jones Beach where we went often. But my heart went to Elinor.

A funny thing was that I had a good buddy, Johnny Hooper, who was at the party where I met your mother. Elinor later told me she had asked him what kind of guy I was. His answer as far as I can remember was "He treats a lady like a queen, and a floozie like a floozie," or something like that. I believe that intrigued Elinor and she wondered how I was going to treat her. Elinor was a lady.

Working one night at the 110th precinct as the "95" man (a rule permitting the lieutenant on desk duty to have a patrolman assist with clerical functions) Elinor called me. She had been at a wedding and said she had caught the bride's bouquet. Was that a hint?

I remember very well that New Year's Eve before we married. I was working a 4 to 12 shift. I managed to get off an hour early. I remember getting off the bus at 221st Street in Queen Village where she lived. I had phoned Elinor. She saw me running down the street. She met me. At just midnight we met and kissed for Happy New Year. We knew we were in love.

Elinor and I eloped. We were married May 29, 1948. She was Catholic and knew her parents would not approve of her marriage to a non-Catholic, particularly a man who had been married before. I had married Edna in the Lutheran Church, in February 1940, by the Rev. Frederick Preuss in Glendale, Queens.

We eloped to Greenwood, Connecticut and were married by a Justice of the Peace at his home; a beautiful home called "On Top of the Rocks."

We moved to an upstairs apartment in my parents' home. It was cheap; only $32 a month rent. It had an old-fashioned coal stove in the kitchen. Later we re-modeled that kitchen. Elinor took good care of my mother. We re-decorated my parents' downstairs apartment.

We lived there almost ten years until you were born, Betty. You were named Elizabeth Diane Spreen, Elizabeth after Elinor's mother. Just when you were born we had bought Elinor's boss's house on Oak Street in Floral Park, Long Island. You came along July 1, 1958. We waited a long time for you, ten years, little Princess. But you only weighed 5 pounds, 1 ounce. We had to leave you in the incubator at the hospital for two weeks. That was tough on your mother. But finally we brought you home to our new house in Floral Park.

Love, Dad

Bedtime Stories

Dear Betty,

You asked me to try to remember the bedtime stories I told you when you were a little girl. I'll bet you remember the names Thundercloud and Dancing Star. I do, too! I think I can remember some of those stories.

I used to call this one "Thundercloud, Dancing Star and the Buffalo Hunt."

Thundercloud was a brave young Indian warrior, the son of the Chief. One day all the young braves were to go out hunting the buffalo. This was Thundercloud's first hunt.

There was a lovely young Indian maiden with shining hair and dark brown eyes. Thundercloud had been noticing her for many moons. He did not know if she liked him too. But when he got on his pony and rode away, he saw that she smiled and waved to him. That pleased him greatly.

A few days later the braves came back after a successful hunt and Dancing Star went out to meet them. But Thundercloud was not among them. She cried out, "Where is Thundercloud?"

The other Indians said they did not know. During the buffalo stampede they lost sight of Thundercloud and his pony. They searched for him in vain.

Dancing Star was frightened and sad. She got on her pony and rode out to look for him and she rode and rode, anxiously looking for her young brave; the young brave she had smiled and waved at. She knew that she liked him.

But where was he? She searched for several days and almost gave up. Just then, she heard a faint sound. It came from a small wooded ravine nearby.

Dancing Star ran over to Thundercloud and hugged and kissed him. She was so happy. She bandaged his wounds. (I guess I said "boo boos" then.) She put a splint on his leg and helped him get on his pony. Together they rode back to their village.

The chief and everyone else was very happy and thanked Dancing Star, and so they began a beautiful romance.

I believe I called the next story "Dancing Star, Thundercloud and the Picnic."

Dancing Star and Thundercloud became sweethearts. They were much in love with each other. One day they decided to have a picnic on the shore of Gitcheegoomi Lake, which is near the shore of Hiawatha Lake, I think.

Dancing Star put out a blanket for their picnic. Thundercloud went out into the woods to get firewood to roast their deer meat. All of a sudden Thundercloud heard Dancing Start scream in terror. He came running back but stopped short! Why? Because he saw that Dancing Star was so scared. About six feet away from her was a great big rattlesnake.

Thundercloud quickly took an arrow from his quiver and took careful aim at the snake. If he missed, the snake would strike and Dancing Star would become very sick or even die.

He let go of the arrow and it struck the snake squarely in the head. The snake jumped but in a few seconds lay dead.

Then Thundercloud reached over, picked up Dancing Star in his arms, and kissed her tenderly. Dancing Star returned the kiss with tearful eyes.

She knew that Thundercloud had saved her life. She said, "Thundercloud, you are a great Indian brave. You shoot straight and true and I love you."

I probably called the next story "The Swim at the Canyon Waterfall."

One day Dancing Star took her pony for a ride in the country. She went to a beautiful spot by a canyon waterfall. It was a wonderful place to go swimming. She got off her pony and walked to the small swimming hole where she was going to swim. Just then she noticed that Thundercloud was there and swimming near the waterfall.

Dancing Star felt very mischievous. Seeing Thundercloud's clothes on a nearby rock, she grabbed them and hid them behind several large rocks nearby.

Thundercloud noticed her standing there and smiled. Dancing Star ran and stood on a very large rock and laughed. "Ha ha! Thundercloud, I hid your clothes."

Thundercloud did not know what to do. Then he saw that the large rock she was standing on was very slanted. He then splashed a lot of water on the rock and Dancing Star slid on the slippery rock and went into the water.

Thundercloud said, "Ha ha! You are all wet, too." Thundercloud kept splashing Dancing Star until she told him where his clothes were.

Then he made her hide her face while he scampered out but I think she peeked a little.

Thundercloud dressed quickly, got on his pony, grabbed Dancing Star's pony, and rode away. Dancing Star had to walk almost a mile to get to the village in her wet clothes, and she was peeved. Thundercloud turned around and brought her pony back.

Dancing Star thanked him and asked why he came back. He said, "Oh, I was just horsing around."

Here is the last little story. Thundercloud and Dancing Star were very much in love and they were married. There was a big festival with much dancing in the village. The Chief gave his blessings to both.

Dancing Star and Thundercloud were very happy. They wanted to have a baby and waited for many moons but no baby arrived.

Finally, after a long, long time, a beautiful baby arrived. Thundercloud and Dancing Star wondered what to call her. Then they decided to call her "Princess Running Late."

And that is the story of Thundercloud, Dancing Star and their lovely daughter. I hope you like it as much as you did when you were my little Princess.

Love, Dad

Rising in the Ranks

Dear Betty,

I know you've asked about how I rose in the ranks of the New York City Police Department. So here's a little information about that for you.

After World War II, I returned to the Police Department, and having completed the necessary period of service to qualify, took the competitive examination for sergeant. Some 7,000 officers competed for a few hundred openings. I finished second on the list and got my promotion in 1948. I took the next examination and was promoted to lieutenant in 1951.

I began to teach other police officers in 1952, when I was assigned to the Police Academy as an instructor. I reorganized the Recruit Training Program, and instituted a new master lesson plan system, which remained in use for many years. The following year I was assigned to institute and develop a training program for the New York City Housing Authority Police.

In 1954, the Department selected me to be the first New York police officer to attend the Southern Police Institute, a nationally known professional school which offered a three-month course for police administrators with heavy emphasis on human relations training.

Subsequently, I was delegated to conduct promotion courses for officers preparing for the examinations for sergeant, lieutenant and captain. For the next three years, I conducted seminars and symposia on police tactics and field operations for all superior officers.

In 1958, I was promoted to captain, the highest rank in the New York Police Department for which a written examination is taken.

Higher ranks are awarded at the discretion of the Police Commission. I was also made precinct commander that year.

In addition to command responsibilities, I continued to receive teaching assignments. I lectured at the Police Academy's in-service training courses for the career development of fellow members of the Department, and conducted a special training course for plainclothesmen and their superior officers within the borough of Brooklyn on more effective enforcement of public morals laws.

In 1961, I was assigned to the Confidential Investigations Staff, a unit reporting directly to New York's "top cop," the Chief Inspector (whose rank is comparable to Chief of Police or Superintendent in other cities.)

A short time later, also in 1961, I was appointed to act as liaison officer between the Police Department and the Department of Parks, an assignment that lasted five years and led me into two areas that had an important bearing on my future. One was direct involvement in what contemporary thinking would call the "public relations" aspects of police work. The other was the development of a new concept of police patrol, initially for use in parks, but which sustained experience indicated had a broader application to general police work. It was the adaptation of a relatively new vehicle, the motor scooter, to police use.

I was promoted to deputy inspector in 1962, and chief of operations in 1965 with the rank of inspector. I retired a year later. One of my two departmental citations was for jumping into the East River in 1953 to rescue a drowning man. The other was for arresting a man for attempted murder in 1949 when I was on vacation in Florida.

I need to write you more about how the scooter idea germinated.

Love, Dad

Why Scooters?

Dear Betty,

I thought I'd tell you about the scooter idea. In fact, I wrote a paper about it for the *Journal of Criminal Law, Criminology and Police Science* in 1966, a journal published by Northwestern University School of Law. The title of the paper was "The Motor Scooter—An Answer to a Police Problem."

In police history, foot patrol has always been considered the "backbone" of the police effort. As we wrestled with how to extend the range of activity of available police personnel at minimum expense, we realized that we could purchase six scooters for the price of one radio car. A two-man car eats up manpower but a one-man car has been assailed as increasing the hazard to the operator. It became clear that the scooter patrolman equipped with a two-way radio could cover more territory at less expense.

Finally, in the spring of 1964, nine scooters were put into service on an experimental basis in Central Park in Manhattan, and Prospect Park in Brooklyn. Eventually the scooter concept received the personal endorsement of two successive police commissioners, Michael J. Murphy and Vincent L. Broderick. However, resistance to change within the department slowed down its general acceptance, in spite of an accumulation of evidence as to its expanding possibilities.

Robbery and other crimes dropped significantly in the two parks during a four-month trial period, but the program continued on a token basis until September 1, 1965, when 50 more scooters were put into service in 17 precincts, still primarily for park patrol. Recommendations were solicited from the precinct commanders, and the results were evaluated. Each of the 17 commanders reported favorably, and requested that the program be continued.

During the visit of Pope Paul VI on October 4, 1965, the scooter patrolmen were invaluable to commanding officers of sectors along a motorcade route lined with over a million persons. The scooter men served as reconnaissance scouts, inter-sector messengers, and as liaison officers when communications were severed or overtaxed.

Beginning October 20, 1965, the program was tested for general street patrol in 15 selected precincts, and again was received favorably. During the electrical power failure on November 9-10, 1965, during the height of an evening rush hour, several million persons stalled in transit. However, the scooter patrol maintained immediate, direct radio communication with precinct station houses. One scooter was sent from Manhattan to Maspeth, Queens, over a jammed Williamsburg Bridge for emergency radio equipment, an impossible task for an auto. The scooter went and returned promptly.

During the paralyzing citywide transit strike January 1-13, 1966, public transportation was nonexistent. Scooters were in constant demand because they could cut through traffic blockages, even riding on sidewalks when necessary. Besides quickly unlocking vehicular congestion, they could survey problem areas and report to precinct commanders. In the vicinity of bridges and tunnels, when traffic lanes were reversed to expedite the flow of vehicles from major roadway approaches, the scooter men were utilized most effectively. They also delivered messages and supplies through otherwise impassable locations.

The Tactical Scooter Unit became a team patrol because they could keep in touch by radio. They operated either as partners or as a group according to the need. From this point on, the use of scooters became an accepted part of New York police operations, some 700 being acquired and put into operation by the time I decided to retire from the Department in 1966. I'll just quote from my article when I described Team Patrol.

> The new scooter patrolmen operated either as partners (team) or as a group (unit) according to need, and always under the knowledge, direction, and control of the local precinct commander via two-way radio.
>
> The teams are encouraged to develop various patterns of street patrol—to be systematically unsystematic. One such predetermined pattern was worked out for two men to ride parallel avenues. The pattern is to proceed three blocks, turn into a side street, meet, and continue on to exchange avenues; two blocks later the same procedure; then after one block. This results in two faces on an avenue rather than one, adds interest for the men, increases alertness, and makes for an illusion of omnipresence.
>
> The scooter patrolmen improvise on and change their patterns of street patrol much as baseball or football players adapt set plays to meet rapidly changing conditions.
>
> Within a precinct, teams can be organized for group operations; precinct units can quickly be welded into a swift, highly maneuverable and unpredictable crime fighting force.

The advantages of scooters were that they greatly extended patrol coverage, permitted better police observation, could move easily in congested areas, freed radio patrol cars for response to major incidents, were economical, could be quickly mobilized, reduced the fatigue of foot patrol, increased the morale of and stimulated recruitment, provided a visible crime deterrent, established rapport with juveniles, and were well received by the community.

I am so pleased when I see the bicycle patrolmen in most big cities these days because they are using the same concept, except for the ability to move faster with less physical expenditure. Some places like Florida, New York City and university police (UCLA and Stonybrook SUNY) use police on motor scooters. Of course they are used in other countries like Italy, Luxemburg, Brazil, etc.

There is also a new vehicle called the Segway that is being tried out by various police departments such as Boston, San Diego and Atlanta. The Atlanta Police Department bought six Segway Human Transporters, electric-powered gyroscope-equipped, two-wheeled transporters.

Unfortunately, they sell for $4,950 currently, which is difficult for departments with budget constraints.

Love, Dad

Jackie Kennedy and John John

Dear Betty,

Here is an interesting sidelight regarding the scooter program I instituted, first in Central Park, then other parks and later all the precincts in the city.

When we first started in Central Park, I was concerned regarding safety so I laid down some strict rules about operation of the scooters. They were not to chase cars. Scooters were slow moving protective vehicles, not motorcycles.

One day a scooter cop came back to my office at the 22nd Precinct in Central Park to tell me this story.

A pretty lady had come over to him and asked if her young son could have a ride. He told her no, he was not allowed to.

Some reporters were there and told him that was Jackie Kennedy with her son John John who was about four years old.

I said to the officer, "Why the hell didn't you at least put him on the bike for pictures?" At that time we could have used that publicity to get our scooter program off the ground.

That was, of course, after the death of President Kennedy. Mrs. Kennedy had moved out of the White House after November 22, 1963, into a Georgetown house with her two children. The Washington, D.C. area was too depressing for her and too filled with memories. She moved to New York City in September 1964 so this event happened sometime after that.

As you know, Jackie married Aristotle Onassis in 1968, but when he died in 1975, she returned to the United States. She worked as an editor in New York from 1978 until shortly before her death in 1996.

Unfortunately, her son John had a tragic death in an airplane crash with his wife and sister-in-law. Only their daughter, Caroline, survives the family. It seems very strange to look back on people who seemed so vibrant at the time we had knowledge of them.
Love, Dad

How I Learned to Learn

Dear Betty,

You are probably wondering about how I got the education that you know I got. Well, I'll tell you.

I had received two more promotions, being appointed to Deputy Inspector in 1962 and Inspector in 1965. At this point, I stood two rungs short of reaching the top of the police executive ladder in the New York Police Department. In 1964 and 1965, New York had its second World's Fair, and I served as the Police Department's Coordinator of Police Services with the World's Fair Administration.

The total number of men under my command in this assignment reached as high as 3,000. The most difficult single event of this assignment was providing for crowd and traffic control during the unprecedented visit of Pope Paul VI. As I mentioned earlier, police scooter men demonstrated their versatility during the Pope's trip.

With the rank of Inspector went command of the Police Department's Bureau of Operations, in effect the tactical direction of all police on day-to-day street duty. While I held this command, a massive electrical power failure, November 9-10, 1965, and a citywide transit strike, January 1-13, 1966, taxed the resources of the New York City Police Department to the ultimate degree. I was commended because again police scooter men, originally my project, proved themselves in a variety of emergency uses.

For me, 1966 was a milestone year in more ways than one. It marked the completion of 25 years of service as a police officer, which allowed me to consider the possibility of retirement from active duty with a nice pension. Only 20 years were needed to apply for retirement benefits, which were ½ pay. At the age of 47, with your mother and you, I considered my alternatives.

As I had moved up the ladder from rank to rank, I had become increasingly aware of the need for further education as a basis for still further professional advancement. So at 35, the "Serutan" age according to some of my wisecracking friends, I became a college freshman, attending classes during off-duty hours, while still handling the full-time responsibilities of a police lieutenant.

My "alma mater" was a branch of the City University of New York, which was then called the Baruch School of Public Administration, forerunner of the present John Jay College of Criminal Justice. In a sense, it was a step backward, for I had previously served as a part-time faculty member at the Baruch School.

The New York Police Department had persuaded the school to start some experimental courses in police science for officers in 1954. Since I was then an instructor in the Police Academy, training recruits and preparing officers for promotional examinations, I was invited by the Baruch School to help out as a lecturer.

But the more I delved into the theory of police science, and the increasing complexity of the problems faced by police in our cities, the more I felt my years of practical experience needed the leavening of study and reflection on related social sciences, communication skills and teaching methods.

I began taking general academic subjects at the Baruch School in Manhattan for my "major" in Police Science. The Baruch School was renamed John Jay College, and I received my bachelor's degree there in 1966.

Meanwhile, I had become convinced that intra-departmental politics had put a halter on further personal advancement beyond my current rank of Inspector. With my degree in hand, I decided to exercise my 25 years and out retirement privilege since I had already stayed an extra 5 ½ years.

I looked forward to "doing my thing" in policing as a teacher rather than as a command officer. To acquire further teaching credentials, I enrolled in the first post-graduate program at John Jay, in pursuit of a master's degree in police administration. Simultaneously I accepted consecutive teaching assignments, spending a year at a branch of the State University of New York at Farmingdale, Long Island, before becoming a professor at John Jay. By the way, I created and taught a course there called "Civil Rights and Human Relations."

To class after class of New York area police officers, I explained the principles of police administration, the problems of civil rights and human relations as they affected police work, and the increased demands for professionalism in police work. I enjoyed the teacher's role, and the feeling of being in a position to make a broader contribution to the advancement of policing by reaching the command officers of the future. I enjoyed the academic atmosphere.

I still yearned to complete my master's but that, my dear, still lay just ahead.

Love, Dad

New Hope for Policing

Dear Betty,

I prepared a paper for a Political Science class in 1967. I wanted to give them some specific information about how modernizing police departments had created more problems than it solved. You will see how I tried to give some historical information without wanting to be too boring. I'll just summarize it for you.

Nowhere in city government has the demand for citizens' grievance machinery been more insistent than in connection with police administration. The mechanism most advocated in recent years has been a civilian "review board" apart from the police authorities.

A 1966 referendum in New York City voted down a review board leaving disciplinary control in the hands of the chief police administrator. While 63% of the total vote cast was against the establishment of any outside review board, 65% of blacks and 48% of Puerto Ricans voted for such a board. The vital nature of the process of criminal justice has seemed to focus the attention of those concerned with human rights upon the manner in which the police treated minority group members. While over a million and a quarter persons in a way expressed and gave a vote of confidence to their police, over three-quarters of a million did not. The police must serve both groups.

One thing we can do now, however, after the stimulus of the review board controversy, is to look at ourselves; both in past and present police performance and perhaps come to a possible theory as to where the future hope of policing may lie.

Crime was increasing at a rate almost seven times the rate of population growth. Why, as police are moving upwards to professionalism, does crime also inexorably continue upwards, at even a greater rate? Why, as police become more motorized and equipped with the latest electronic and communicative devices, does crime also become more of a problem? Why, as police become more and more specialized and adept in crime investigations, juvenile work, traffic and vice control, do crime and delinquency continue to rise and police scandals do not diminish?

The greater majority of people seem less and less concerned about their police, their agents of "regulation and repression." I have a theory that about 10% of people really like and admire police officers; about an equal number despise and hate them; and the balance of about 80% couldn't care less. If true, is this because the policeman of today is alienating himself from the people he serves?

The change in semantics of a policeman's role from that of a "policeman" to that of a "law enforcement officer" is a point in question. The higher sounding phrase "law enforcement officer" imparts a punitive or repressive thought. Yesterday's "policeman" with his old-time rapport has become today's "law enforcement officer," impartial but also impersonal.

It also seems that we have become more estranged from the general public. A great proportion of our tremendous budget outlays seem to benefit only a small proportion of our population. The average law-abiding person rarely meets or sees a police officer because he is average and law-abiding.

Further, policing is changing from the concept of "police service" to a cold, impersonal "enforcement of laws and ordinances," removing it from a preventive to a punitive connotation. Policing should rest on service as an interested neighborhood police protector with a de-emphasis on "law enforcement."

Many militant civil rights groups have combined "Bull Connor tactics" in Alabama and "po-lice" to give a most sinister allusion to the present meaning of the world "police" among their followers and sympathizers. The proper image should be one of a man who is responsible for peace keeping, crime preventing, protecting his neighbor and mine from harm and unlawful infringement of his human rights. The policeman, as the watchful protector for every individual in our society, is the true guardian of the "blessings of liberty."

Because of the growing complexity of police tasks, in recent years police administrators have divided operations in terms of purpose, method, clientele, time and area. This has resulted in specialized divisions such as Traffic, Juvenile, Vice and Detective divisions. The Patrol Division, long regarded as the backbone of policing, was devitalized and demoralized. Specialization divides the department into separate forces that sometimes operate independently of each other. Specialists are prone to ignore work that is the primary responsibility of some other unit and citizens are sometimes shunted from one specialist to the other in search of service.

Unfortunately, today the glamour and reputation of specialists has caused the most important division, patrol, to look uninviting to officers. This is not only unfortunate but it is ruining police performance and effectiveness in the field where it counts most—the protective and preventive services. Further, the specializations grab the cream of police officers from patrol, giving credence to the thought "you're not in if you're out in the field."

One advance, the automobile, is today perhaps the worst culprit in the present alienation of the police officer and the public he serves. Ever since August Vollmer, historically regarded as the father of modern policing, held that the patrolman on foot was obsolete and showed how motorization amplified enormously the striking power of the force, police administrators have emphasized the use of the automobile.

Since Vollmer, police administrators have expanded the advantages of rapid response by car and the enhancement of two-way radio communication. This is no doubt an effective police weapon. However, radio cars are almost entirely engaged in responding to calls rather than preventing calls. In a radio car it is difficult to stop, talk and get to know people.

The Los Angeles police drive into some ethnic neighborhoods as if they were in occupied territory. The city is so huge and sprawling that almost all patrol work is done by officers in cars rather than by men walking beats.

In New York City it is the exception when one performs his daily tour in his home precinct neighborhood. To quicken his sense of responsibility for friendly policing, he should be allowed to perform his duties there as often as possible. To keep him in his command precinct more often, better means of scientific deployment is necessary. Being allowed to know and be known in his precinct should make the better professional.

Unless we de-emphasize the cold, mechanical improvements of recent professionalism, policing will continue to become Gestapo-oriented; cynical, hardened and alienated. Crime will rise and rise. The people will pay and pay. All that is necessary is for the police to return to the people and allow the people to return to their police.

My dear daughter, you probably can't appreciate the fact that we were only two generations removed from the atrocities of Nazi Germany and I wanted to avoid a repeat of those tactics.
Love, Dad

PART II

Detroit Police Commissioner

o o o o o o o o o o o o o o o o o o o o o o o o o o o

"Life affords no higher pleasure than that of surmounting difficulties, passing from one step of success to another, forming new wishes and seeing them gratified. He that labors in any great or laudable undertaking has his fatigues first supported by hope and afterwards rewarded by joy."

—*Samuel Johnson*

The Detroit Riot

Dear Betty,

I woke up the morning of July 23, 1967, to find every television station reporting on a riot that was developing in Detroit. The morning newspapers didn't have the story yet but the evening newspapers did. Over the next four days the horror of death and destruction in one of our American cities dominated everyone's attention. I'll give you some of the highlights since you were too young to understand or follow it at the time.

I'll describe the police raid that triggered the riot in some detail elsewhere. The public became agitated by the police raid and began to attack policemen who were hauling in those arrested. As police retreated under the attack, more were called in and soon a full-blown riot was occurring.

Soon all available local police and fire units were called into action, the burning, looting, and disruption were uncontrolled. Mayor Jerome Cavanagh and Police Commissioner Ray Girardin notified Michigan State Police in the early morning. This was in addition to notification of the FBI, Sheriff's Office, Road Patrol, and other agencies.

The Mayor requested 200 Michigan State Troopers by 2:00 p.m. the first afternoon. Some 360 State Police Troopers arrived in the late afternoon and the National Guard committed to send troops. The Mayor issued a proclamation for a curfew from 9:00 p.m. to 5:50 a.m. Bars and theaters were ordered to be closed across the city.

By July 25th, 14 had been killed, damage was estimated at $150 million, 731 fires had broken out, over 800 were injured, 1,663 people had been arrested and snipers, looters, pillagers, fires, and destruction continued.

President Lyndon Johnson ordered 4,700 Army paratroopers into Detroit riot areas Monday night as Negro snipers launched an offensive that stretched from the West Side to Grosse Pointe borders.

The President ordered Defense Secretary Robert McNamara to "take all appropriate steps to disperse all persons engaged in acts of violence and to restore law and order."

Johnson's personal emissary, Cyrus Vance, immediately ordered 1,800 federal troops to aid Michigan National Guard men and State and Detroit police, who were running dangerously short of ammunition in gun battles with entrenched snipers.

The nation watched these events unfold on television and read newspapers in stunned disbelief for four days. Newsmen had to run the gauntlet of snipers and police battles and some were injured.

Pressure built up in Congress on the fourth day for a bipartisan Senate-House investigation of the riot. The President stayed in close contact with Cyrus Vance. The press reported that Mr. Johnson slept only five hours and was awakened three times with riot reports.

Senator Robert Kennedy said that the nation's welfare system had broken down and called for a private enterprise attack on ghetto housing. He said, "Wherever violence and mob action break out, it must be stopped forthwith."

Michigan Governor George Romney reemployed his original state of emergency on the fifth day and ordered a curfew to keep "spectators, gawkers and amateur photographers" from impeding the usual flow of traffic and efforts to clean and restore public facilities in the west side riot area.

President Johnson made a radio-television address to the nation the fifth evening on the subject of civil disorders. United Auto Workers President Walter Reuther pledged the help of 600,000 Detroit labor union workers in "removing the scars" torn in Detroit by four days of rioting.

Meanwhile Lt. Gen. John Throckmorton, in command of federal troops in Detroit, said, "We hope to complete our job in the very near future and phase out the military."

On the sixth day, Governor Romney demanded the creation of metropolitan school systems for full integration and statewide open housing to prevent new riots in Detroit "or something even worse."

That was what the nation knew by the end of July 1967 and that was what I saw and read at the time.

Well, that last information now, at the end of 2002, strikes me strangely. Only this week, the Census Bureau issued a report stating that black people remain the most highly segregated minority group in neighborhoods across the United States, despite progress in integration over the last 20 years. The bureau said the five most segregated metropolitan areas were Milwaukee, Detroit, Cleveland, St. Louis and Newark, New Jersey.

The article quoted John Logan, director of the Lewis Mumford Center at the University of Albany in New York. He said blacks moved into the five most segregated metropolitan areas including Detroit in the 1920s when laws enforced segregation. "That established a pattern of segregation that has proved durable. The patterns are being reproduced in the suburbs. It's not just that the old city ghettos have been maintained but a tradition of segregation was established and is being re-created in the present."

As you can imagine, I was very disheartened to read of so little progress. It set me to thinking of what more could have been done in Detroit after the riots. But now I will write you concerning my part in this human drama.

Love, Dad

I Was Courted to Be Detroit's Top Cop

Dear Betty,

I know you are probably wondering how I got to be the Police Commissioner of Detroit. That was where I went out of the frying pan into the fire. All of a sudden, the opportunity was thrust at me of having the authority and responsibility to put into immediate practice some of what I had been preaching at John Jay. I'll tell you how it happened.

Early in May 1968, with the completion of my master's degree requirements still a month away, I was attending a graduate seminar in New York University on decentralization in government, education and police work.

I didn't really know about "headhunters" but I soon learned. I guess when the word "head-hunting" first appeared in an English dictionary, it referred to a particularly gruesome kind of warfare between certain primitive tribes.

"Headhunting," American-style, is an urbane but intensive talent search, with some of the competitive aspects, if not the bloodletting of tribal warfare, and some of the same qualities of stealth and persistent stalking that prevailed in the jungle.

The object of the hunt in civilized America may not lose his head in the same way as the primitive victim, but he may sometimes wonder, when the hunt is over, whether he didn't stick his neck out just a little too far.

Most headhunters in America are professional personnel experts who satisfy the needs of business clients for fresh or additional executive talent by discreet but probing searches. Most victims of this kind of headhunting are rising young men with M.B.A. degrees, a growing record of performance, and a fair degree of visibility within their profession.

When the headhunters catch them, I would assume they normally find it a highly rewarding and remunerative experience, and they wonder why it took the hunters so long to find them.

But consider this kind of quarry: male, white, age 48, profession policeman, two degrees (both acquired at the end rather than the beginning of his career), and currently in a pressure-free working retirement setting as a college professor. What kind of headhunters would be interested in prey like that?

In my case, they were a trio: the mayor of Detroit, an ex-police commissioner, and a university administrator. Very skillfully, I was marked, baited and lured, until finally my head was on their pole.

In the process, however, although I may have lost my head, I ended up a willing victim, performing a function that served as a career capstone and gave me a privilege granted to few men. That position was being able to execute, however briefly, the ideas and dreams of a lifetime, or at least of my adult lifetime.

I was present as one of several guest panelists at a seminar. On the panel with me was one of my former bosses, Vincent Broderick, who had served as New York City's Police Commissioner. After the panel discussion, he stopped me in a corridor outside the conference room.

"Did they call you from Detroit yet?" he asked me.

"Detroit?" I said. "You mean Chicago, don't you?"

An industrial firm had been in touch with me previously about going to Chicago to head up a public service project that involved working with youth.

"They're interested in you as police commissioner in Detroit," Broderick said.

All I could think of when I heard the name "Detroit" was the image of a desperate, riot-torn and racially uptight community. That was the image I had gotten from the New York news media.

I started to laugh.

"Why would I want to be police commissioner in Detroit?" As soon as the words were out, I was sorry I'd said them.

Commissioner Broderick was a man I admired and respected very much. His jaw dropped. He waved aside the flippancy, and began to talk to me earnestly about the magnitude of the opportunity that existed in a city like Detroit for a dedicated career professional to render an important public service, not only to the city but also to policing as a profession.

He said many things about my own past record that indicated a degree of recollection and awareness that surprised me. He paid me some stimulating compliments. He said he had only superficial knowledge of the Detroit situation, but in terms of department size, he pointed out it was no larger in numbers of personnel than some of the commands I had held in the New York City Police Department. There was nothing in the Detroit picture, he said, that my experience did not qualify me to handle.

At the end of our conversation, when I still seemed quizzical, he finally said, "This is too important to settle in a few minutes. Why don't you just send me a resume, and I'll see that it's put into the proper channels. Then you can go from there."

I was not deliberately trying to appear difficult, but it just seemed to me that a "retiree" who was looking forward to a second career in teaching had every reason to study with caution any proposals that promised to abruptly sidetrack his planning for the rewards of some quiet years.

I decided to take your mother out to dinner that evening, at an attractive restaurant in the Lynbrook, Long Island area where we lived. I waited until after cocktails to raise the question.

"What would you think about my being police commissioner in Detroit?" Elinor's chin dropped even farther than Vincent Broderick's. While I was waiting for her to respond to the idea of my becoming a police commissioner, her mind was racing past the question of the job to the question of geography.

"What? Not Detroit!" she gasped.

I guess we'd both been brainwashed by what the Eastern news media carried about this city, which neither of us had ever seen, but which after 18 months neither of us wanted to leave.

After her initial startled response, Elinor and I discussed the subject on a "let's take a second look" basis, and as a result, I did prepare a resume which I forwarded to Broderick.

But I was too busy completing my master's thesis and teaching my classes to spend much time wondering whether my resume would draw any further response or not.

On our 20th anniversary, May 29th, your dear mother put in 12 hours typing a draft of my master's thesis.

A month passed since my corridor conversation with Broderick, and nothing more had occurred. I dismissed everything from my mind except graduation, and my first summer in years free of special assignments and special duties. We planned a pleasant family vacation in the Catskill Mountains at a handsome resort reserved for the New York Police Department people. It was on property willed to the Department by Hetty Green, an odd recluse famous 60 or 70 years ago as the "Witch of Wall Street."

I submitted the final draft of my master's thesis on June 7, 1968. I received the first master's degree in police administration to be granted by John Jay College. I was only mildly interested to note that the commencement speaker, a partially gray-haired gentleman named George Edwards who was seemingly no older than I, was a former police commissioner from the city of Detroit.

He was a poised and effective speaker, and impressed me particularly when he took pains to praise the endurance and sacrifice of the wives and families that had made it possible for the John Jay graduates to finish their courses and earn their degrees, all on family time, while fully employed. In other words, my dear, he knew I hadn't spent enough time with you and your mother.

With graduation, my teaching commitment also had ended for the summer, and our Spreen family began to pack for a Catskill vacation, which was to begin on Monday, June 17, 1968.

Thursday, June 13, was a warm, pleasant day and we decided to drive the few miles from Lynbrook to Jones Beach, one of the fine seashore playgrounds on the ocean side of Long Island. You and your mother were seated inside the car, and I was just closing the garage door when I heard the outside buzzer that indicated the telephone was ringing inside the house.

"Never mind that, let's go," said Elinor.

I paused. "Oh," I said, "I might as well answer it. It might be important. It'll only take a minute."

At the other end of the line was a man named Julius Edelstein, whom I knew as the vice-chancellor of the City University of New York. I knew he had served as a city official and advisor to New York's Mayor Robert Wagner. At the time I did not know he was also an acquaintance of Detroit's popular young mayor, Jerome P. Cavanagh.

Edelstein quickly told me he was speaking on behalf of Mayor Cavanagh, that my resume had provided interesting reading in Detroit, and that he would like to see me in person about the Detroit situation. He invited me to call at his office in Manhattan the following Monday.

I thanked him for calling, but told him I couldn't possibly make such an appointment, since I was leaving on vacation with my family that very day.

He was flexible and persuasive. He suggested that I just drop in during the morning, on my way out of town. I insisted that nothing was going to interfere with our first family summer vacation in five years, but I finally agreed to stop by, in my own mind determining that once the amenities had been observed, I would politely decline and proceed to the Catskills.

You and your mother were waiting impatiently when I returned to the car. I've never had much of a poker face, and Elinor was studying me as only a wife can do. I finally said, "Guess what."

From that lame beginning, we talked about Edelstein's call all the way to the beach. I assured your mother that I had promised nothing except to pay the man the courtesy of making a call, and that nothing would disturb our vacation plans.

The following Monday morning, I called on Dr. Edelstein at the midtown Manhattan offices of C.U.N.Y. After about an hour of earnest conversation, he put a telephone call through to Mayor Cavanagh in Detroit. "I've got the man for you," he said.

Edelstein was so persuasive and convincing that I agreed to take the next step, which was to go to Detroit, see the city, and meet the people there for myself. However, I was more than taken aback when Mayor Cavanagh asked if I could be in Detroit the very next day. I could understand his eagerness to settle a problem that had been plaguing him for nearly a year, but I had a problem too, of summer vacations deferred, that had been a source of buttoned impatience to my family for five years.

We finally agreed on a compromise. I would begin my vacation, and after getting the family settled at the Catskill resort, I would take time out for a quick trip to Detroit before the end of the week.

So that afternoon, only half a day behind schedule, our family group finally headed north in my five-year-old Buick sedan. You may recall that besides you and your mother, the group included your mother's mother, Elizabeth Fallon, and my nephew, Kevin, who was about your age.

The Police Recreation Center involved about a 150-mile drive. It is near one of the highest points in the northern Catskills, 4,000-foot Hunter Mountain, in Greene County, a few miles west of the Hudson River. There is a comfortable resort hotel and all the attractions of a woodsy summer resort, including a lake for swimming and boating. I relaxed with all of you on Tuesday and Wednesday, and then headed back to New York City Thursday morning, after assuring your mother that I was just going to Detroit to talk.

"I haven't said I'd take the job," I tried to point out. But your mother knew me very well. She knew it was more than a casual interest that was tugging me to Detroit.

Well, that was how they courted me.

Love, Dad

What I Knew About Detroit

Dear etty,

Detroit had a terrible reputation at that time because of the riot, which began on July 23rd, 1967. Regardless of what one calls it, it was the most devastating and severe riot in America in the 1960s. Detroit's riot of 1943 was also terribly shocking in that era. In 1943, a false rumor announced from the stage of a nightclub helped spread racial fighting that began on Belle Isle. That riot left 34 dead.

Let me tell you about the riot of July 23, 1967, a day that changed the City of Detroit forever. It started with a routine "blind pig" raid in the black community at an "after hours" joint for a liquor violation. A "blind pig" is a gathering where alcohol is sold without a liquor license. It may be in an illegal saloon, a speakeasy, or just a place of illegal occupation. People greedy for profit and fun just turn a blind eye to illegalities.

On Twelfth Street, an after hours club run by a group called "United Community League for Civic Action" was selling alcohol without a license and sold to minors as well. A tip led a sergeant to the site on Sunday morning, about 1:45 a.m. About 73 Negro customers and the bartender were arrested. During the next hour, squad cars and a paddy wagon ferried the arrested to the police station but not fast enough as a crowd began to gather.

Then it began. They allowed John Conyers, now a Congressman, to stand on a car with a bullhorn to try to get the crowd to disperse. He was the wrong man. They should have activated their new Tactical Mobile Unit (TMU) to respond and arrest the original few agitators. They needed to act fast before it festered.

Having served as police lieutenant in the well-known Bedford-Stuyvesant district of Brooklyn, and later as Captain of the Brooklyn morals squad for over three years, I led many such raids with my plainclothes officers.

Detroit's police made an unfortunate mistake in allowing some of the participants and hangers-on to remain in the area on that fateful Sunday morning. That was not good police tactics. In New York City, even though in technical violation of rules and regulations forbidding males and females to be placed in the same patrol wagon, we quickly removed participants from raided "after hours" joints to the police station (or station houses) for booking and incarceration. No stage for them on the streets! No time or opportunity for them to preen, prance or mouth off!

However, the police stuck to the rules and carried males in one vehicle after another, and females in others, thus extending the time for the crowd to gather. The crowd began to taunt the police and jive with friends arrested, who were awaiting a paddy car ride. Suddenly, as a vehicle pulled away, a bottle smashed a squad-car window. Then it began.

Police Commissioner Girardin had ordered police not to use guns. Soon looters knew they would not be shot at and took advantage of the situation. Rocks, bottles, looting, arsonists, Molotov cocktails, snipers, and hoodlums attacked police and firemen trying to restore order. Over the course of four days, 14 square miles of Detroit were gutted. By Tuesday, people stayed home from all jobs in the affected area. It took 15,000 law enforcers from local and state police, the Michigan National Guard, and federal troops to restore order to the city.

It was the bloodiest uprising in half a century and the costliest in terms of property damage in U.S. history. The result was 43 dead, 347-467 injured, 1300 buildings destroyed, 2,700 businesses sacked, 3,800 arrested, and 5,000 left homeless. Damages amounted to $500 million.

Mayor Jerome Cavanagh had looked at the city from a rooftop and said, "It looks like Berlin in 1945."

Also, as an aside, the dreadful riot of 1943 could have been contained if Detroit's then police commanders had blocked off the Belle Isle Bridge, thereby containing the incident to Belle Isle and not allowing it to spread to the mainland and the streets of the city.

With this history in mind, you can see why I was worried about whether to accept the position. But, as you know, I did accept it.

Love, Dad

Why I Became Detroit's Police Commissioner

Dear Betty,

I've always wondered if I would have accepted the position as Detroit Police Commissioner if I had known the problems that lay ahead. I'll try to tell you how I was thinking at the time.

I interrupted our vacation at the Catskills to leave Hunter Mountain very early, and caught a morning flight out of LaGuardia Airport that put me in Michigan before lunchtime. Cliff Owens, a police aide to the mayor, met me at Detroit's Metropolitan Airport, 30 miles from downtown. On the smooth but fast half-hour drive over continuous expressways, Owens told me he'd been instructed to pass me off as a magazine feature writer if accosted by newsmen.

However his mission was to get me into the mayor's office as inconspicuously as possible, which he did, without detection; a nice trick considering my six foot five-inch size.

Owens, who was in plainclothes, was more than simply a policeman. He was friendly and articulate, and to me seemed to exemplify the highest type of police officer. Some say New Yorkers are "provincial" and cannot recognize the good qualities of other people or other regions. Perhaps subconsciously I had such a feeling about the New York Police Department; that it consisted not only of New York's "finest," but also the nation's "finest."

My exposure to Cliff Owens, both then and until his untimely death a few months later, convinced me New York had no corner on top cops, and if Owens typified the Detroit police, they didn't have to take a back seat to anybody. A commissioner with such men in his department would be fortunate indeed.

I saw the name "Ford" on one of the expressways, which didn't surprise me. Then I saw another sign with what I thought was the name "Dodge" on it. I wondered if all the famous Detroit carmakers had streets named for them until Owens corrected me, and pointed out that the name was "Lodge," in honor of one of Detroit's former venerable councilmen.

The expressway dipped below the surface as we approached downtown Detroit, and spilled us out on a broad riverside boulevard a block from the mayor's office in the City-County Building, a new 20-story building in gleaming white, aluminum and glass. We took an elevator up to the 11th floor, stepped down a corridor, and into the mayor's suite of offices by a back entrance.

Owens left me alone in a small simply furnished room with a couch and a few chairs, and an adjacent private lavatory. I thought about my past career and the plans Elinor and I had made together for our future, and I said to myself, "What the hell am I doing here?"

Although only a few minutes slipped by, the passage of time seemed longer than it was until a door opened and Mayor Cavanagh came in. A slightly plump-faced but boyish six-footer; the mayor had a touch of Jackie Gleason roguishness about him, which relaxed me immediately. He was affable and forthright, and after a few minutes invited me to have lunch with him, so we could talk at length in private, away from the office.

We left by the back way again, and drove east along the Detroit River to a private marina near the mayor's official residence, a large riverside home called the Manoogian Mansion for the businessman who had donated it to the city. We boarded a comfortable cabin cruiser, and five of us, including an aide to the Mayor and a man and wife team who operated the boat and served us lunch, headed out into the river.

I admired the tight cluster of new and old tall buildings that dominated the Detroit skyline, and the lower profile of the buildings of

Windsor, Ontario, on the Detroit River's south shore. The sky was clear blue and the sun warm; even the poet Lowell could not have enjoyed a rarer June day.

We sipped a gin and tonic, and sampled a platter of cold cuts, potato salad, and two different kinds of bread, both delicious, the likes of which I have been unable to match since. It was enough to sway anybody, especially an ex-immigrant from a frame-flat neighborhood in one of New York City's crowded suburbs.

The Mayor described the city, its people and government in general terms, and outlined the problems and needs of the police department. Both the depth of his information and the clarity of his expression were most impressive. He spoke frankly about the 1967 Detroit Riot, and about a two year-old scandal that had involved some police officers of rank with the proprietor of a restaurant in Detroit's "Greektown."

I asked him what he personally wanted from the police department, as a matter of policy, and he told me simply, "a fair, effective and efficient department."

I asked him if he believed the police commissioner should run the department free from political influence or interference from other city officials.

I was concerned, because I felt that my retirement from the New York Police Department was influenced importantly by my observation of the influence of politics on the New York police executives. I wanted any administrative responsibility of my own to stand or fall on the performance or lack of performance of police responsibilities, not political responsibilities.

Mayor Cavanagh said he believed that once policy was understood, his department heads, including the police commissioner, should have a free hand to stand or fall on the basis of their personal performance.

We had already talked for about four hours, and as we looked at each other, I think we each sensed a degree of personal commitment to each other.

I knew I liked Mayor Cavanagh. I hope he liked me. I also knew that wasn't all there was to the story, but I liked what I'd seen of the city, and what I understood about the police department and the quality of its men. I'd also heard and seen enough to realize that Detroit offered me a personal opportunity to promulgate the kinds of action steps that just might convince a few people that the urban policing problem might be susceptible to solution at the local level if the local man had the ideas, and the moxie to try them.

I told Mayor Cavanagh that I shared his beliefs as to police policy and objectives, and that I thought with his backing I could make a contribution to solving Detroit's problems. He stuck out his hand, and I shook it. As of then, I was Detroit's police commissioner, although the people of Detroit didn't know it, and your mother didn't know it.

Our leisurely cruise ended, and the boat snorted up out of trolling speed to a powerful surge for the home base. Approaching the marina, we saw signs of some kind of disaster. We were waved off for what we eventually discovered was a fire at the dock we had initially used. Perhaps that was an omen of the hot times ahead. We returned by way of another docking area, and journeyed on to the Manoogian Mansion, where the Mayor asked me to stay overnight in a hotel. He wanted to announce my appointment, with me present, at a press conference in the morning.

I had anticipated an in and out visit with no overnight stop, so I had brought no additional gear with me. However, that was the least of my problems. My biggest challenge was to explain my decision to your mother.

The Mayor's aide picked up some toilet articles. The Mayor and I checked our waistlines and he provided an additional accommodation. When I appeared at the press conference the following day, I was wearing his underwear, his shirt, and his tie!

I had a steak dinner that evening with Cliff Owens at the Motor Bar of the Sheraton Book-Cadillac Hotel, and went out to call upon the retiring Detroit Police Commissioner, Ray Girardin, at his home.

No two people could have been more different physically. Commissioner Girardin, a native Detroiter with a great sense of devotion to his home city, was a man of slight build, not much older than I was chronologically, but with a face incredibly lined and wrinkled. He had been a career newspaperman, partly with the *Detroit Times*, a Hearst newspaper that had folded dramatically. He had once covered the police "beat" and as a result had tremendous personal rapport with the newsmen working police headquarters.

He was most generous with information about the commissioner's job, and particularly about relations with the local press. He seemed genuinely relieved that someone had finally appeared to assume the burdens of the commissioner's responsibilities.

Back at the hotel, in the solitude of my room, I placed a phone call to my wife at the Hunter Mountain Resort. I should have known I couldn't surprise your mother.

"Honey," I began.

"I know," she said. "You took the job."

I can't remember what I actually said to her, but I did tell her how impressed I was both with Detroit as a city, the Detroit police as a department, and Mayor Cavanagh as a charismatic city official.

I also reminded her of something we'd talked about many times before. I was concerned that policing in America was in trouble, importantly because too much of what police did was not acceptable to the American public. I felt I could make policing acceptable to those who needed its services. I thought I could do something to improve community relations, and help remove the problem of policing as a thorny issue in American society.

I'd said it to Elinor before, but I repeated what Vincent Broderick and Julius Edelstein had been wise enough to point out, that I had an unprecedented opportunity to put into practice the things I myself had theorized about for so long in New York, and preached in my college classes.

So those were the reasons that made me accept the position.
Love, Dad

Seconds Thoughts About My Decision

Dear Betty,

The night I made the decision to become Detroit's "top cop," I called your mother and told her that I was sorry to even think of taking another summer away from family concerns. But then I gave her a positive consideration: I couldn't take office for 30 days because of the Detroit 30 day residency requirement.

It was a dark and stormy night.... This is supposedly how the writer begins a mystery novel. Snoopy, too, which you know because you read the comic strip "Peanuts." A mystery is, in effect, usually a tragedy with murder and violence involved.

It was not a stormy night on June 20th, 1968. It was a hot, sultry mid-summer night as I tried to sleep in my room in the Sheraton Book-Cadillac Hotel in the city of Detroit. Sleep did not come for a while. It was still a mystery to me why I had made that fateful decision. Earlier, when shaking hands with Mayor Jerome (Jerry) P. Cavanagh, I had agreed to become Detroit's next police commissioner. The next day would be the press conference.

The constant wailing of police sirens interrupted my dozing. About 2:00 a.m. I looked out of my hotel window onto the streets of Detroit, the city that would become home to me and my family; a city that had suffered the worst riot in American history less than a year before.

"What have you done?" I said to myself that night. "This is Detroit, the city that you saw engulfed in flames last July watching on television from New York."

"What the hell are you doing here?" I opened the blinds to take a look at the rooftops of downtown Detroit. I didn't know it until later, but your mother was as restless as I was. Along about the same time of the morning, she and her mother encountered each other in the suite at the Hunter Mountain Resort. They consoled each other drinking rum colas (with whisky instead of rum.)

I suppose I was also motivated to accept the position because my orientation toward life is like that old saying, "Success is when preparation meets opportunity at the crossroads." I thought I was prepared, here was an opportunity, and maybe I could be successful.

I had many thoughts that night about the nature of law enforcement in which I had served for over four decades. Elected officials, selected supposedly in a democratic manner, represent the people. They deserve some thinking about. Also many groupings of people fall into what might be called self-interest or pressure groups. All this affects the quality of life in cities like Detroit, indeed in communities all over the United States. Additionally, our media, which report and interpret our daily events as we move through time, affect our thinking.

I certainly have quite definite opinions in some areas. Who would not after all these years in the practice and calling of law enforcement? My later introduction into the real world of politics as an elected sheriff, and two and a half years association with the media as a columnist for the *Detroit News*, have added more and firmed up others.

I have spoken before many groups and organizations. That, and many years of teaching college courses in law enforcement and administration have given me additional insights into the attitudes, impressions and opinions of many concerned individuals. That night I hoped that my birth sign of Libra would assure that a fair balance will be struck.

It seems to me that unfortunately too many of our nation's great controversies resolve themselves or are resolved into yes or no positions. Today, there is too much rigidity, either, or, for or against. Yet, many times there really are no clear-cut sides. Gray areas often overshadow black or white. There is middle ground to be explored.

Our firmly molded either/or attitudes are often the cause of our tensions or our problems as we seek to live in a peaceful society. Our either/or attitudes can cause the death of our cities, our communities, and our neighborhoods. Many of us do not seek or examine the middle or neutral ground.

Rigid lines for or against, whether black or white, male or female, Democrat or Republican, abortion or not, capital punishment or nay, create more heat than light, exacerbate rather than alleviate, and so society begs for answers to the problems of drugs, escalating crime, racism, sub-standard education, and the like.

There is right or wrong on almost all sides of issues, on institutions, on almost anything. I hope to bring these out about policing, politics, people (both individually and in groups), and also about the chroniclers of the day-to-day events concerning them.

Perhaps from my perspective, as a man who came to Detroit on a hot summer day, my thoughts that night in a lonely hotel room and the events that followed, you may understand why I was second-guessing my decision.

Love, Dad

The Announcement That I Was Detroit's Top Cop

Dear Betty,

At six in the morning when my selection was to be announced, June 21, 1968, I had a call from the lobby. It was James Trainor, the Mayor's press secretary, a former city editor of the *Detroit Times* and a skilled public relations man. We met for him to prepare a press statement for the Mayor's news conference announcing the long awaited selection of Detroit's new Police Commissioner. I had mixed emotions ranging from thoughts of Puck's expression, "What fools these mortals be" to "Hey! I have the courage and the know-how and the desire to do this most important job and I will do it."

We had breakfast together, while he extracted enough from me about my personal background to build a basic press release for the upcoming press conference.

He left me, and I returned upstairs to get properly dressed and to compose myself. I made some notes for myself on a three by five card, which I still have.

Then, driven by Cliff Owens, the Mayor's chauffeur, I was taken to the City-County Building, moving as unobtrusively as possible to the Mayor's back room. Waiting there, I admired a lovely picture of the Cavanagh family, the Mayor, his lovely wife and eight fine-looking children. I remarked to him, "What a beautiful family", little aware of the difficulties that would precipitate the breakup of that family I so admired on the Mayor's wall.

Then the press conference June 21st, the longest day of the year, in the middle of Detroit's long summer began at 10:00 a.m. Hundreds of reporters crowded into the conference room, all anxious to see and take the measure of the man Cavanagh, after nine months of searching, had picked to do this impossible job.

As usual, the television people were the most conspicuous. Detroit had two major daily newspapers, and their representation of two reporters and two photographers barely matched the personnel concentration of a single TV station, with its news commentator, cameraman and one or two equipment handlers. Five TV stations were represented, and several radio stations. And this was in the midst of a newspaper strike.

AP and UPI had representatives; also the *New York Times* and the *Wall Street Journal, Time-Life,* and *Newsweek,* all of which have full-fledged bureaus in Detroit.

The Mayor was there, along with Commissioner Girardin. The Mayor opened the conference by saying he had scouted the entire country, and he had found the best man. I hoped the press believed him, because I felt he had contacted eight or nine other candidates before he got to me. I knew by this time that Julius Edelstein had talked to two New Yorkers in addition to me. Before I had finished these considerations, I discovered the Mayor had completed his introduction and the floor was mine.

I wish I had had the presence of mind to ask for a tape of that conference. I remember that a volley of questions was directed at me. I remember a few of my answers. Evidently they and the Mayor were satisfied with them.

Prompted by my three by five card, I started out solemnly. As a teacher, I had a penchant for tricks or strategies to make my students remember points I expected them to retain. One of these was the use of acronyms, or words concocted from the initial letters of principles I wanted to confirm in their minds. One of my acronyms was building around the word "Police." I interpreted it to mean *Protectors Of Liberty,* for the *Individual,* and for the *Community,* and for *Everyone* equally.

I got as far as *Protectors Of Liberty*, when I was interrupted by a question from the floor, and that was the end of the acronym and the point.

It ended, finally, and I returned to New York, but not before registering at the Park Shelton Hotel, a residential apartment building in Detroit's Library-Art Institute cultural center district, to establish a legal residence in the city to meet the 30-day requirement.

After the conference, on the flight back to New York, my mind danced wildly from thoughts of my waiting apprehensive wife, your mother, who had learned of my decision to accept the challenge only hours before, to wondering what the future was holding in store for us all.

As soon as we hit La Guardia airport, my car sped me back to the New York Police Recreation Centre. There your mother, your grandmother, and you were agog, frantic with questions like; "What happens now?", "What about our home in Lynbrook?", "What is Detroit like?", "What is the Mayor like?", etc.

Many New York police officers and their families now knew that one of their own, vacationing with them, was to undertake a most exciting and adventurous challenge. They all wished me well, and plenty of luck.

The Spreen family enjoyed the rest of its vacation, with no further interruption except for a trip to Central Park in Manhattan at the request of one of the Detroit TV stations, which sent a team to get some local color on the new commissioner in his native habitat.

I played some tennis, my favorite recreation, and enjoyed being with you and all of my family. For we all knew I wouldn't have much time for that henceforth.

Love, Dad

Reactions to My Appointment

Dear Betty,

When we returned from the Catskills, each time I mentioned to someone that I was leaving the following month to take over the post of Police Commissioner of the City of Detroit, there was always a quick upward thrust of their arms, coupled simultaneously with an explosive gasp, "Not Detroit!"

Later, I titled one of my speeches to Detroit's people, "Why Not Detroit?"

An appointee to a position in the City of Detroit required a minimum of a month's residence in the city. I had established an official residence and therefore, would be sworn in as Police Commissioner on July 22nd, one day before the anniversary of the riot, (or insurrection, as some put it).

Meanwhile, back in New York, packing and organizing for our exciting adventure in Detroit, we were surprised to receive a call from TV Channel 2 in Detroit. Could they come in to New York and do a half hour TV interview and story about the Spreens? I know you recall that.

Anchorman Joe Weaver, his ace cameraman, Sig Siegel and crew did come, and did a story that was shown to the people of the greater Detroit area. They later told me they had talked to quite a few people including New York City police members about me. Joe said, "We couldn't find anyone to say a bad word about you, and we tried."

Of course, Joe Weaver is the same guy who later, in a hallway press conference at the City-County Building, stern-facedly said, "Commissioner Spreen, did you know that your predecessor Ray Girardin, before he took the job of Police Commissioner, was seven feet tall and didn't have a line in his face?" That burst my seams when he came out with that. You may remember that Ray Girardin was probably about 5 feet, 6 inches and often was referred to as "Prune Face."

I met with Ray Girardin at the Park Shelton just before being sworn in by Mayor Cavanagh. Ray was very cordial, friendly, and helpful. I believe he also was quite happy to be relieved of his burdensome responsibility. I'm sure the years as Police Commissioner, coupled with the riot of 1967, had taken a toll on him.

Joe Loesche, the Aide to the Police Commissioner, also visited and introduced himself to me at the Park Shelton before the swearing in. I found him a cheerful buoyant man with an air of confidant "joi' de vivre" about him. Joe turned out to be invaluable to me as this newcomer from New York, who knew no one in the city or its police department.

Cliff Owens, who had temporarily been assigned to me by the Mayor, also impressed me as a gentle warm human being. He was of great help to my family and me. I was shocked and saddened when some months later he was stricken by a fatal heart attack early one morning after his arrival for a tour of duty at the Mayor's office. We felt a great loss.

My day, July 22, 1968, arrived. Johannes Spreen, once a little immigrant lad landing at Ellis Island from Germany, who later joined and served as a cop in the New York City Police Department, would today take the helm as Police Commissioner of the fifth largest city in America. This city was struggling, badly shaken by the disastrous events of a year past, to right itself. This was a city that before those chilling events had been looked upon in the pages of national magazines as a model city, during the halcyon days of its young Mayor, Jerome P. Cavanagh. Love, Dad

Preparing Myself for Detroit

Dear Betty,

I had a month before starting my new job as Police Commissioner, so I gathered as much information as I could about Detroit and its past history.

The most pervasive fact confronting a new commissioner of police in Detroit in the summer of 1968 was that the city had suffered through one of the most serious urban riots in American history the previous summer, and fear of a repetition hung over city officials and police.

But it was not the only city in the nation that had felt the tremors of civil unrest and the heat of racial passion. And as far as I could see, the seriousness of the crime situation was typical of major cities generally, and not peculiar to Detroit.

Appraised from the police point of view, Detroit's profile included such features as these.

The city was the nation's fifth largest in population.

Its police department was also the fifth largest.

Detroit ranked fourth nationally in the total number of crimes known to the police, a circumstance ascribed by some analysts to the understatement of totals reported from Philadelphia, a city which stood slightly ahead of Detroit in most other statistics, rather than to a disproportionate amount of crime in Detroit.

In certain types of serious crimes, including murder, robbery and burglary, Detroit ranked third.

Like some other major cities confined within geographical boundaries, the population within the city limits had been shrinking in spite of a massive growth in the suburbs.

Within the city proper, black citizens accounted for more than one-third of the total population. Black pupils accounted for more than one-half of the public school population. But black officers accounted for only about six per cent of the police force.

I then took a look at the crime trends. As was true of many cities, Detroit's crime rate was rising. And as far as anyone could tell, racial tension remained high.

On the opposite side of the coin, as far as I could see, in spite of a few bad apples widely publicized locally, the Detroit police force was fundamentally sound.

Most city officials seemed to me to be alert and responsive to the problems. Detroit may not have been a graft-free city, but it seemed considerably cleaner than my recollections of New York.

Organized business leadership in Detroit had a consistent "track record" of broad community concern and deep involvement in the solution of community problems.

As far as the racial pulse of the city was concerned, while more blacks than whites were disadvantaged economically, most blacks as well as whites were enjoying a generally high level of economic prosperity.

While the city's problems were serious, it also had some important assets, and the picture was not totally dark.

The memory of the 1967 riot overshadowed all approaches to crime control. A concerted civic effort to unravel the causes of the riot and deal with them had already produced some healthy results and had created an ongoing mechanism aimed at keeping channels of communication open between all segments of the community.

This mechanism was an unusual organization called New Detroit, Inc., which began as a temporary committee of concerned citizens. It was launched out of a meeting called by Michigan's Governor George Romney, and Detroit's Mayor Jerome P. Cavanagh, on July 27, 1967, the fifth day of the riot. Some 150 attended the meeting, and organized a committee of 39 people.

An established civic assistance organization financed by private funds, the Metropolitan Fund of Detroit, provided an initial staff structure and housing. Eventually New Detroit incorporated, expanded, and developed the capacity to obtain as much as $10 million a year from major business donors in Detroit. They invested the money in projects principally designed to help disadvantaged and minority groups in a variety of areas such as housing, education, employment, community services, recreation and others.

New Detroit came to be operated by a cadre of paid staff, a substantial number of volunteers from private industry who served a fixed period (six months) and were paid by their normal employers for their time. They had a board of trustees of such breadth that it permitted ADC mothers, black ghetto militants, and neighborhood improvement leaders to discuss problems and issues face to face with the established political and economic leadership of the city, including the heads of the major auto companies.

As I took office as commissioner, New Detroit was pointed out to me, and accepted by me, as a significant civic resource and a remarkable indicator of the city's capacity to develop its own means for bettering communication between citizens and stimulating self help.

It was a tremendous idea and an exceptional organization. Much to my regret and to the detriment of the police department and the city, I eventually ended up in public disagreement with some of the leadership of New Detroit over the organization's approach to helping the police. I'll explain more about that later.

Love, Dad

Detroit's History

Dear Betty,

I told you about New Detroit earlier. Now let me tell you about Detroit. I realized it was simply a fresh manifestation of what the Frenchman, Alexis de Tocqueville, had noted nearly a century and a half earlier in his book, *Democracy in America.* He wrote about the American predilection and capacity for organizing locally to handle emergencies when they arose.

De Tocqueville pursued his investigations into the warp, woof, manners and mores of this interesting new nation on the west side of the Atlantic in the 1830s. Detroit was little more than an outpost of civilization, a few thousand people, situated on one of the major commercial bottlenecks of the Great Lakes. The traffic of Lakes Superior, Michigan and Huron all funneled into Lake Erie through the strait (etroit) on which the French first built the Fort D'Etroit in 1701 as a fur trading post.

Like most American cities, Detroit put the problem of effective policing on the back burner until well into the 19th century. At that time, population increase and a civic disturbance of crisis proportions generated the creation of a full-time paid police force.

For the first century of its existence, Detroit was a garrison town, and keeping the public peace was handled by the military. This fell to the French military until 1760, and the British military for the next 36 years.

The explorer Antoine de la Mothe Cadillac built the first "Fort of the Strait" on the body of water now called the Detroit River. Trappers and farmer/settlers who gathered around its wooden palisades were protected by a small contingent of French soldiers. The military commandant dealt with any crimes that occurred, sending suspects back to the capital of French colonial America in Quebec for trial and punishment.

Wolfe's victory over Montcalm at Quebec, which settled the French and Indian War and ended French rule in North America, occurred in 1756. The pace of treaty-making and adjustments to this decisive fact was such that it was 1760 before a British garrison finally took over from the French.

After the American Revolution, concluding with Cornwallis' surrender in 1781 and the Treaty of Paris in 1783, an even lengthier delay took place before actual control was handed over. The British garrison simply stayed and stayed, and apparently did a conscientious job of policing.

From this period, a quaint record still remains of certain ordinance violations in town, which were reported by the British lieutenant in charge of the guard to the American civil magistrate: "cow straying, hogs running loose, a citizen galloping in a no-galloping zone, and a cart parked in the street illegally overnight."

The new American government in 1787 passed the Northwest Ordinance establishing the framework of government for the Great Lakes territories beyond the boundaries of the original 13 states, including Detroit. An American territorial government and civil laws were created, while still the British garrison stayed on. It was 1796 before the British Army finally yielded its occupancy of Detroit to the community's first American military commandant, Col. John Hamtramck.

Detroit was officially incorporated as a town by the territorial assembly in 1802, and authorized a single law enforcement officer, a marshal, who was appointed by the territorial legislature. A huge segment of the Northwest Territory, larger than the present state of Michigan, was designated a "county," and named in honor of General "Mad Anthony" Wayne, who had defeated the Indians at the Battle of Fallen

Timbers, near the present Michigan-Ohio boundary. As peace officers for this vast region, a sheriff and a few constables were named.

This handful of "peace officers" was inadequate. It was the first of many expedients tried by the citizens of Detroit in 1804, when a night watch of five men was employed, to watch out for Indian attacks and fires. The night watch lasted three months. A disastrous fire wiped out the town the following summer.

Another temporary watch was tried in 1825, after a "firebug" scare.

The night watch was revived again in 1833, after citizens rioted to prevent the local sheriff from returning two runaway slaves to their Southern owner.

Another watch experiment in 1835 disintegrated when half of the complement of 12 men was found drunk and disorderly the first month.

An attempt by citizens to enforce morality without due process of law occurred in 1841, when the town marshal was persuaded by local civic leaders to tear down a notorious whorehouse. The disorderly house owner took the case to court and the marshal had to pay damages.

In 1859, downtown merchants became disturbed and hired a private patrol to protect their businesses. Finally in 1861 a police "commission" of three was created. The commission's weakness was laid bare in 1863. In March of that year during the Civil War, a black man accused of attacking a child was tried. The accused man was subsequently pardoned after a review of the evidence. But the trial incited a riot, which ended up in widespread arson and attacks on blacks in general. The small force of 25 men authorized by the police commission, poorly organized and ill-trained, was unable to cope with the situation.

A city alderman named John J. Bagley then went over the heads of the other city fathers and appealed to the State Legislature, which eventually passed the Metropolitan Police Act, founding the present police department in 1865.

Whether they were conscious of it or not, the legislators were following the example of London, England, where Sir Robert Peel had organized the first metropolitan police force in the Anglo-Saxon world in 1829. Similar departments in American cities had begun with Philadelphia in 1833, New York in 1844, Chicago in 1851, Cincinnati in 1852, Baltimore and Newark in 1857, Providence, Rhode Island, in 1864, and others.

As you can see, the police department was brought into being because of a civil disturbance during the Civil War. A city charter written during World War I dictated the present organization. It included an appointed civilian commissioner overseeing a department headed by a professional chief, the superintendent.

And that, my dear, was where I fitted into the picture.

Love, Dad

What I Found in Detroit

Dear Betty,

When I came to Detroit in July of 1968, I knew I was taking office as a "crisis" commissioner. Things had to be done, and done quickly. In addition, the Mayor who appointed me, Jerome P. Cavanagh, indicated that he would probably run for re-election the following year, but his uncertainty told me I might have only 17 months to finish whatever I started.

There was even an atmosphere of crisis about my appointment, since the city had been searching for a police commissioner for nine months. Something like nine candidates turned down the job before I was appointed, including the man who subsequently succeeded me, Patrick Murphy, another ex-New Yorker whom I had known for years.

After I was sworn in on July 22, 1968, the eve of the first anniversary of the Detroit riot of 1967, I "celebrated" the anniversary the following day out on Twelfth Street, the black business avenue where the riot had started. Mayor Cavanagh and I together dedicated a mobile recreation facility for the neighborhood kids, a huge truck trailer filled with water as a "swim-mobile," sponsored by one of the local television stations.

The day was sunny, and the kids were happy, splashing in the water. That night it was a different story.

That night, 300 miles away in Cleveland, there was a shootout between black men and police officers. Seven were killed, including four black civilians and three policemen.

Whether or not the black community felt a seismic tremor from that shootout across Lake Erie, I do not know. But my second night in Detroit was not many hours old when I was down on Twelfth Street again, this time in the darkness of the summer night, inside a scout car full of concerned police top command officers. We cruised slowly up the six-lane-wide street following a sweep of police cars, each with four heavily armed officers.

Even I, who had not seen the riot of 1967, could feel the tension in the air, in the eeriness of the too-empty streets, the rows of storefronts, the expressions on the faces of the Superintendent and the precinct commander riding with me, and the rigidity of their bodies as they stared out the windows.

Any doubts that I'd had about the wisdom of coming to Detroit as police commissioner surfaced right then.

But the few people on the streets dispersed, as the loudspeakers on the scout cars asked them to. Trouble that night was limited to some isolated fire bombings and reports of looting. Here and there a few scampering packs of youngsters were sighted, who disappeared before the police patrols.

Our command car halted, and we had a standup staff conference on the pavement in the middle of Twelfth Street before returning to headquarters. I got to know a lot of the ranking officers in the department in a hurry that night.

The police alert lasted four days, and there were a number of arrests, but there was no repetition of the disaster of 1967.

You and your mother were scared for me that night but proud of me, too.

Love, Dad

The Night I Stifled a Riot

Dear Betty,

One night, I ran into a little problem and the press gave me a little positive coverage. Here is what the *Detroit Scope Magazine* wrote on August 3, 1968, in an article called "He Walked Down 12th Street to Stifle a Riot."

"Caught in the delicate balance between sufficient force and restraint, Police Commissioner Johannes Spreen gave a commendable performance of agility last Thursday morning during the 12th Street incident. Beginning about 12 p.m. with a group of youths breaking windows and setting two cars on fire, the activity slowly mushroomed until a tactical alert was ordered at 2:30 a.m.

"Commissioner Spreen, Superintendent John Nichols, Dept. Superintendent Charles Gentry and Sgt. Harold Liggett, aide to the commissioner, arrived on the scene at 2:45 a.m. By then there were seven fires—two suspected arsons and three started by Molotov cocktails.

"Bullhorn in hand, Spreen walked the uneasy streets urging residents to return to their homes. He remained upon the scene until the tactical alert ended at 6:43 a.m.

"In all, there were 16 arrests, mostly for breaking and entering and one for assault on a Tactical Mobile Unit officer. The officer, uninjured, managed to seize his assailant inflicting only a minor abrasion on his forehead.

"Peace returned with the dawn and the weary commissioner departed 12th Street where the riot seeds were planted last July. Spreen has probably not seen the last of 12th Street, a place where scattered minor incidents mark a return to normalcy. Let's hope that when necessary he can match the way he gently nipped last week's riot."

Betty, if only things had always been that easy. But they just weren't.

Love, Dad

Blacks, Whites and the Golden Rule

Dear Betty,

The experience of stifling a riot on 12th Street convinced me, if I needed any further convincing, that as police commissioner I had to give first priority to dissipating the crisis atmosphere that hung over police community relationships, and warped or hindered police decisions and operations.

Some crisis situations are unavoidable, but a sustained crisis atmosphere curdles individual police attitudes, twists behavior, hurts the community and helps the criminal.

The tragedy of most crises, however, is that they seem to build up out of an accumulation of trivia, to be triggered by trifles. The 1967 Detroit riot grew out of a routine "blind pig" raid.

The Bible gives us a Golden Rule for doing good and avoiding evil, which if followed, would forestall human crises. But when a crisis atmosphere does develop, there's another gold quotation in the Bible that more people should follow. As James, one of the mystery-authors of the New Testament, puts it: "Let every man be quick to hear, but slow to speak and slow to anger, for the wrath of man worketh not the justice of God."

Or in the language of the New Generation, "Cool it."

How can a police commissioner in a modern city today help to "cool it?"

First by practicing the golden rule of James himself, and second, persuading others to follow it, starting with the police, and enlisting the help of all concerned individuals and groups of good will, particularly the media of public communication.

When I ended my term of office as Detroit's police commissioner on January 6, 1970, 17 months and two weeks after being sworn in, I had seen six more crises or near crises develop, all with explosive potentialities. These were the "Happy Riot" following the 1968 World Series, the George Wallace political rally of October 29, 1968, a fracas between off-duty police and black teenagers November 2, 1968, the murder of a police officer and the wounding of his partner by armed militants of the Republic of New Africa March 29, 1969, the anti-Viet Nam War "mobilization" of October 15, 1969, and a series of attempts in December 1969 by anonymous phone callers to provoke a confrontation between Detroit police and local Black Panthers.

The most serious were the police teenager fracas, in which police were the accused, and the Republic of New Africa shooting, in which police were the victims.

There were undoubtedly inappropriate reactions from police officers in their handling of this incident, but the RNA was as serious a threat to the peace and stability of Detroit as the riot of 1967. Since the near boiling point of that shooting and the police reaction, a much more serious event than the "blind pig" raid of July 23, 1967, both police authorities and most responsible citizens took a deliberate "cool it" approach which contributed to a noticeable simmering down of the crisis atmosphere. Citizen participation in the anti-war mobilization, and police response, were both characterized by restraint, and as far as I could tell, mutual respect.

The Black Panther incident was kept from developing into a confrontation situation by police restraint, and "fail safe" checks initiated by police to know Black Panther phone numbers. I know it sounds silly to just call people and talk to them to enlist their help, but that turned out to be very successful.

Love, Dad

Detroit Was Watched by Baseball Fans

Dear Betty,

I told you about that fateful night, July 23rd, 1967, when the Detroit riots began. Let me describe it from the standpoint of people who were watching the Detroit Tigers play the New York Yankees. As people tuned in to see the game on television, little did they know that three miles away from the Tiger Stadium, there was much unrest. Willie Horton and Earl Wilson were black Detroit Tiger players, but generally black baseball players were not altogether welcome. There was a 30% unemployment rate for blacks in Detroit and it was not Lyndon Johnson's "Great Society."

As the game progressed, black clouds of smoke and fire appeared on the horizon. The Tigers split a double header with the Yankees. Buildings and homes began burning that night over a 25 square mile area. Baseball concession stands closed early. Airlines cancelled flights. The Mayor issued a curfew. Governor George Romney sent in federal troops and President Johnson sent in 5,000 troops.

For baseball fans, Detroit was winning but there was still the final game to be won. There were 15,000 empty seats because fans were afraid to come out. The home team was trailing but rallied in the 9th inning, only to lose in over time.

So 1968 was going to be the chance for the Detroit Tigers to break back. Martin Luther King, Jr. and Robert Kennedy were assassinated in the spring of 1968, and many thought there would be fights again.

But it was the year of the Tigers. We set a home attendance record and Detroit was called Tigertown, U.S.A. It was between the St. Louis

Cardinals and the Detroit Tigers. The Cardinals had led the series until the final game, which was played in St. Louis. Jose Feliciano sang the *National Anthem* and although some might have found his version too modern, I thought it was just right. The "City on Fire" shut down to watch the game.

The stadium was filled to capacity. The Tigers finally won their first pennant since 1945. Mayor Cavanagh, using the V for Victory, said the win saved the city. When the Tigers won it, black and white fans gathered at the airport to greet the winners. It seemed like life was back to normal again. But I knew the problems that still lingered. I'll describe them for you in my next letters.

Love, Dad

I Wanted the Police to Be Professional

Dear Betty,

You remember how much I valued professionalism. I hadn't been at my post in Detroit long when I gave a talk on the subject. I called it "Police Professionalism." Here was the gist of what I tried to say.

I believe that relationships between the public and the police pervade the entire spectrum of police activities. Of late, these relationships may have been sensitive and thorny, and one of the major goals of my administration is to continue the work that has been done to remove questions about these relationships from the firing line of concern. We would hope that there would be no question regarding the methods of this department or the actions of its officers. We hope that our actions and methods will be accepted by Detroit's citizens as professional and proper.

Some of the members of the Detroit press have dubbed me "Detroit's Top Cop." This is very flattering but it describes what I think all of Detroit's police officers should be; that is, tops in performance, tops in training, tops in efficiency, and accepted by the community as tops. As a matter of fact, the way in which I like to view my job as Detroit's Police Commissioner is just one of some 4,700 "Top Cops."

We need to do everything possible to bolster the many good cops, not talk so much about hanging the few bad ones. I have said that I will not tolerate unprofessional conduct. There is no room for bias, bigotry, or brutality in police work. This means that any officer who cannot give a fair shake to each citizen must be shaken from the tree. We cannot afford to have any rotten apples.

But the problem of police in a democratic society is not merely a matter of obtaining newer technological and scientific equipment nor of recruiting men who have to their credit more years of education. What must occur is a significant alteration in the ideology of police, so that police professionalism rests on the values of a democratic legal order. It is vital to recognize that order is not the ultimate end of government in a free society.

Properly understood, this end is perhaps best expressed in the phrase "law and justice in an orderly society." This way of putting it captures the idea of the American dream for all our people, implying equal protection of the law and respect for the rights of all persons. Every citizen in a free society is entitled to be treated as an individual on the basis of his individual acts, and not as a group.

Professionalism in police work is measured by a number of gauges. It includes firmness, fairness and impartiality in the performance of police duties. It involves courtesy and consideration, even compassion, in dealing with people. Loyalty, integrity, and strict adherence to a code of ethics are part and parcel of the professionalism. Additionally, professionalism means self-respect as well as pride in the uniform and the badge of a police officer.

Professionalism involves first, the duty to serve mankind generally rather than self, individuals, or groups.

Second, there is a duty to be fully prepared for service before entering active practice.

Third, there is a duty to work continuously to improve skills by all means available and to freely communicate professional information.

Fourth, there is a duty to employ full skill at all times, regardless of personal gain, comfort, or safety, and to assist fellow professionals whenever necessary.

Fifth, there is the duty to regulate practice by the franchising of practitioners, setting the highest practicable intellectual and technical standards, judging fellow professionals solely upon considerations of merit, being constantly alert to protect society from improper and unethical practices through swift and ready disenfranchisement.

Sixth, there is the duty to zealously guard the honor of the profession by living exemplary lives, recognizing that injury to a group serving society injures society.

And finally, there is a duty to give constant attention to the improvement of self-discipline, recognizing that the individual must be the master of himself to be the servant of others.

Regarding professionalism, J. Edgar Hoover, Director of the Federal Bureau of Investigation said, "If every officer and law enforcement agency must suffer in some degree from charges made against other officers, we cannot afford to take a passive view, shrugging the matter off as none of our business. I believe that it is the duty of every officer in every law enforcement agency to take a personal interest in maintaining a high standard of conduct within his organization."

I have talked a great deal about the officer's personal role in acting professionally and in achieving professionalism. Police administrators also have an important part in this endeavor. We must give police officers the training, which is essential to professional performance.

In Detroit, Common Council did not provide training after Police Academy graduation so I started "Seven Minute Seminars" by video with private funding.

Training encourages the development of the professional ABCs: Attitude, Behavior, and Conduct. Our men are well-selected, well-qualified, and well-trained and we want to make every effort to give them *more* training, *new* methods, and *better* machines so that they can do the job that must be done.

I do want to emphasize that although our recent recruiting efforts have been successful, we still need more good men. Send me your best. We offer an opportunity to *all* young men in the community to become part of a profession with pride. We need the finest young men to maintain the level of professionalism so necessary in modern police work.

Police officers are men with as much brain as brawn. Increasingly in the future we will need men and women trained in such diverse fields as sociology and psychology, in chemistry and physics, in computer technology and systems analysis, in communications engineering, and in highly sophisticated criminological and investigative techniques. In and of itself, police work is a satisfying, rewarding, and challenging career and it offers a great opportunity for service in the interest of humanity.

Well, my dear, you see the direction I was taking. But there were some rotten apples and they had to be dealt with.
Love, Dad

The Best Policing Prevents Crime

Dear Betty,

You might be interested in my speech about preventing crime by making policemen part of the community again by using scooters. I will paraphrase it for you.

Progress toward police professionalism has thus far emphasized the scientific and technological advances in the field. Important as these are, we may have unintentionally proceeded along a mistaken path to professionalism. We have become more efficient, but perhaps also more cold and impersonal. In fact, the emphasis on scientific advancement may tend to embody the police officer with the characteristics of *Dragnet* Sgt. Joe Friday's bureaucratic "just the facts, ma'am," impersonality.

I see two trends in this progress, which may indicate that we have been traveling on the wrong road to professionalism. Policemen have become over isolated and over-specialized. The result may be that we have lost sight of the essence of the police function, which is the reduction of crime and community tension through *preventive* efforts.

We have placed the majority of our patrol force in impersonal vehicles with flashing lights and screeching sirens, and we have asked this force to respond as quickly as possible to calls for help. Thus, we have isolated the policeman from the people he serves. When a policeman does have contact with people, we forced him to act as a controller or regulator of a situation that has already occurred.

We need to take a new direction on the road toward combating crime and violence, and that is a road toward the people. I introduced the scooter in New York and while it may not be the final answer, it seems to be the best means presently available. It offers greater range and mobility at less manpower expense than foot patrol. It allows for greater observation than a car, since the patrolman has 360-degree visibility and moves at less than auto speed.

I believe that scooters make our patrol force part of the community again. It also gives us a chance to pay as much attention to crime before the fact as to crime after-the-fact.

That was the gist of what I told them in Detroit, and I think a lot of them probably laughed. But look what has happened across the country. The trend toward community policing has police and security forces perhaps not using scooters but using bicycles and doing the very thing that I was advocating. So it must have been a pretty good idea.
Love, Dad

The Police Role

Dear Betty,

I thought it was important for the people to see the true role of the police. So I gave a public speech to bring out the protective nature of the police-citizen relationship. It included these ideas.

I believe that the police officer occupies a most important role in today's society. To most citizens he represents the front line of defense against crime. He, more than anyone else, is symbolic of the governmental establishment because he is in constant and daily contact with each of the various segments of the population.

Every police-citizen contact necessarily involves a measure of intimacy. Police action can affect a citizen's dignity, self-respect, sense of privacy, or his civil rights. Thus, by his actions, a police officer brings to the police profession, and to government itself, the commendation or the condemnation of the citizenry he serves.

No doubt, the police are condemned by the nature of their work to bear the brunt of resentment against authority. This is an era in which traditional ideas and institutions are being challenged with increasing insistence. The poor want an equal opportunity to share in America's wealth. Minority groups want an end to any form of discrimination.

The urban policeman tends to become a pawn between those forces of the community pressing for stricter law enforcement and those who charge "police brutality" at every turn, between those who demand that he "get tough" and those who admonish him to respect the rights of individuals, between those who insist that he prevent crime and stop riots and those who insist that he be reasonable in the use of force.

Not only is the policeman thus called upon to serve incompatible ends; he is often frustrated because he has to deal with ills resulting from the social and economic failures of the community. Thus, the policeman has become the visible symbol of the shame of society.

It saddens me, having been a police officer and as Police Commissioner, to see that the police have become such a thorny issue in this so-called crisis of law and order. As the most visible symbol of government, police officers get most of the blame for our failures and little of the credit for our successes. Of course, the police do not enact the laws they enforce, nor do they judge or punish the persons they arrest.

It is a formidable assignment to perform efficiently and with discretion the complicated law enforcement and community service tasks the police are expected to perform. In urban areas, the very places that perhaps need and want effective policing the most, there is much distrust of the police. Policemen are sometimes sneered at or insulted in the street. Sometimes they are kicked or spit upon. Citizen hostility toward the police is just as disruptive of law and order as police indifference to or mistreatment of citizens.

Police work today must strike out in new directions if it is to cope with the problems and issues confronting our society. "Law Protection Officer" is perhaps a more suitable term than "Law Enforcement Officer." The police officer is a fellow citizen concerned with the protection and safeguarding of his fellow citizen's rights. The policeman is the watchful protector for every individual in the community.

What may be needed is a full-scale selling campaign to salvage the term "police," and present it to a concerned community in a new and acceptable version. Perhaps I can best illustrate this by an acronym that may well spell out a new spirit of law enforcement in Detroit.

I like to think that police, P-O-L-I-C-E, stands for Protectors Of Liberty, for the Individual, for the Community collectively, and for everyone Equally.

The police officer is a protector of liberty. He, more than anyone else, protects society from the deeds and threats of persons or forces that might be repressive or harassing. Practically, liberty is the freedom to do the things you want to do as long as you don't infringe on the freedom of others to do likewise.

While policemen everywhere must still be proficient in the bringing of a lawbreaker before the bar of justice, the emphasis should be placed on their responsibility for peacekeeping, crime prevention, protecting neighbors from harm and unlawful infringement of human rights.

Frequently the policeman is called upon to handle civil rights demonstrations, anti-war protests, "legalize marijuana" love-ins, open housing marches, labor disputes and freedom rallies. The policeman can take only one side and that is on behalf of the law.

The police officer protects you as an individual. You should regard him as your protector against the forces of evil. The police officer is the one to whom you turn in time of trouble. He is there to protect and serve the community, all of the individuals who make up the community. The E in police stands for "everyone equally." This means that the police officer is the protector of liberty for everyone regardless of race, creed, color or what have you.

A policeman is much like the umpire in a baseball game. He is there as an impartial arbiter and we expect him to call the plays as he sees them. And we have to respect his judgment even when he calls the shots against the team we're rooting for. He is the expert on the rules. And he has the best possible viewpoint from which to see the action.

It seems to me that the only alternative in policing is that either we do the job or we live in an armed camp. Either we do the job professionally and have it accepted by the community, or we had better purchase tons of armored vehicles and get them out on the streets.

I want to repeat the assurance that I have made to the people of Detroit; that we will fight crime and we will do it in such a manner as to gain acceptance by all citizens. Let everyone know that we will not back away from those few who threaten the lives and property of the law-abiding majority in this community. We plan to give our men, who will be well selected, well qualified, and well trained, every method and machine at our disposal to help them accomplish this task. I am glad to say that I have seen some changes in the direction of my thoughts in many communities across the country in the past several years but so very much work is still needed.

I was proud of my words but they must be followed up with good deeds.
Love, Dad

Second Police Car Bombed

Dear Betty,

This letter may remind you of how high the tension was during the time I was police commissioner. The *Detroit Free Press* wrote this on September 7, 1968, under the title "All-Night Sentinels Ordered: 2d Police Car Bombed."

Love, Dad

> The second dynamiting of a Detroit policeman's private car within a week prompted police officials Friday to order an all-night guard on parking lots at all precinct station houses.
>
> Commissioner Johannes Spreen said that ordering the surveillance was 'robbing Peter to pay Paul,' in light of his recent order that police will no longer respond to calls on family squabbles and minor crime.
>
> He said he has ordered Deputy Superintendent Charles Gentry to study the possibility of using volunteer police reserves for the guard duty, but he declared: 'In the meantime, we will give police precincts all the additional security, particularly in the nighttime, that they need.'
>
> The latest blast, at 2:50 a.m. Friday, destroyed a 1965 Plymouth owned by Patrolman Richard Lloyd.
>
> Officers said the explosion probably was generated by 10 to 12 fuse-lit sticks of dynamite. It demolished Lloyd's car and blew one tire over a group of trees and into Nardin Ave., a block away. It also blew a five-inch crater in the asphalt driveway.
>
> A car parked next to Lloyd's auto was damaged extensively, and several other cars in the lot suffered lesser damage.
>
> The blast came a week after a similar explosion struck a car in Detroit's Woodward Precinct.

Scooters Nab Rape Suspect

Dear Betty,

Sometimes there was good news to report and the press was often cooperative. I needed the press to commend officers on scooters because some cops wanted a "macho" image and thought scooters were too sissified for this. The *Detroit Free Press* printed this story on October 24, 1968.

Love, Dad

> Apprehension of a suspected rapist by two scooter rangers led Police Commissioner Johannes Spreen Wednesday to express 'gratitude' for the performance of police scooter units.
>
> The incident in Grand Circus Park occurred Tuesday night when a girl's screams brought the two scooter patrolmen to the scene, Spreen said. They followed the assailant and caught him two blocks from the park.
>
> The Rangers were working with special Area X teams recently instituted.
>
> 'Since Monday, scooter operation in two precincts clearly demonstrates that the people are talking to the scooter rangers and the rangers are talking to the people. Their records show they have made 202 to 927 street contacts a day,' Spreen said. This would be impossible with scout cars,' Spreen added.
>
> He said the rangers had made more than a dozen arrests, had issued numerous tickets and had investigated 31 persons.

Youths Commit Most Crime

Dear Betty,

When I was in Detroit, one of our biggest problems was how to deal with young people. I spoke to the police about my ideas and started off with the population distribution at that time. Here's a condensed version of what I said.

There is much unrest in America today, particularly in the nation's largest cities. This is a time when traditional ideas and institutions are being questioned and challenged with increasing ardor. The police are faced with a special problem resulting from the fact that almost half of our population is under 25 years of age.

This generation has been described as perhaps the most passionate, dedicated and discontented generation since the 1930s. They seem to be activist, agnostic, radical, frightening to their parents, heartening to their fellows, as well as an entire simmering subculture.

Some of these descriptive words mean that young people are concerned, that they are questioning some of our traditional ideas and institutions. If our ideas and institutions cannot stand up to these questions, then they must be changed in a progressive but orderly fashion. For the measure of this country has not been how much dissent it can suppress, but how much it can tolerate; not how rigidly its institutions defend themselves, but how gracefully they yield to wise change; not how much we fear our young people, but how much we trust them.

Our younger citizens are becoming increasingly involved in national problems: in their idealism, they have seen ambiguities that exist in our communities and have become disenchanted with the enormous gaps they see between American ideals and American achievements. The feelings of discontent that arise out of these discoveries affect young people in the suburbs and on college campuses as well as in the slum areas.

A small but voluble minority has allied with radically militant protest forces. The common denominator that links these people seems to be a loss of faith in the American dream. Young adults and minority group members charge that this loss of faith was inspired by parents, teachers, and clergymen who taught them the American dream but failed to practice it. When these people attempt to justify disruption as a means to an end, they claim that the civil rights movement made protest legitimate, the Viet Nam war made it popular, and the slowness of change through traditional channels makes it a practical necessity.

There are two striking facts about American crime. Boys and young men commit most crimes and most crimes are committed in cities. The communities' social institutions have not found ways to motivate young people to live moral lives. Some have not even recognized their duty to seek such ways. Youth who have not received love and strong parental guidance, or whose experience leads them to believe that society is callous, are people with whom the community is ill-prepared to cope. Boredom corrodes ambition and cynicism corrupts those with ethical sensitivity.

Adolescents are at a notoriously sensitive age and are ready to see themselves as victims of police harassment. Abuse of authority, real or imagined, may seriously impair their respect for authority and produce deep resentment. Police professionalism demands that youngsters receive the treatment that is neither unfair nor degrading, just as any other citizen.

The policeman is symbolic of the government and this invites the rebellion of youth against the establishment. In Michigan, the individual police officer has the right to use his discretion when he contacts a juvenile. Good instincts can tell a policeman that a crime may be about to happen. He can choose whether to pass by, stop for a few words of general banter, ask juveniles some questions about themselves and where they are going, or send/take them home. If a violation has actually occurred, the officer may take the youngster into the precinct for further questioning.

Clearly, it is with young people that prevention efforts are most needed and hold the greatest promise. For every youngster we can salvage, we may have prevented future crimes. For every step we take to combat juvenile delinquency, we may save one youngster from a life of adult criminality. We have a responsibility to help our future citizens through the difficulties they face in maturing and to help make them responsible, law-abiding, interested and involved adults.

I hoped, my dear, that this speech might help the police officers recognize their role in preventing youngsters from becoming criminals. I know from their reactions that some began to think more carefully about their contacts with youth. Oh, that it might continue.
Love, Dad

Police Boss Needs Two Heads

Dear Betty,

When I was the Detroit Police Commissioner, I was helping to promote the department's "Police and Youth in Sports" program. I turned out to do my thing dressed in sweats and sneakers. I noticed that a boy, about 10 or 12 years old, was giving me a close inspection with a puzzled look in his eye. As soon as he realized I was looking at him, he said:

"Are you really the Commissioner?"

"Yes," I said, "I really am."

He stared at me again. "Well, you sure don't look like a commissioner."

I asked him, "Why do you think that?"

"The Commissioner in Batman doesn't dress like that!"

Of course, I laughed and said that I dressed differently on different occasions, to do all the things that a commissioner had to do.

"After all," I said, "I don't have Batman to help me." Many times I wished I did.

The boy's question was a provocative one. I began to wonder what would a modern day urban police commissioner really look like?

He'd need at least two heads. One would accentuate the positive and the other would counteract the negative. He'd have to wear many hats and be prepared for quick changes. He'd need about six arms to keep in touch with the white community, the black community, the police, the mayor's office, the City Council and civic organizations.

He'd need a magician's wand and a bag of tricks to make bad turn into good, and to make essential resources materialize out of thin air. He'd need the sense of balance of a tightrope walker, and the patience of Job, and a sense of humor to fall back on when everything else failed. At times, a disappearing act would be most appropriate.

He must live by the Golden Rule and the Ten Commandments, uphold the Constitution of the United States and the Constitution of the State of Michigan, operate in accordance with the ordinances of the city, and protect the rights of all citizens by monitoring obedience to the laws of the city, state and nation by the people of his community.

To accomplish his mission, he must recognize and deal with the external pressures of politics, people and groups and their personal, racial, social or economic biases; including those who want to help and those who want to hinder.

He has parallel internal pressures to manage, including politics with the police department, the problems and frustrations of the individual police officer and the special concerns of the police organizations.

He has to establish and maintain the necessary equilibrium of money, men, materials, machines, new methods, and personal motivation. The better-educated, intellectually inquisitive citizen of today is questioning the application of police power. The sharpness of the current Law and Order debate reflects the general confusion over the excessive or inadequate employment of that power. It is the commissioner's role to help bridge the gap between conflicting views of the proper exercise of police power, and to provide the necessary citizen-oriented policy control over the police department.

The very word "police" is derived from an ancient word that meant "citizen" and "city." The policing function is derived from the effective exercise of citizenship and of government, and is for the benefit, not the oppression, of people.

Police power is the power of government to ensure the general health, welfare and safety, and to protect the freedoms and rights of all by guarding against abuses of individual liberty. This power has always been carefully limited under our Constitution. Today's police commissioner has to be able to apply our traditional public philosophy of limited police power to be sure it remains both limited and effective.

How can he best do this? By pointing out to the community the discrepancy between what it expects from its police and how it equips them to meet those expectations; pointing out to police the discrepancy between the professional ideal and the conventional levels of performance; working within the department to upgrade police performance; and working with the community to upgrade community awareness of the power, problems and promise of their police.

You can see how the little boy's question about Batman's police commissioner set me to thinking. I wonder where that little fellow is today.

Love, Dad

My Response to an Incident

Dear Betty,

Incidents always occur. I issued this statement to the Common Council on November 7, 1968, about an alleged incident at Veteran's Memorial Building on November 1st and 2nd. They wanted to bring in outside investigators like the state or the F.B.I. I wanted the opportunity to investigate first and after my investigation, we suspended nine policemen and fired three.

Love, Dad

> If the facts as alleged are true:
>
> Then I can only express abhorrence and dismay at the actions of a handful of officers. I am further saddened by the knowledge that if this matter is not resolved quickly, fairly, equitably (with the principle of equal justice firmly in mind) that this can seriously reflect on 4,700 other police officers, who were not there, were not on the scene, and I am certain are not in sympathy with such actions.
>
> The point that is missed by some police officers is that they occupy a unique position in society, because they are sworn to uphold the law, to provide protection of life and property, and to protect the human and civil rights we enjoy in a land of liberty, therefore, they certainly cannot be above the law.
>
> The police officer has taken an oath to uphold the laws of the land. When such a man, selected by society to represent them, violates the rights of others, he in effect violates our trust in him and also our rights. It diminishes all of us, and certainly public confidence in law is seriously weakened. We must have the confidence of the public in the just and orderly processes of law or else respect for authority will become an illusion never to be grasped.

Not only can we not break the law but also there is accountability to our fellow members of the police profession, not only in this city but all throughout America.

If the facts as alleged are true:

Then some off-duty police officers engaged in unlawful and improper conduct and actions.

The Detroit Police Department cannot and will not tolerate any unlawful actions on the part of individual officers (whether on or off duty)!

A crime committed by anyone is reprehensible, certainly the more so when committed by someone sworn to prevent crime and to protect his neighbor and fellow citizen.

The constitution of the United States and the State of Michigan and laws duly adopted guarantee to everyone equal protection under those laws.

None of us want an officer or officers who could have committed such acts as alleged.

There is no room in this department for such a man, no department can possibly rise above him if his actions are condoned and allowed. I have the utmost faith in the overwhelming preponderance of the men and women in this department, in their high caliber and their excellence. This department must be maintained so that we can continue to strive for a profession with pride.

I ask that any member of this department or anyone that was at the affair to come forward and bring it to the attention of District Inspector James Bannon. I have issued an administrative directive to all members of the department to this effect.

This department, including the leaders of the various department organizations and I, are as anxious as anyone else to find the truth and deal with it as quickly as possible.

I feel that this department can and will conduct a full, fair, complete and impartial investigation and I want that opportunity.

Grand Jury Probe of Incident

Dear Betty,

The next day, November 8, 1968, the following article appeared in the *Detroit News* on the incident I just wrote you about. They were going to give me a chance to handle this my way.

> The Wayne County prosecutor's office hinted today at the possibility of a grand jury investigation into charges that off-duty Detroit policemen attacked a group of Negro teenagers after a dance last weekend.
>
> But James H. Brickley, chief assistant prosecutor, emphasized that such a development would have to await the results of a probe headed by Police Commissioner Johannes Spreen.
>
> 'We would look into any evidence of criminality,' Brickley said, 'if we were satisfied that the appropriate law enforcement agency was not investigating.
>
> 'This happened less than a week ago, and Mayor Cavanagh and Commissioner Spreen have indicated they are giving this matter top priority. It would be inappropriate for us to inject ourselves at this particular stage and this particular moment.
>
> 'But it may well turn out to be a proper case for the grand jury if we run into reluctant witnesses although we have no evidence of that at this time.'
>
> State Senator Coleman A. Young, Detroit Democrat, said parents of some of the children involved 'either already have or soon will' request that Wayne County's new 23-member grand jury investigate the fracas which allegedly occurred early Saturday outside the Veterans Memorial Building.
>
> At least four Negro youths charged they were attacked and beaten by officers.

The youngsters were attending a church-sponsored dance while policemen were attending a function of the Detroit Police Officers Wives Association on separate floors of the building.

The Police Department investigation has run into criticism by some city councilmen, Young and several Negro leaders in Detroit.

Brickley, however, indicated that the department's investigation has not had time to produce results.

'I am confident,' he said, 'that both Mayor Cavanagh and Spreen, by what they have said in this case as well as by what I know to be their past performance, will do everything within their power to see that this matter is thoroughly and honestly investigated.

'I also am confident that if they find they are foreclosed from further investigation, that they will ask us to use the grand jury for whatever investigative power it has.'

The grand jury, which will begin operating next week, has the power to subpoena witnesses and take testimony under oath. It is presently charged with investigating charges of criminal activity in the Highland Park Police Department and the slaying of a State Police detective last summer in Inkster.

Well, Betty, you can see that my 100-day honeymoon was over.
Love, Dad

Who's the Boss of Detroit Police?

Dear Betty,

This interesting article by David Cooper in the *Detroit Free Press* on November 10, 1968, picked up on many of my problems. How can one person please the police union, the press, the politicians, the people and the police all at the same time?

Love, Dad

> Detroit faces a growing crisis over control of its police department and policemen. Some city officials fear a Detroit version of Robert McNamara's 'Battle of the Pentagon' with the national's military establishment.
>
> Mayor Cavanagh concedes the crisis exists. So do Negro leaders, but they are not certain Cavanagh will exercise enough authority to cope with it.
>
> The announcement late Saturday by Police Commissioner Johannes Spreen that department investigators have identified the off-duty police who beat Negro youths after a police dance at the Veterans Memorial last Saturday may help alleviate some of their fears.
>
> But the broad question remains: Who runs the department? The police themselves or the City of Detroit? The City Charter makes it clear who is supposed to run the Police Department: The civilian authority or the City of Detroit.
>
> Recent events, however, have shown that Mayor Cavanagh and his new police commissioner, Johannes Spreen, are having difficulty asserting their authority.
>
> Item: Private directives from Cavanagh to Spreen in August about police recruiting of Negroes turn up mysteriously in the

hands of a hostile city councilman, Philip Van Antwerp, who uses them to criticize the mayor for causing 'low morale' among police.

Item: Cavanagh admits that these same orders to Spreen on Negro recruiting are not followed by the Police Department.

Item: Shortly after Spreen names Marvin Brown, a Negro, as his top aide for community relations, Van Antwerp obtains material from police personnel files on Brown's record as a police recruit over a decade ago. Van Antwerp used the material in an effort to undercut Cavanagh and Spreen.

Item: During the recent bitter election campaign over a proposed change in the policemen's pension system, Spreen asks his 4,700 troops not to put bumper stickers opposing the change on city cars, or to campaign against the proposal while in uniform.

Item: As high-level police officials try to investigate the alleged beating of Negro teenagers by off-duty policemen, Cavanagh complains that the police are not cooperating with the probe. Again, Spreen had to issue a formal order to policemen requiring them to step forward with the information.

Item: The police union becomes more bumptious and demanding. The police longed to defeat the pension change at the polls Nov. 5. The union lost narrowly in the election; the pension change was approved by voters. City officials heaved signs of relief, mainly because the union's political muscle had been weakened somewhat.

Sources close to the new commissioner say Spreen, since taking office last summer, has tried not to ruffle the feathers of the department's rank and file. Rather he has attempted to gain the confidence of his men.

The question in the minds of some city officials is whether Spreen has tried too hard to woo the police rank and file and in the process not clearly shown that he is the boss.

The commissioner showed Saturday he wants to command the department. The question now is whether the police rank and file will let him.

Prosecutor May Try Police in Beatings

Dear Betty,

This article by Herbert H. Boldt came out in the *Detroit News* on November 14, 1968. We reacted extremely quickly to name, picture, and suspend all officers charged with offenses against the black youth.
Love, Dad

> Nine suspended Detroit policemen face trial board action and possible criminal charges in the beating of several Negro youths after a Nov. 1 dance at the Veterans Memorial Building.
>
> The suspensions were announced at a press conference yesterday by Police Commissioner Johannes F. Spreen who said they were based on a 'thorough and painstaking' departmental investigation of the incident.
>
> Spreen withheld details of the incident, which has increased tension between the Police Department and the Negro community, but he said it followed a 'series of confrontations' between the off-duty officers and the youngsters, some of whom are members of prominent Detroit families.
>
> Both groups had been attending dances on separate floors of the building in the Civic Center area on the Detroit River. Spreen said words were exchanged between the officers and the youths, but he declined to elaborate.
>
> The suspended officers included two sergeants and seven patrolmen. In response to a question, Spreen acknowledged the possibility of more suspensions. 'But,' he added, 'we feel at this point we have done as much as we can. The identification ability of the witnesses is about exhausted.'

He said the suspensions, all on the general charge of 'conduct unbecoming an officer,' were based mainly on identifications by the victims during several showups.

Spreen and Bannon emphasized that the degree of involvement in the incident varied among the officers and that some, while not actually striking the teenagers, may have stood by and watched, without intervening.

Since an officer is required to take positive action when he sees a crime, Spreen said those who were involved in a passive role could be disciplined by the Police Trial Board and yet remain free of criminal charges.

Bannon said three persons were injured in the assaults, suffering minor cuts and bruises.

Derrick Tabor, 17, son of a minister, received hospital treatment for several bruises on his face and below his waist. He said he was beaten and kicked by eight white men after someone with a gun had ordered him to halt in the building's parking lot.

Hospitalized overnight was James Evans III, 17, whose father, James, director of the Fisher YMCA filed a $140,000 lawsuit in Wayne County Circuit Court against 10 unnamed policemen; five officials of the Detroit Police Officers Wives Association, sponsor of the dance; and Carl Parsell, president of the Detroit Police Officers Association.

Two other youths said several men smashed their car as they cowered inside, and then plastered the vehicle with 'Wallace for President' bumper stickers.

City Councilman Nicholas Hood said his 15-year-old son was among those who were menaced by the off-duty officers.

The Police Department investigation was conducted under increasing public pressure and amid 'foot-draggin' and 'whitewash' charges.

'There is a natural reluctance on the part of any group,' said Spreen, 'to incriminate its own members. But there was movement on this from the start. People did come forward and this made the showups possible.'

The nine suspensions, effective yesterday afternoon, will keep the officers off the force without pay pending a trial board hearing or disposition of any criminal charges.

Under trial board procedure, a policeman can be fired from his job if convicted.

The board is made up of three department executives, including the chief inspector. The hearings are similar to courtroom trials, but the rules of evidence are relaxed somewhat.

Police Serve Three Publics

Dear Betty,

There are complexities in police work. I always felt torn in so many directions. I, and other police executives, deal with three publics. The first is the small percentage of criminals. The second is the vast majority of law-abiding citizens. The third is a new public: protesters, picketers, dissenters, and demonstrators. Police methods in the past have been geared toward the smallest sector, the criminal element.

The small percentage of criminals has attracted the largest amount of police effort. The development and refinement of the response function by means of a radio-equipped car has been directed at what I like to call "crime-after-the-fact." This is what law enforcement has come to mean.

The policeman's role has been that of the catcher of crooks. When he deals with people other than criminals, he assumes the role of regulator. He acts with efficiency, impersonality, and is often cold and like "Big Brother." He sees so much of people at their worst that he may develop a negative, cynical attitude about human nature. Ironically then, we demand of him that he implement successfully our community relations programs.

The second public, the great majority of law-abiding, decent citizens, has been largely neglected in thinking about police methodology. Our role in terms of this public is as guarantors and protectors of their freedom to live in peace and safety. But we haven't enough rapport with them. The police officer must be given the opportunity to get to know this public on a person-to-person basis.

The third public (protesters, picketers, dissenters, demonstrators, and the disenchanted) is a relatively new phenomenon. The police role in terms of this public has not yet been clearly defined. It seems to be a problem of the tyranny of a minority. When we are there to keep the peace, we try to be sure that the rights and freedoms of all those involved are protected.

Lack of police methods to deal with this third public has resulted in unplanned, abortive, uncoordinated, and unsophisticated police response. We've all seen televised examples of the type of unplanned confrontations, baiting and deliberate provocation, which we may be called upon to deal with more frequently. Since we haven't met with unchallenged success in handling such incidents, we must be doing something wrong. It is our job to find out what our mistakes have been and to develop techniques that will correct them.

Well, to this day, I am uncomfortable when I see mishandling of major incidents by police departments everywhere.

Love, Dad

How the Community Can Help

Dear Betty,

I don't know how many times I have found that cities wanted to turn everything over to the police and didn't realize their own responsibilities. I tried to show them their role in a talk one time. Here's what I tried to tell them.

I said that effective law enforcement is impossible without citizen interest, support and participation. This means more than the familiar "Support your local police" bumper sticker implies. When a citizen asks me the question, "How can I, as a citizen, help you?" I usually say, "Keep on asking that question. Your continual show of interest in the day-to-day operations of our department is as essential to crime reduction as the capture of criminals."

As Edmund Burke, the British political philosopher once said, "The only thing necessary to the triumph of evil is that good men do nothing."

The police officer that performs his duties day after day conscientiously with dedication and integrity doesn't expect even so much as a pat on the back. He expects very little for doing his job well. The fair, impartial and effective manner in which he conducts himself should earn him the respect of the community. We owe him this much. Your respect for and confidence in our officers is part of your support.

We listen carefully to the voice of the community. We welcome suggestions and ideas because we learn much from questions and comments. We ask that when we are wrong, you correct us; that you offer us your best counsel and advice; and that when we are right, you are behind us.

We would like to encourage our supporters to be vocal and enthusiastic. One of the most important things a citizen can do is to evaluate police operations in his own mind, discuss them constructively with his friends and neighbors, and then let his voice be heard.

One very important way you can express your support is to back us when we request whatever additional men and equipment we may need to do our job well. Efficient and effective police service is really a bargain. We are willing to pay for it when we are sure that we are receiving a good return on our investment. The costs of police service are highest when we pay the price in lives and property lost or destroyed or with our personal freedoms to live in peace and safety.

Citizens can participate on the law enforcement team by providing us with extra sets of eyes and ears. Our department is constantly vigilant and we would hope that you call us whenever you see or hear something that is suspicious. If you have any information that you think the police department should be aware of, call, write or report it so that proper police action can be taken. A citizen can even help by appearing in court as a witness.

After listening to my ideas, it seemed that many citizens tried to participate more. I was happy that we began to capitalize on the fact that police and the community are teammates with common goals.

Love, Dad

Civilian Review of Police

Dear Betty,

During the months I was the Detroit Police Commissioner, one of my saddest duties was to suspend several officers pending further investigation of charges against them. A civilian review board would certainly have been an easy out for me. I would not have had the responsibility of being the defense, prosecution, judge and jury. But I questioned whether we wanted to take the easy way out.

Our department had strong internal disciplinary procedures, which, fortunately, it was not necessary to invoke often. But I sometimes thought the community didn't remember that our system of government rests on the belief that a man is presumed innocent until he is proven guilty. And secondly, every person has the right to be judged as an individual on the basis of his individual acts, and not as a group.

Outside review boards imply inadequate police leadership since review boards can only exist where police or police leaders fail. Such clamor for review over police says that law enforcement cannot qualify as a profession because of the inability of its practitioners to establish and enforce standards of conduct among themselves.

I always said that we had no objections to civilian observers. We have nothing to hide. We would hope that observers would be knowledgeable about police procedures, that they would not interfere in the lawful performance of police duties, and that they would take precautions to protect themselves in volatile and dangerous situations.

The voices in Detroit were loud and clear in their advocacy of an outside review of police actions. But have we heard loud and clear approval of Civilian Review Boards from cities that have them? In the long run, I felt that the community should realize that the vast majority of police officers were as anxious as anyone to remove unprofessional officers from their midst.

I proposed the formation of an "Observer Corps" made up of representative citizens whose reporting of situations would "Tell it like it is" to both the police and the community. I suggested that this corps be called out at crowd control situations. We want to have the Monday morning quarterbacks at the line of scrimmage during the game.

Although I thought citizens should be concerned about the police department, I questioned what could be gained by establishing a civilian review procedure based on negativism or a no confidence vote in the police.

I hoped that we could do everything possible to heighten the confidence of the community in the police department.

Love, Dad

The Cost of Crime, Tension and Congestion

Dear Betty,

I always thought that the most important method of reducing crime was to prevent it by ameliorating conditions that drive people to commit crime and that undermine the rules erected by society against anti-social conduct.

I used to try to help people understand the costs of crime, tension and congestions. I told them that society insists that individuals be responsible for their own actions. The criminal justice process operates on that assumption. However, society has not devised ways for insuring that all its members have the ability to assume responsibility. It has let too many of them grow up untaught, unmotivated and unwanted.

Crime is by no means a simple phenomenon. Victims and practitioners of crime are people of all ages, incomes, and backgrounds. Crime trends are often difficult to determine. The causes of crime are legion. Cures for crime are likely to be costly and complex.

Crime costs all Americans money. At the time I was police commissioner, it was estimated that the annual cost of crime was $27 billion. Public expenditures for police, courts and correctional systems were estimated at more than $4 billion annually.

Crime has other costs as well. The cost of lost or damaged lives, of fear and suffering, and of the failure to control events. How do you measure the pain and suffering of the victim of a vicious assault? What is the cost when community tension requires the National Guard to restore order? What happens to the family of a man killed or critically injured in an auto accident? How do you estimate the price of freedom to walk the streets without fear or travel the highways in safety?

The most effective crime deterrent is the certainty of apprehension and the certainty of punishment. This means that the "fear of being caught" can be used as a crime preventive; we assure the criminal that the police will be there or just around the corner when a criminal act is committed. And this will heighten the confidence of law-abiding citizens in their police department.

Taxpayers must realize that it is cheaper to prevent crime and to provide fair and efficient police service than to pay the price in terms of lost or damaged lives and property or freedom to live in peace and safety.

When community tensions overflow, riots occur like the Detroit riot of July 1967. The lives lost, the property damaged, the families displaced, cost Detroit dearly. But the psychological cost of lost pride and damaged reputation was also high.

Another enemy is congestion, which clogs the streets when accidents or mechanical breakdowns occur. It was estimated that motor vehicle accidents cost the country $10,700,000 in 1967. This was in addition to the 50,000 people killed and almost two million injured in accidents yearly. These costs justify the expense of helicopters, motor scooters, and other vehicles to quickly get to the scene of accidents, take control, and alleviate problems.

Betty, I can only say that these costs and numbers have risen. We do not have the answers yet.

Love, Dad

Project C.O.P.: Community Oriented Policing

Dear Betty,

My concept of the Scooter Patrol had worked so well in New York City that I tried to introduce it in Detroit. I explained that it offered a unique opportunity to prevent crime and reduce community discord. The Scooter patrolmen had all the advantages of the old-time neighborhood cop on the beat but they also had the mobility and communication necessary to police the modern metropolis. The teamwork concept was introduced because the men patrol in groups on scooters.

The teamwork, scooter and portable radio transceiver infused new interest into the mundane chore of patrol. I was convinced that it would restore respect and rapport between police and people, thus allowing us to emphasize crime prevention as much as to report a crime after the fact.

The Scooter patrolman was an attraction that drew children like magnets. He could stop and chat, and learn the habits and problems of the area he patrolled. He was seen as a friendly person and fostered the image of a helpful person. Additionally, the scooter provided 360 degrees of visibility and could move more rapidly than a patrolman on foot.

The Scooter Patrol seemed to work out well in the five districts in which it operated in Detroit. But it was not expanded after I left. I don't know if any police department anywhere in the United States uses it, but its cousin, the bicycle patrol is used.

Love, Dad

My "Love-In"

Dear Betty,

I arrived in Detroit with no illusions about my position as a commissioner with a probable time limit of 17 months to get things turned around. The tension between the police and the black community was more serious than crime itself. Many things played a part in the problems of Detroit, which began because of civic disturbances during the Civil War.

A civilian commissioner, appointed by the mayor to oversee a department headed by a professional chief called Superintendent, was rather rare in city law enforcement. The city had a good record for citizen group action to meet local problems, a community-wide annual charity drive, a civic-oriented auto industry, a peppery chamber of commerce, and a New Detroit organization formed especially to revitalize the city after the 1967 riot.

I decided on a "wild idea" which was principally to get the cop out of the car and back face to face with the public. I couldn't leave him on foot so I put him on a scooter. Of course there were family troubles in a low-income housing project, and the first police death of the year. Cars were "bombed" at two police precincts.

Besides all that, I had the personal problem of finding a home, relocating you and your mother. I had to feel out the department command and try to build a knowledgeable and dedicated staff. There was the first "rumble" with the local politicians, before the Common Council on the screening of police phone calls. I tried out a direct approach to the people, with a public statement on our future plans.

The public baseball pennant fever helped to keep the summer quiet, but the celebration of an ecstatic world series triumph bordered on a riot, albeit a happy one.

My first crisis during the 100-day "honeymoon" came from a "cop watcher." He complained after disturbances at a George Wallace political rally. The police were caught in the middle. Within four days, the roof fell in as police were accused of terrifying and beating black teens as off-duty police and their wives and the teenagers held simultaneous dances in the same downtown building. A Common Councilman's son was involved. The police command was chagrined when early reports of the trouble were stifled in the precinct. We had to sift statements for the truth. Police morale dipped to a new low and crime figures started to rise after a brief lull.

Then there was a "Poor People's March" held the month before I came to town. The march was a strange case of provocative militancy, which was eventually "rewarded" by national publicity. Police patience wore thin after hours of commendable restraint. I was to resolve it. I struggled to demonstrate fair play and community concern by holding a recruiting drive aimed especially at blacks. It paid good dividends but just as I was about to announce a new budget, black politicos escalated a minor flap over a black teenager resisting arrest into a charge of "police brutality." This was coupled with a police officer murdered trying to stop a robbery.

I tried to decide what to do. I issued a document unique in police annals, an almost poetic dissertation on "love and crime." It called for a 100 day "love in" to unite the community and establish a moratorium on criticism of police until reforms could take effect. You'd have been proud of your dad.

Love, Dad

An Article About "My Love-In"

Dear Betty,

Bob Talbert of the *Detroit Free Press* wrote on February 21, 1969, "Spreen's Love-In: Here's Why We Can't Afford Not to Join." I thought you might be interested in what he had to say. I surely appreciated his support.

> Spreen's intention is to humanize the cop. He's taken some imaginative steps in this direction by demilitarizing the prowl car with his scooter-patrol Rangers, men with first names and faces that smile, who laugh with the man and woman on the street.
>
> Commemorative dates have had a funny role in Spreen's six months in Detroit. On June 21, the longest day of the year, someone tried to talk the New Yorker out of taking "the toughest police job in the country." Spreen says, "I had to take the job then. I wouldn't have taken the job if I'd thought policing in this country was perfect. I know it's not. I know it needs to change.
>
> "I was almost 49 years old and eligible to retire. I had a whole new life planned with my family. Is that bad? But policing was in trouble. My entire career I've had ideas about how it should be, how it could be. Detroit was the place to make policing a profession once again. To give it respect."
>
> On July 22 Spreen took office, inheriting a department's troubled past, and an immediate riot anniversary confrontation the next day. He slept at headquarters the first four days he was in office and found "you make friends quick in the fox holes."
>
> Right away the word got around that here was a positive man who had told the power structure that "if you want a negative commissioner you'd better hire someone else." Respect was the first thing people said about Spreen.

Along with the riot anniversary trouble on 12th Street, Spreen found he had verbal snipers and uncompromising critics who wanted action yesterday, not today or tomorrow.

The critics, the would-be cronies, the crowds, the public and the criminals haven't let up. In six months he's had 366 requests to speak or appear somewhere every meal and evening. He's caught it from all sides and angles, from the Sheila Murphys and Donald Lobsingers and Lou Gordons and James Del Rios and John Conyers and George Crocketts.

He took his family, wife Elinor and 10-year-old daughter Betty, to Florida for a few days over Christmas. Remember this is the family that was looking forward to having a retired Daddy home full-time. And yet he was criticized for giving his family a few days away from it all.

So Big John Spreen has now asked us for love.

He deserves this much at the very least. The man has some dramatic, innovative things to show us about what can happen when policing really works. But he didn't have them yesterday because he wasn't here yesterday.

If we give him the time today to show us, he will give us a tomorrow that works.

During this "Love-In" period the best thing we can do is get to know our policemen. Invite them into your homes, your offices. Get to know them socially as people with first names and faces.

So what is this love that Johannes Spreen is talking about? He says:

"It's caring about your neighbor so you report an assault you witness upon him or his home. It's caring about your city so that you don't want to see it suffer. It's doing your thing well within the law and within the bounds of propriety. It's putting your personal desires and politics second to your concern for your city.

"It's helping to professionalize your police rather than policing your police. It's your never getting tired of asking what can we do to help. It's wanting to change things with calm, cool reason and considered judgments, not with destructive 'to hell with it' attitudes. It's having faith in people and police officers and the hope we can all live together in a better Detroit. It's making the policeman 'my man' not 'the man.'

> "It's believing that a miracle can work in this city. The miracle of those silent, uncommitted citizens of our city speaking out and committing themselves. That's what love is. That's what it can be. That's what it must be."
>
> Spreen has laid it on the line. You and I can't afford not to join his "Love-In."

Betty, dear, I think he understood where I was coming from.

Love, Dad

Love and Crime

Dear Betty,

People asked me to print up a document based on my original "Love and Crime" statement. I revised it and this version has most of the same words that I used when I first presented it to the City of Detroit. I hope you like it.

> The problem of crime is complex and difficult and requires competent, well-trained, acceptable, professional police and sheriff's departments to cope with it. But, if I had to pick one thing that could really do the job and solve the problem, it would be love.
>
> Love! What is it? It can be called a hundred different things, and the young don't have a monopoly on it. We seniors over 30 know about love also, and we are, hopefully, balanced by our experience. Maybe we can teach the younger generation a few things about love and work together for a pleasant and peaceful future.
>
> What is this love that can cut down crime and cancel community tensions? What is this love that can do more about crime than all your law enforcement agencies, vigilantes, guns and tanks? Let's try to define it:
>
> - If it's caring about your neighbor so you report an assault you witness upon him or his home, that's love.
>
> - If it's caring about your community so that you don't want to see if suffer, that's love.
>
> - If you care about your fellow citizens no matter what their hue, that's love.
>
> - If you care enough to willingly serve your country and your community, that's love.

- If you are concerned about the conditions that can tempt man to harm his neighbor, and you want to see them alleviated, that's love.
- If you get concerned about crime and do something constructive about it, that's love.
- If you feel that there are things wrong, injustices, evils in this world, and you earnestly wish to do something about them, that's love.
- If you want to change things that do not seem right to you, calmly, coolly, with considered judgment, rather than with a destructive "to hell with it all" attitude, that's love.
- If you do your thing well, within the law and within the bounds of propriety, that's love.
- If you put your personal desires and politics second to your concern for your community, that's love.
- If you concentrate more on helping to professionalize your police than to complain about or ignore your police, that's love.
- If you can take a negative and help turn it into a positive, that's love.
- If you follow the principles of honesty, truthfulness and fairness, that's love.
- If you use consideration, care, courtesy and compassion in your dealings with all you meet, that's love.
- If you live according to the Golden Rule, the Ten Commandments, or your moral, ethical or religious beliefs, that's love.
- If you consider the feelings of the other person as an individual who is with you on this small spinning speck of dust called earth, that's love.
- If you have faith in people and in your police, that's love.

- If you have hope that we can all live together in a better world, that's love.
- If you offer charity to all your fellow men, that's love.
- If you believe there may be a spot in heaven for all, regardless of their race, color or creed, that's not only love but heaven on earth.

Well, dear, people thought these words were certainly strange coming from a policeman. That was my goal, to say something very strange and hope that people would pay attention and realize we were the good guys.

Love, Dad

It's Hard to Row Against the Current

Dear Betty,

It seemed like there was one problem after another in Detroit. When the Common Council indicated resistance to the police need for additional financial support, I went to the public with another first in American policing. I called it the "Buck Up Your Police" fund drive. A private foundation offered additional financial help. A small team of officers was organized to counsel with businessmen to protect themselves against crime; thus the nucleus of a police information service was begun. A special drug-use detection service was created to aid parents, called "Analysis Anonymous."

Fortunately, when the governor visited the Department, he found that things had apparently begun to turn around for the better. But just about then, another crisis emerged.

Two white police officers challenged a squad of rifle-toting black militants near midnight, outside a church building rented to the "Republic of New Africa." The challenge was met by rifle fire resulting in one dead officer and another seriously wounded. Police rounded up more than 140 people at the meeting, after surrounding the church building. Many shots were fired.

Here's a little background about the Republic of New Africa. First, I have to tell you that during World War II, many Southern blacks moved to Detroit in search of jobs as autoworkers. As the number of black autoworkers more than doubled, whites often protested by staging "hate strikes." A black attorney named George Crockett became head of the UAW's Fair Practices Committee, which attempted to root out factory-floor racism. So the atmosphere between blacks and whites was charged in "Mo-town." By 1968, he had been appointed judge.

The Republic of New Africa (RNA) was formed in March of 1968 in Detroit because of this atmosphere and because of the riot of 1967. The RNA called for the United States government to hand over five contiguous states in the South where African people could form their own independent nation (Louisiana, Mississippi, Alabama, Georgia and South Carolina). Imari Obadele, co-founder of the RNA, said the teachings of the late Malcolm X inspired the republic movement. Charles Howard, a civil rights activist and lawyer was named the minister of state and foreign affairs and was to appear before the United Nations as an official emissary of the RNA. The RNA maintained a uniformed, armed legion for self-defense as members carried out their political activities in the Deep South. Their aim was to create the separate nation by plebiscite, a vote of the people. As an aside, I was told that the F.B.I. had labeled both Howard and the RNA as communist or Marxist.

So March 29, 1969, around 11:00 p.m., some RNA members armed with rifles were at the New Bethel Baptist Church where Rev. C. L. Franklin had apparently rented a room to them. As police tried to enter, they were shot at.

As those at the church were arrested, Rev. Franklin and Judge Crockett showed up at police headquarters. Crockett set up court in headquarters and released all but two of the 142 RNA members who were charged with the murder and shooting of two police officers outside the church, claiming that evidence to hold the suspects was inadmissible because police had ignored their right to counsel while requiring them to submit to gunpowder tests. Incidentally, the street on which New Bethel Baptist Church is located has been renamed C. L. Franklin Boulevard.

A storm of public controversy arose over police "attacking" a black church filled with men, women and children (one baby and two other juveniles). A black legislator called a black judge who "held court" at police headquarters. Charges flew between the judge and the county prosecutor over the "premature" release of suspects. The police were caught in the middle and the city was divided worse than ever.

Black youth picketed police headquarters while off-duty members of the Detroit Police Officers Association picketed the court building at opposite ends of the same block. On-duty police kept the two groups apart. Legal opinion supported the legitimacy of the black judge's decisions, while cases were prepared against shooting suspects. The community simmered and a grim funeral was held for the dead officer.

I had to row hard against the current. I finally authorized a problem identification study of the police department by an outside counseling firm. I thought the conclusions might support my recommendations to the Common Council about department needs. The budget deadline was approaching and I was running out of time. So I decided to make a major address to the business community outlining the dimensions of the crime and tension problem. I outlined police needs and asked for support. But it was too late.

The Council was not impressed. They voted for economy rather than increased funds for police. Meanwhile, the city's Commission on Community Relations made a provocative and one-sided attack on department recruiting. That was in the midst of the most effective recruiting campaign the Department had ever employed. With a lack of support by the public officials to whom I had to report, I wondered how effective I could be.

Then another police officer was shot to death. You probably remember how disturbed I was as I weighed whether to stay on as commissioner.

Love, Dad

Detroit Police on the Rebound

Dear Betty,

I decided to stay on as commissioner and see Detroit through a "cool" summer. A local mayoral campaign featured the city's first serious black candidate. Police recruiting efforts were intensified. A black command officer received a new promotion to the highest rank ever held by a black man in the Detroit police department. It was long overdue.

A video camera figured in a quick arrest executed by a helicopter. I used the little bit of good publicity to secure a little help from private dollars. Then I sought "rapport" to help flatten out the rising crime curve and improve relations with the community.

I increased the scooter force. I authorized use of on-the-job training in all precincts using video cameras, another "first" in American policing. I appealed to the New Detroit organization (the group formed out of the ashes of the 1967 riot) for funds but was only granted money for studies, not for things of immediate use. So I authorized a second brief study by a national police group to lay the groundwork for a long-term study recommendation. I instituted a new citizen's complaint procedure. We also inaugurated a citywide "Police and Youth in Sports" program. The summer stayed "cool."

I added a "third dimension" and then a "fourth dimension" to policing in Detroit. These involved using private funds for a helicopter and equipping an underwater recovery team. The "Buck Up" campaign concluded after raising almost $50,000.

No matter what we did, trouble continued to surface. Two police officers involved in the Veteran's Memorial fracas with black teenagers were back in the news, seemingly "exonerated." An unusual "incident" in a Westside park created another rumble of "police brutality," this time it was whites versus whites. The city and police prepared for anything on the Vietnam War Moratorium Day but the demonstration passed in relative peace and harmony. The police and the city breathed a sigh of relief but then another police officer was shot and killed.

Some voices began to cry out for me to publish allegedly critical studies of the police department, which I was accused of "suppressing." I became tired of needling over the police department "studies" question and decided to concentrate on crime. I mobilized extra strength to protect the major Christmas shopping areas, particularly the heart of downtown for the final months of the year. I consented to a third preliminary study of the department by an outside consulting firm, and agreed to release two previous study reports when the third was completed and an analysis returned.

The mayoral campaign neared its climax. The election campaign concluded in a narrow defeat for the black candidate. The new mayor announced he was "evaluating" the various appointive posts, including that of police commissioner. My contact with the new mayor was polite but infrequent and guarded.

"Operation Downtown" Christmas protection continued with weekly reports to the public. Anonymous phone callers attempted to provoke a confrontation between police and a Black Panther affiliated group, but were foiled by police "failsafe" precautions.

The third department study was completed and a report was made verbally and privately to me. I summarized the contents of all three studies, criticized those who had been pushing for what they thought might be "sensational" disclosures, and with some reluctance, announced the completion of my service as commissioner. I withdrew from consideration of reappointment.

I know that you recall my final days as police commissioner. There was a mixture of relief and sadness that I had not been able to accomplish more. But I learned some important lessons, which I'll describe later.

Love, Dad

Tightropes a Top Cop Must Walk

Dear Betty,

Here are some of the things I learned as Detroit's Police Commissioner. A modern metropolitan police commissioner has to walk many "tightropes" to get things done. That was necessary to reach an understanding with the many special interests and sub-communities within the total community, many of whose interests seem to conflict with those of others.

My three main "tightropes" involved the white community, the black community, and the members of the police department themselves. To these there is another sub-community that requires another set of considerations: youth.

Today's police mission is response, when it ought to be more carefully aimed at prevention of crime. The patrol function is the principal police deterrent method, and today's methods are not working.

For all around betterment, police agencies today need improved recruiting, in numbers and quality and in minority representation. They need standards and incentives for upgrading the individual officer, better educational opportunities, higher educational requirements, better training, and increased use of civilian employees for a variety of "non-police" functions.

Halting crime and easing tensions are the responsibility of all the people, not just the police. It takes a team effort. The cost of crime is on the increase in America today, both in economic and human terms. Police systems and methods need reforming, but police reform alone is not enough.

Public attitudes, confidence in the structure of our government, reform of the entire criminal justice system, and personal rejection of public disorder as a legitimate means to accomplish social ends are all aspects of the problem and its solution.

Some criticisms of past recommendations on policing, a new vision of police service and some ideas for the future emerged from my experience. I'm gradually sharing them with you.

Love, Dad

Police Youth Program

Dear Betty,

We had some nice news coverage when we opened a new Police-Youth Program. The *Detroit Free Press* story explained my role at the kick-off in an article on October 11, 1969. There was a nice picture of me with a caption, "A 30-game winner he's not, but Spreen obviously enjoyed his baseball outing."

Love, Dad

> Police Commissioner Johannes F. Spreen, renowned for his tennis game, Friday struck out Detroit Tiger outfielder Willie Horton and tossed wavering forward passes to former Lion back Dick (Night Train) Lane on the Kern Block.
>
> The athletics were staged to kick off a physical-fitness pentathlon that is part of the Detroit Police Department's Police and Youth in Sports (PAYS) program.
>
> The pentathlon, five events to test the fitness of Detroit's youth, will be held at ten sites around the city Oct. 18.
>
> Participants will compete in a walk-and-run race, sit-ups and their choice of three others; pull-ups, standing broad jump, push-ups or softball throw.
>
> Spreen said he hoped the PAYS program would help 'bridge the communications gap between the youth of this city and the Establishment.'
>
> The pentathlon was the second youth-oriented program Spreen started Friday. Earlier he spoke to about 50 people at the Detroit Citizens Center. The Center is directing the distribution of 25,000 handbills outlining the city's curfew law.
>
> The law requires that children 11 years old and younger may not be on the streets between 10 p.m. and 6 a.m., 12- and 13-year-olds between 11 p.m. and 6 a.m., and 14 to 16-year-olds between

midnight and 6 a.m., except Friday nights when the curfew is 1 a.m. to 6 a.m.

Spreen said curfew violation could 'lead a child in the wrong direction; to crime, narcotics addiction, eventually to jail or a slab in the city morgue.'

Manpower Requests

Dear Betty,

Clark Hallas of the *Detroit News* wrote an article called "Spreen bid for help falls on irate ears" on November 11, 1969. This article clearly and distressingly showed the problems between politicians and police administrators. Obviously the press love to report on controversy and friction between groups.

Love, Dad

> When the Detroit City Council closed the budget last spring, denying some of Police Commissioner Johannes F. Spreen's requests for more manpower, they told him: 'The Council's door is always open.'
>
> Yesterday, in a bitter exchange between councilmen and the commissioner, the Council appeared to slam that door.
>
> Spreen was before the Council to request an additional two district inspectors and eight more inspectors.
>
> But he had barely taken his seat when Councilman Philip J. Van Antwerp, a longtime Spreen critic proposed:
>
> 'Let's hold this in abeyance until after the new mayor takes office to see whether we need more Indians or chiefs."
>
> Sparks continually flew during the discussion, in which the Council took Spreen's request under advisement with no promises that he would get the additional supervisory personnel.
>
> At one point, Spreen and Van Antwerp, seated next to each other at one end of the table, became embroiled in a shouting match which required the gavel of Chairman Robert Tindal to silence.
>
> Van Antwerp lashed Spreen's specialized units, asserting 'This is all manpower that should be used out on the streets,' and accused the commissioner of letting 50 scooters sit idle.

Councilman Louis C. Miriani chastised Spreen for asking the Greater Detroit Chamber of Commerce to purchase radios for the scooters instead of submitting a request for funds through normal city channels.

'I did; on Jan. 10,' Spreen said, 'and the request was denied.'

Miriani then indirectly blamed Spreen for Detroit's rising crime rates.

'You've been here 15 months and crime has been going up,' Miriani said. 'When can we expect it to stop? I'm not laying the blame on anybody,' Miriani said.

But before Spreen could answer, Miriani persisted. 'Will crime keep going up?' he asked.

Spreen finally answered, 'Yes, it will until we can get more manpower and equipment.'

'I don't want to get into an argument because I don't have any PR (public relations) people to blow my horn,' Miriani snapped.

'I don't either,' Spreen replied hotly.

Spreen told the Council the supervisory personnel were needed because 25% of the total force and one-third of the squad car contingent have less than two years' experience.

He credited specially assigned supervisory personnel on duty during last month's Vietnam moratorium rally in Kennedy Square with helping to avoid violence.

Spreen said the department's recruiting was 7% ahead of last year at this time and that in October 28% of the recruits were black.

However, Spreen, whose request for 1,700 additional patrolmen was denied by Council last spring, conceded that the department had gained a net total of only 133 new men since a year ago.

He blamed a requirement that policemen live within the city for 40% of manpower losses and another 40% on better jobs. Retirement and other reasons account for the remaining 20%, he said.

This, coupled with Spreen's admission that 176 funded departmental positions remain unfilled, seemed to irk the Council, which drew some criticism when it said Spreen could not recruit 1,700 patrolmen in a year.

Van Antwerp, a retired Detroit police inspector, said he had heard from 'several sergeants and lieutenants' that police cars are tied up for lack of manpower.

When Spreen started to respond, Van Antwerp barked: 'Don't give me any excuses.'

Spreen said at least four district inspectors were a 'priority in order to free district inspectors for field work.'

After the hearing, Spreen rapped Van Antwerp, commenting, 'He's been out of police work for a number of years. I think he could use some boning up on police administration'.

New Detroit Had Old Problems

Dear Betty,

It was recommended that studies of the Detroit Police Department methods, management, community relations polices and procedures be undertaken which would cost $367,000. I felt that would be wasteful unless consideration was given to funding improvements concurrently with the study.

On February 28, 1969, I prepared a statement of community relations needs, general operations and management needs, as well as training, equipment, and program needs including the cost of needed equipment (over $25,000).

I concluded the statement with these words:

> In Summary, we feel that priorities should be placed on immediate improvements in police service. The role of action programs must be emphasized. In essence, the Department should benefit from available knowledge immediately. Delay in adopting improved procedures should not be tolerated in the hope that something better will become available in the future."
>
> On March 11, 1969, New Detroit sent Mayor Cavanagh and the press a joint statement about their proposals for a $10,000 study of police management and a $57,000 study of police-community relations, with another $300,000 set aside for the project. Their position stated, "All recent studies of community attitudes in Detroit show a continuing deterioration of relationships between the police and substantial numbers of the citizens they serve.

Their statement described a 24-member Advisory Committee to set up the study which included eight members recommended by me, eight persons representing the concerns of black citizens, and eight persons representing the city administration, New Detroit Inc. and other community interests.

On April 3, 1969, I addressed New Detroit, Inc., at a meeting. The gist of my address was to ask for an immediate $150,000 to bring in police and academic experts to look at executive and administrative operations for a week, to lease and equip a two-story building for recruiting and community services, and to lease and equip another building for police-youth athletic programs adding a special bus for these activities.

I also mentioned that I thought as police commissioner, I might have been asked for my views on what areas should be studied or at least been advised of the study areas prior to reading about it in the press. I wanted to make it clear that the police recognized some of their problems and were already correcting them with programs that had not been mentioned in the New Detroit statement.

On August 14, 1969, I gave a talk at the monthly meeting of the New Detroit Committee. I made it sort of an annual report on the past year's work stating that my number one priority had been to increase positive communication between police and citizens. I told them of the successful 1968 recruiting campaign, which had attracted more black officers than ever before. I described the success of the Community Oriented Patrol on motor scooters enhancing face-to-face contact between police and citizens, and being used to give new recruits good first experiences under the supervision of very professional officers. I summarized the personal involvement generated between people and police in the Buck Up Your Police project.

I also explained how the Love-in, the Public Information Center, the Counter Crime Clinic, and the counseling of would-be victims on how to avoid potential robbery situations were paying off. I told them about the opening of the new recruiting center and the youth center and the addition of training through seven-minute videotapes at roll call.

Then I got into the New Detroit funds for a study of the police department. I explained that my academic research background made me value studies but I believed in immediate action and immediate funding of things such as educational and recruiting incentives, additional training and operating equipment, consultants, outside examination and testing methods for recruits, and funds to sustain successful programs like Police and Youth in Sports, educational materials, police work reference books, videotapes, and closed circuit televisions.

All in all, I felt that New Detroit left much to be desired. I had problems with the committee of 24. The eight members who were to represent concerns of blacks included Senator Coleman Young who was a racist. Later when he became Mayor of Detroit, whites fled the city.

Love, Dad

Was the First Year a Waste?

Dear Betty,

After a year as Detroit Police Commissioner, I was getting frustrated that nothing was changing. Michael Madenberg of the *Detroit Free Press* wrote an article on July 17, 1969 called "Spreen Calls His First year a Near-Waste." Here is what he said.

Love, Dad

> A dejected Johannes F. Spreen Wednesday called his first year as police commissioner 'almost wasted.'
>
> Looking a bit haggard after a long morning meeting with Detroit Police Officer's Association (DPOA) spent fighting for things that are needed for a professional police force, he said, 'This city can't get off the ground to give the police what they need.'
>
> Spreen spoke of his often stormy relations with Common Council and his quieter but no less substantial differences with New Detroit, Inc.
>
> 'People here have a commissioner. If they don't want to support me they should get a new one.'
>
> In an hour-long interview, Spreen stressed support. 'Common Council,' he said, 'didn't listen to me. Why? I'm appointed by the mayor, and the council hates the mayor so much maybe they transferred it to me.'
>
> As for New Detroit: 'We asked them for $10,000 for 30 lousy scooters. We never got scooters from New Detroit, we got them from the Chamber of Commerce. We are making movement, but it's no thanks to New Detroit. We asked them for help and didn't get any. New Detroit is hepped up on studying police attitudes. I think they're barking up the wrong tree.'
>
> Spreen seemed stung by the implied criticism of his judgment resulting from budget disputes with Common Council, and his

differences with New Detroit over the civic group's $367,000 appropriation for a study of police management and police-Negro relations.

Spreen recently brought in the International Association of Chiefs of Police (IACP) to do a 'problem identification survey' of the Police Dept. New Detroit agreed to pay for the $3,000 study.

A four man IACP team completed the five-day survey last week, and its director, Roy McLaren, said a full-scale examination of police management is 'an absolute necessity.'

Spreen agrees. He has never opposed a management study he says, but: 'I don't want a six-volume study on my desk and no money to back it up. You can study and study and study, but there comes a time for action.'

Spreen made it clear he doubts any study will reveal problems not already 'obvious.'

'I am a professional,' Spreen said. 'Should I wait for studies to tell me what I already know, and not only me, what top professional people in the department know; that we need a new building, that we are short of personnel, that we need better training?

'I am only one so-called expert,' he said, his tone bitter, 'and many people in this town, including New Detroit, don't think I'm that much of an expert.'

So he invited the IACP study and asked in other consultants, because 'If I can bring in five consultants who all say the Detroit police are short-handed, that the building stinks and so forth, then maybe we can get some help'.

The Press Said I Cried

Dear Betty,

On July 19, 1969, the *Detroit Free Press* ran an editorial called "Spreen Plays Cry Baby and Vents His Spleen." I'm going to tell you what they said and then tell you what I replied, although they never printed my response.

Love, Dad

> Police Commissioner Spreen must have had a terrible day Wednesday. He probably stubbed his toe getting up, cut himself while shaving, found the toothpaste was squeezed in at the top, the toast burned and the coffee cold and so hi-ho off to a jolly meeting with the Detroit Police Officers Association.
>
> Following these disasters he sat down and had himself a good cry in public, remarking in effect that nobody loved him and he might just go out and eat worms.
>
> His cup of sorrow for the day was not yet full. There was a hint from the Commission on Community Relations that the examinations for Negro police recruits were loaded against them. The DPOA went to court to permit police to live outside naughty Detroit. A candidate for mayor said he favored a civilian trial board to oversee the police.
>
> So Thursday Spreen backed up another truckful of wrath and unloaded it on Richard Marks, director of the CCR, though the commissioner had not read Marks' report thoroughly.
>
> For all his vexations, Spreen is not entitled to the luxury of wallowing in a swamp of persecution. Even if he was wronged, his reactions were non-professional. The office of commissioner is a sensitive one and has always been wreathed in lightnings and swept by mighty winds. Spreen's problems certainly came as no surprise.

> And Spreen's disenchantment with New Detroit Inc., the CCR and Common Council are equaled by the feelings of many in those groups about Spreen.
>
> New Detroit Inc was not founded to buy scooters for the police department. The CCR did not beat up the kids at the Veterans Memorial. Common council has not felt quite the same about Spreen since he rented a recruitment headquarters on the west side without telling the council about it.
>
> The commissioner did not get all the new patrolmen he wanted, but he got some of them, and council okayed his request to promote 109 men into higher rank just a few days ago.
>
> He got 30 scooters from the Chamber of Commerce, a strange place to acquire them but an interesting expression of civic concern. His Buck Up the Police campaign has brought in nearly $50,000 from people whose budgets are as tight as the police department's.
>
> Spreen is a competent police executive. His love-ins and poetic outbursts have been refreshing. A majority of Detroiters respect him, want to help and would have a hard time finding another man with his background and skills.
>
> So let him turn off the water works, quit lashing out at everybody in sight and get about his tasks, chiseled profile into the hot wind.

On July 22, 1969, I wrote this letter, which I wish they had printed.

To the Editor:

I was somewhat surprised at your editorial of July 19th. I felt it was over-reactive and perhaps somewhat defensive.

None of those early morning catastrophes happened to me on Wednesday as you so picturesquely described. If, as you claim, I cried in public, may I say I do not cry for myself but for this city and all of its people and their police? May I add, I would stand on my head in Kennedy Square if it would help Detroit.

Wednesday, though negative, was not necessarily a day tougher than others. All days, as you point out, are tough for a Police Commissioner.

However, last week your pages reported much of the negative re: the Police Department. Yet, there were also positive things going on. I believe there should be a balance achieved.

On July 17th, your article by Mike Madenburg regarding the New Detroit studies also depicted only the negative and did not point out any of the optimistic views and positive movement ahead that I expressed.

I did not say the entire year was wasted.

I did say perhaps half of the first ten months could be called "wasted" (in quotes) but *not really* because plans and efforts are now working out and are in stages of completion.

My favorable remarks about recent cooperative actions of Common Council regarding the Recruiting Building and the new supervisory positions were not mentioned in your interview report, but I did mention them.

This is the problem as I see it and why I say I "cry" (your term) for our city. The negative, the controversial, the heated exchanges, the charges and accusations are given top priority it seems, but the positive, the constructive, the efforts to improve are many times forgotten.

I have now been here one year. When I arrived, I established certain priorities. They included *Recruiting* the best men possible; *Training* so as to provide opportunity and knowledge of professionalism, and *Protecting* by patrol methods and manpower so equipped and utilized as to assure the best possible service and protection for all people.

Certain projects were started, among them Scooter Patrol (Rangers); television training (video-taped Seven Minute Seminars at Roll Calls); a helicopter (for patrol and traffic coordination); and People-Police teamwork (through our Counter Crime Clinic and Public Information Center.)

This past week the hard work and efforts of so many in the Department were beginning to come to fruition as plans were actualized. However, there was no mention in your paper of the Police Department's efforts in this regard, but quite a bit of space was devoted to some people's accusations again the Department.

I cite for example:

Thursday, July 17th: Our Public Information Center racks, purchased by the people through the Buck Up Your Police project, were announced as available the next day in all precincts. I feel that citizens, armed with proper information, can defend themselves by knowledge of how to decrease the would-be criminal's opportunity. I believe this is so important that perhaps 5 or 10% reduction in certain major crimes is possible without adding another man or piece of equipment to the Department. Yet, no mention was made by you.

Friday, July 18th: At the 16th Precinct, we announced that with the 6th and 16th Precincts completed, all precincts now had a Ranger team (scooters) for preventive patrol and constructive neighborhood rapport.

We also announced that our year's work on training had culminated in our new video roll call training sessions. The first of the seven-minute seminars was shown this day.

The Public Information Center racks were now in all precincts and were prominently displayed where they were.

Yes, we 'cried' this day also that all this received no mention in your paper. Yet page one was devoted to a large picture of a girl in a bikini. While we certainly don't expect our Public Information Center display racks to be placed on page one, perhaps page D-12 or space next to the obituary column might have been possible.

Saturday, July 19th: I was amazed and amused at your editorial (the subject of this letter.) Scanning further through your pages, I was not too surprised to find that nothing of the positive regarding what had happened in the Police Department the day before appeared anywhere.

This is what happened the day before:

In the A.M. Friday

- Scooters in all precincts completed and announced

- Roll call video training started and announced
- Future projects and events for following week announced
- Public Information Center rack available and displayed

In the P.M. Friday

- Graduation of a class of 52 new patrolmen and 2 policewomen
- Promotion of 92 men to higher ranks including Lieutenants, Uniformed Sergeants, Detective Sergeants, and Detectives
- Announcement of assignments of some supervisors and all of the new patrolmen to the "Cool Pool" in effect Monday following
- Announcement of new deployment of Detective Sergeants on field duty with Uniformed Patrol for instantaneous investigations.

Yes, I am somewhat disenchanted but I am not discouraged. I believe the positive can be also pointed out for the good of our City along with the negative. Equal justice requires equal space. That is why I "cry" for this City and if that is what it takes to attain teamwork between the people, their police and their press, I will so continue.

Sincerely, Johannes F. Spreen, Commissioner

P.S. Should you be interested in any further information regarding last week's or this week's police programs or announcements, we will be glad to furnish you complete information through our Public Information Center!

Cops, Corporations and the Community

Dear Betty,

I was asked to address the National Industrial Conference Board's Conference on Crime and the Corporation at the Waldorf-Astoria in New York City on June 26, 1969. I was excited to have the opportunity to speak to so many corporation heads and wanted to give them my best possible recommendations.

I started off by telling them that it is no longer enough for corporations to provide jobs, goods, services and a fair return on investment. They are expected to shoulder the assortment of social and economic burdens, just as policemen are expected to not only catch criminals, prevent crime, cool off community tensions and assure that citizens live in peace and safety. I explained how the police department and the corporation might work together. I gave them examples from my own experience. Here's what I told them.

As you know, I'm a New Yorker. I moved to Detroit just about a year ago to become police commissioner. Detroit was the nation's fifth largest city and the police department was the fifth largest. However the city ranked fourth in the total number of crimes and in certain types of serious crimes it ranked third. The year before, the city had suffered one of the nation's most serious civil disorders.

Also, like some other major cities, Detroit's population within the city limits had been shrinking, in spite of massive growth in the suburbs. Within the city proper, black citizens accounted for more than one-third of the total population. Black pupils accounted for more than one-half of the public school population. But black police officers accounted for only about six percent of the police force.

On the plus side was a fundamentally sound police force, alert and responsive city government officials, a high level of economic prosperity for blacks and whites and a track record of community involvement by organized business.

I was hardly on the job a day when an officer was shot in a family quarrel. A sergeant was dead and two patrolmen wounded. It so happened that the police were white and the family was black. I was quickly on the scene but by the time I got back to my office, a story was bouncing around the national newswires that Detroit was up in arms after another racial confrontation. I had to call a press conference in the middle of the night to get the matter straight.

Later a major police recruiting campaign was under way, importantly promoted by the Detroit business community. Other incidents occurred that disrupted police community communications, however. One involved the New Bethel Church where two police officers were investigating a group of men with rifles. One opened fire on the officers. One policeman was killed and another wounded. Police responded to the officer's calls for help to find about 140 people meeting in the church. There was more shooting but no more killing. The fact that the police response involved a black church with women and children antagonized many blacks and put an end to a love-in that I had organized to cool tensions between police and the community.

There has been recognition, both by community leaders and the police, that preserving order is secondary to the total community role of minimizing the conditions that lead to crime and confrontation. There is recognition that superior training and equipment, higher professionalization of the police force, and a larger role for members of the black community on the police force would contribute to easing community tension.

Within our police force, we have undertaken to build on what already has been started, to provide more modern means of communication, reporting, preventive patrolling and taskforce response to control the rising level of crime and community tensions. One of our new groups is the Counter-Crime Clinic. It operates out of police headquarters and is manned by a special group of trained officers. Our aim has been to conduct it like a medical clinic. We are using it to bring together groups of citizens and police for the purpose of studying, discussing, evaluating and prescribing remedies for specific crime problems.

In all of these efforts, the help of the business community has been outstanding. The 1968 recruiting campaign involved the Chamber of Commerce and the donated time and talent of some of the best business and advertising brains in the city. Detroit business and industry subscribed more than $60,000 in cash for out-of-pocket costs, and donated about $400,000 worth of advertising space and time.

The program these people came up with was based on the theme, "It takes a big man," and was superbly effective. It attracted the largest number of police recruits in the city's history, and for the first time ever, the number of black recruits matched the black share of the city's population; 35 percent.

In Detroit, funds raised by the Chamber of Commerce made it possible to begin an experiment with the use of motor scooters for neighborhood police patrol. The idea had been tried successfully in New York. The whole purpose of the scooter is to put the police department back in the business of preventing crime instead of simply reacting to it after the fact, by creating a visible presence on the block and in the neighborhood.

A follow-up campaign to involve citizens in direct support of their police was conducted for us by the Detroit Jaycees. We called it "Buck Up Your Police," and asked citizens to show their support by contributing a buck. This campaign has brought in more than $40,000 in a couple of months, bought us over 100 more scooters, and also some valuable videotape equipment for each precinct to improve our training methods. But the most important aspect of this campaign has been its effect on police morale. Police discovered that there were thousands of people who cared about them.

You can specifically help your own police departments in many ways, but most importantly by helping to build rapport between police and the community. Don't seek or expect instant answers from one or two corrective measures. It takes a broad-front approach, a systems approach, and neither you nor your police can do it separately.

In Detroit, I have taken steps to organize a special advisory bureau of businessmen, top men from the auto industry and other major concerns, who will serve as an adjunct of our Counter-Crime Clinic. I could call this business advisory group Concerned Corporation Consultants. I've asked the former board chairman of the Burroughs Corporation to act as the organizing chairman.

Our intention is to have this group of businessmen meet regularly once a month, to hear a report on the crime picture and current problems and progress of the police, so that they might advise us out of their experience and provide such other help as they might be willing and able to provide through their community influence and contacts. We are trying to open and maintain vehicles for communication between police and the community that never existed before.

I don't have to tell this group about the importance of communications. Business executives who are experts in public communication have a special opportunity to promote the cause of police and citizen rapport. Get to know your police and help them work more effectively with the news media so that good stories get equal play with stories about the few who do wrong.

If you help your police put their best foot forward, you'll help build a better economic and social climate, you'll contribute to rapport between the community and the men in blue, you'll improve the quality of your police department, you'll help police recruit better individuals, and you'll insure a modern police department for your community. I believe a modern police department is created by the seven M's of good management: Money, Manpower, Material, newer Machines, better Methods, increased Motivation and all of this promptly enough to beat the final M—the Moving finger of time. Tomorrow is too late!

Betty, the immediate reaction from the group and later letters and calls helped me realize that my comments were very useful to these businessmen. I had learned a lot but my time as Police Commissioner was quickly running out, as you will see.
Love, Dad

War on Crime Shows Results

Dear Betty,

Just a few weeks before I left, we began to see good results on our crime statistics. The *Detroit Free Press* wrote this article on November 24, 1969.

Love, Dad

> Operation Downtown, a combination of a million dollar computer and 75 extra patrolmen, has reduced the number of reported street crimes downtown during the first two weeks of November from 68 to 45.
>
> The biggest reductions came in assaults and thefts from individuals, which each dropped from 12 to 5. But robberies from individuals (thefts involving a threat of force) rose in the first two weeks of the campaign, which began Nov. 1 and ends after Christmas. All comparisons are made against the same period last year.
>
> Spreen is aiming to reduce thefts, assaults and robberies against individuals to improve the attractiveness of the downtown area as a Christmas shopping spot.
>
> Police figures for those types of crimes in the first two weeks show:
>
> - Assaults against individuals dropped from 12 to 6
> - Larcenies from individuals also dropped from 12 to 6
> - Larcenies from autos dropped from 38 to 25
> - Robberies of individuals rose from six to eight
>
> Spreen credits an array of electronic gadgetry and the doubling of the number of patrolmen with the success of the campaign.

Much of the campaign strategy was worked out by a computer that is fed the details of crimes in the downtown area and predicts when and where crimes will occur on a given day. Officers are deployed on a schedule that will put them in the area where the computer predicts criminals will be operating.

Crime Fighters Offer 'Extra Eye'

Dear Betty,

Just as I was about to leave, various groups were beginning to help the police department. This article by Don Tschirhart of the *Detroit News* on December 3, 1969, described a program that gave hope to the black community in particular.

Love, Dad

"What can an ordinary citizen do about crime? He can be an 'extra eye' for the Police Department, more than 1,000 Detroiters believe.

They are the citizens who have joined the Civilian Radio Patrol and nightly roam residential and business streets throughout the city.

So far the patrols have been credited with solving a holdup, halting a store burglary, assisting at several injury accidents and reporting fires.

'We could use 30,000 such people,' said Police Commissioner Johannes F. Spreen. 'People keep talking about crime in their neighborhood, and these Citizen Radio Patrol members are doing something about it. They are setting an excellent example of what the ordinary citizen of Detroit can do about the problem.'

The project is citywide in scope. There are 15 patrol groups ranging in size from 30 to 300 members each. The volunteers ride in pairs in their own automobiles, reporting any suspicious activity to their group's base station by radio. This information is relayed to Police Headquarters for further investigation by a regular scout car.

To coordinate their activities, the groups recently formed a Citizens' Radio Patrol Council and elected as their temporary chairman the Rev.

Isaiah D. Patterson, founder of the College Park Radio Patrol. Mr. Patterson disavowed any 'vigilante' activity on the part of the patrol. 'We work within strict rules set by ourselves and the Police Department,' he added.

'Our motto is 'Observe, Report, Move,' and the job of our patrols is to look carefully at what is going on, report to the police any activities that do not look right and then move on so that the patrol doesn't get too involved.

'Like the time one of our patrols spotted two young men on the roof of a store on Puritan. As soon as the young men spotted our car with its distinguishing radio aerial, they jumped off the roof and ran. Later police found burglar tools.'

Lt. Arthur Sands, of the 12th Precinct, described the citizen patrols as 'part of the crime-fighting team.' 'I know for a fact that these groups have helped our police team, and all of the scout car patrols are high in their praise of these citizens who give up a night each week to help their neighbors,' Sands said. 'I'm well aware of the recent crime statistics which show crime in our city is high,' he said. 'But I keep thinking that without our patrol the number of crimes committed could have been much higher'."

Political Battles and My Departure

Dear Betty,

When Richard Austin, Michigan's former secretary of state died in 2001, it reminded me of what happened at the end of my term as Detroit Police Commissioner.

It brought back to me the election of 1969, the race between Richard Austin and Wayne County Sheriff Roman Gribbs, when I was caught in a political quandary. Mayor Jerome Cavanagh, who had appointed me police commissioner, had decided not to run again. Mr. Austin named me as his choice for police commissioner if he became mayor. I also knew his opponent.

It had always been my belief that proper police professionalism must be above politics. When asked if I would remain as police commissioner after Mr. Austin's statement, I said, "Both men are eminently qualified. The new mayor will select his police commissioner."

Roman Gribbs won. After meeting with him, I chose not to remain as police commissioner. His term was not noteworthy. What a pity that the city was not ready for Richard Austin, a black man who could have united races and created a better Detroit. I would have been proud to be his police commissioner. But the man who succeeded Gribbs, Coleman Young, exacerbated the racial divide.

Austin went on to be elected five times as the secretary of state. He reshaped the office and changed it from a political patronage office to a more service-oriented operation. I always felt we missed a great opportunity when Richard Austin lost the mayoral election.

I just thought you might be interested in what transpired as I left office.

Love, Dad

The New Commissioner's Job

Dear Betty,

The *Detroit Free Press* wrote an editorial on December 11, 1969, which you might find interesting. In some articles, the newspaper incorrectly stated 1700 police positions were requested but I only requested 1000 to be spread over a two year period.

Love, Dad

> The two reports on the Detroit Police Department that were released by Commissioner Spreen Tuesday should not be used as an excuse to heap coals of fire on the heads of the policemen as such. No responsible person has any interest in tearing down the Detroit Police Department.
>
> But the findings, some of them made by the very authoritative International Association of Chiefs of Police, ought to provide the new police commissioner a charger for his job. They reveal weaknesses in the department's structure, promotion system, morale and physical facilities that impede its efforts to fight crime.
>
> In the past, many police officers have despaired of reforming the chopped-up organizational structure of the department. Even generally good police commissioners, including Commissioner Spreen, have found themselves frustrated about changing it. The strength of the police union, the resistance of the bureaucracy, the force of political habit, all these factors get in the way of an effective reorganization.
>
> But Mayor-elect Gribbs is a man who has had some experience with law enforcement and who ought, perforce, to be in a position to take on the problems of reorganization. He and his commissioner will surely be tested by the need to reshape the command structure, impose better discipline and get better use of his manpower. We would hope that he will select his new commissioner, in

part, on the basis of his commitment to rebuilding the department's bureaucratized structure.

Interestingly, the findings support Mayor Cavanagh's contention, so scorned by Common Council, that Detroit urgently needs 1,000 new policemen. It adds another expensive but potentially crucial recommendation that Detroit build a new police headquarters. The inadequacy of the existing building may be more important than most of us would have thought to any new effort to make the Detroit police more of a spit and polish, highly motivated outfit.

A Happy New Year to Detroit

Dear Betty,

You might enjoy this article because it included comments from your mother. As I prepared to leave the post of Police Commissioner of Detroit, the *Detroit Free Press* wanted to do a story. Helen Vogel published this article on January 1, 1970.

> The Johannes Spreens are wishing their adopted hometown a happy new year and more than that.
>
> Elinor, the retiring Police Commissioner's slender strawberry blond wife, said, 'I wish Detroiters God's speed in the direction they're going.'
>
> The Commissioner nodded his agreement.
>
> 'I hope,' he said, 'that this is the year we reach an understanding that we are all people, the black community, the white community, the police community. I sometimes felt I was caught among the three.'
>
> 'We must understand,' he continued, 'that we're all together here, all Detroiters, on this small spot on the North American continent on a small ball spinning in space.
>
> 'This I would like to see, mutual faith, mutual trust, mutual understanding. I have spoken of love before, ' he added smiling.
>
> 'Of course, we will stay in Detroit,' Elinor declared.
>
> 'I'm looking forward to getting to know my husband again,' said Elinor. In the past 17 months she had been in his office twice.
>
> 'And I'll rediscover my family,' he declared. The couple has an 11-year-old daughter, Betty.
>
> They also hope to see more of Michigan beyond the boundaries of Detroit.
>
> 'I hardly ever get beyond Eight Mile Rd.,' Spreen said.

'In some ways, Elinor knows Detroit better than I do. She's had time to ride around and look. I'm always driven by a chauffeur, and I'm studying notes or something,' he said.

'I have often wanted to do a tribute for the policeman's wife. She has a hard lot,' he said.

'And they never have enough money,' said his wife.

Elinor is not only the wife of a policeman, but the daughter of one and was, for a while, a policewoman.

'Policemen's wives are a breed unto themselves,' she said. 'Not just anyone can be one. They have to be as dedicated as their husbands.'

'They have so much to go along with,' said her husband. He explained that in New York, the working shift changes every five days; in Detroit every month which means an entire rescheduling of the household schedule.

'They must be very empathic people,' said Elinor. 'When their husbands come home from seeing something tragic they must be able to empathize, and they must be astute psychologically and know when to stop,' she declared.

'They do care about these things,' she said. 'They have families of their own.'

'I think policemen make the best fathers in the world. The family is usually a very close one,' she said. Spreen listened as his wife talked. Then he took a deep breath.

'You know a policeman's wife never knows when he leaves if he is coming home,' he said.

His wife nodded. 'They learn to make the best of each day,' she said.

'And,' said her husband, 'if they want to advance, they must study. I took the sergeant's test and the lieutenant's test, and the captain's test, and after that I went back to college. So after work, I had to spend all my time studying.'

'And then,' said his wife, 'after all of that some policeman somewhere does something wrong and everyone says, 'Well, after all, you know he's a cop!'

Spreen would like to see more cops in the community on scooters. 'It's an entirely different thing for both the policeman and the community than cops in squad cars,' he said.

'You can't help but smile when you see a cop on a scooter,' he said.

'And we're mirrors,' said his wife. 'When you smile at me, I smile back.'

All the scooter men are volunteers, specially picked and trained, Spreen said.

He explained how, on Moratorium Day, the scooter men had been mobilized when some '50 to 100' young people out of the thousands who took part became 'troublesome.'

'I shudder to think of what might have happened if we had sent in armed, masked riot police,' he said.

'The scooter cops pleaded, charmed, cajoled the kids,' he said. 'The kids have got their arms around the cop,' he said. 'That's the way it should be with the policeman, always there, helping, aiding, guiding, advising. I want the policeman to feel he is the protector of liberty,' said the retiring Commissioner.

'Happy New Year, Detroit'.

How I Was a "Supercop" On My Last Day

Dear Betty,

After all the stresses and strains as Police Commissioner, my last day on the job was rather upbeat and interesting. Here's the story about it written by Mike Maza on January 6, 1970 in the *Detroit Free Press.* He entitled the piece, "Detroit's Spreen Era Ends in Unveiling of 'Supercop'."

By the way, the "friskometer" nightstick is the same thing as the wand now used in airports on people and baggage to detect metal.

Love, Dad

> In his last day as police commissioner, Johannes F. Spreen Monday sentenced crime-fighting greats Batman and Superman to the out-crowd with a cry of 'Supercop is on his way!'
>
> Supercop, the commissioner told 100 police academy students, will be the technological child of Dick Tracy and Buck Rogers, nourished by upgraded training programs and 'a more competitive salary schedule.'
>
> 'Supercop,' Spreen said, 'would be equipped with a Buck Rogers-like jet belt.'
>
> As hefty Lt. Frank Blount modeled a display version of the belt, obviously straining under its 120 pounds, Spreen said, 'Just think of the range and the patrolling powers a flying Supercop could have…'
>
> 'Why, Gotham City's police commissioner wouldn't even need Batman if he had Supercop.'
>
> Superman's x-ray vision could be replaced by a 'friskometer' nightstick, which was also demonstrated. As the club was moved over an officer-suspect's body, its tip four to six inches away, a

meter in the handle registered each time a piece of metal interrupted its magnetic field.

A pistol, a knife and a wristwatch were found on the 'suspect's' person.

'They only cost a hundred bucks a piece,' Spreen quipped. 'I'm sure we'll have no trouble with council providing funds if the department decides its men should be equipped with the clubs.'

But Supercop will depend on more than technology. 'Today, pink-cheeked college freshmen who ought to know better may call you a 'pig' or worse,' Spreen said. 'The only way police today can meet the high standards of professionalism required by the problems of today is to be as advanced and sophisticated, personally, as today's new materials, machines and methods.'

'The most important element in improving police work remains the human element. And that's you,' Spreen said.

Consultant on Law Enforcement and Protection

Dear Betty,

A month after I left my position as Detroit Police Commissioner I had a new job. Paul Gainor wrote about it on February 11, 1970, in the *Detroit News*. As you know, I wrote articles for the *Detroit News*, taught criminal justice at John Jay College in New York and at Mercy College in Detroit all at the same time. It was a busy but interesting challenge.

Love, Dad

> Former Detroit Police Commissioner Johannes F. Spreen has accepted the new position of 'consultant on law enforcement and protection' in the Oakland County prosecutor's office.
>
> His appointment was announced today at a press conference by Oakland County Prosecutor Thomas G. Plunkett.
>
> Plunkett said Spreen was selected 'to help bring big city experience and the experience of having tried new things' to Oakland County law enforcement agencies.
>
> 'He will be a liaison between the prosecutor's office and police departments in what we think is a unique program to improve communications within the law enforcement community,' Plunkett said.
>
> Spreen will be available to all police agencies of the county for consultation on police services and training, subjects in which he is 'a nationally recognized expert,' Plunkett added.
>
> The prosecutor said he believes Spreen also can help build better police-community relations.
>
> He praised Spreen for 'his ability to communicate and make law enforcement attractive to the community.'

Spreen writes a twice-weekly column for *The News* detailing his experiences during the 18 months, from July 1968 until Jan. 6, he served as Detroit police commissioner.

He said he regards the Oakland County position as 'a new challenge."

'This really is a new road in the criminal justice system," Spreen said. 'There are no real guidelines.'

'My job will be to try to bring about better law enforcement and better protection for the people. I'll be doing whatever I can to make the system better serve the people'.

Part III
Newspaper Columns

o o o o o o o o o o o o o o o o o o o o o o o o o o o

"The next thing most like living one's life over again seems to be a recollection of that life, and to make that recollection as durable as possible by putting it down in writing."

—*Benjamin Franklin*

My Message to Police Departments

Dear Betty,

I wrote an article for the law enforcement journal *Police,* which appeared December 1971. At that time, I was writing news articles and was dividing my time between faculty positions at John Jay College of Criminal Justice in New York and Mercy College in Detroit.

I relished the opportunity to explain my views to police departments across the country because despite the increase in technology and police specializations, the crime rate was increasing at eight times faster than the population rate.

I explained how the new terminology of "law enforcement officer" was punitive and punished the offender after the crime was committed. This was contrasted with the original purpose of the visible friendly policemen who patrolled and thus prevented offenses in the first place. In the modern era, specialization and closed police cruisers prevented the closeness of police to those they were to protect.

What does the victim care, after the fact, that society has been avenged and the law enforced because the criminal has subsequently been arrested and punished? The true yardstick of effective policing is the *absence* of crime.

It seems to me the image of the police officer of tomorrow must be something more than the "get-em," "catch-em," "jail-em" concept of law enforcement. While the professional police officer must be proficient in the means and methods of bringing a lawbreaker before the bar of justice, his primary responsibility should be for peacekeeping, crime prevention, and protection of his neighbors from harm or unlawful infringement of their human rights.

I added that when I was police commissioner, I had the words "Protectors of Liberty" stenciled on the back of every police car. Some thought it was "corny," but in my view it helped make the officer sit straighter and prouder in his car.

Preventive medicine, preventive maintenance and preventive police work may not be as exciting as a spectacular operation, a big repair job or an exciting car chase, but they are more valuable.

I was pleased, dear, that the *Police* issue with my article also had my picture along with the scooter patrol that I developed in New York and Detroit.

Love, Dad

How I Came to Write for The Detroit News

Dear Betty,

I no sooner left the post of Police Commissioner for Detroit than I had a wonderful opportunity to express my views in the newspaper. *The Detroit News* carried my picture and an announcement that I would be writing a column for them and would answer questions as well. Here was the January 25, 1970, column entitled "Spreen to write for *The News,"* by Joseph Wolff, *News* staff writer.

> As Detroit police commissioner, Johannes F. Spreen mixed wit, imagination and a keen sense of how to communicate into his efforts to improve law enforcement and police-community relations.
>
> "Now he's going to use the same talents in a column which will appear twice each week in *The Detroit News*, beginning next Sunday.
>
> "The column—to be called "By Johannes Spreen"—will use personal anecdotes, crises and moments of human drama experienced through his career, to illuminate the promise and the problems of police work in a major city.
>
> "The new feature will appear on Sundays and Wednesdays.
>
> "Some of Spreen's feelings about his 18 months as police commissioner of Detroit will be revealed for the first time. He will tell what it takes to be a policeman in today's society; whether he is a rookie beat patrolman or the head of a department.
>
> "In his first column appearing in next Sunday's editions of *The News,* Spreen, who stepped out as police commissioner here Jan. 6, will describe his personal feelings during the first days after he

assumed control of the department on the first anniversary of Detroit's tragic riot of 1967.

"He will tell of the pressures often placed on a department and its command officers by politics and special interest groups.

"Many of Spreen's columns will answer questions on police work submitted by *News* readers.

"Spreen speaks with the authority that can come only from years as a policeman and a professional who believes crime fighting must continually adjust itself to the changes of modern society.

"The 6-feet-5, 240-pound Spreen who played tennis with inner city youths, did pushups and played basketball with others, began his career as a New York City beat patrolman. During his 25 years there he moved through the ranks of sergeant, lieutenant and deputy inspector before he retired as inspector and chief of operations.

"He is a graduate of John Jay College of Criminal Justice, City University of New York, where he received a Bachelor of Science degree with honors. He later earned a master's degree in public administration.

"He conducted seminars and in service training courses in the New York Police Department and reorganized the recruit training program to what is still being used there.

"Between his retirement from the New York department and his Detroit appointment, Spreen was teacher and lecturer at the State University of New York at Farmingdale, Long Island, on police administration, civil rights and human relations.

"He intends to return to full-time teaching this fall while continuing his column in *The News.*

Well, dear, I seized this opportunity to educate the public, unaware of the next step in my law enforcement career. I am including excerpts from a few of the columns I wrote and some in their entirety.
Love, Dad

What Medals for the Wives?

Dear Betty,

This was my third column for *The Detroit News* and it appeared on February 8, 1970. I know your mother always worried about me, as you did also, so you may appreciate this column.

Love, Dad

I met Mrs. Richard Woyshner for the third time at a funeral home where friends had gathered to help her mourn the death of her husband, a Detroit police officer with more than 22 years' experience. He was shot two weeks ago.

As I thought back to the first time I met Mrs. Woyshner, the events recalled by the process of association spanned my entire term of office as Detroit police commissioner, and brought back the most poignant moments of that year and a half.

My mind went back to Aug. 5, 1968. I was just starting my second week on the job in Detroit, and was still looking for a permanent home for my family. It was in the early evening and my aide was showing me some of the residential neighborhoods. We heard a report on our police radio that an officer had been shot at the Jeffries housing project.

We were on the scene shortly after the first police cars responded. Three officers had been shot, one fatally, while they were investigating a complaint of "family trouble."

That night in August 1968, after the officers themselves had been cared for, our first concern was to notify their families before the news could reach them through other channels.

I heartily support this Detroit Police Department practice. I have never forgotten how I felt as a policeman in New York City, when an officer who lived around the corner was shot. A neighbor, who heard the news on the radio, informed his wife. In spite of all the other things a police department has to do, it still has to remember that a policeman has a family.

Police cars were sent to notify the three Detroit wives and to bring them to the hospital if they wished.

Officers with command responsibility, sergeants or higher, are usually sent on such missions.

Last October 25, for the sixth time, I joined a Detroit police family in grief, when I had to bring word of the death of young Patrolman Paul Begin to his wife and parents.

I still don't know how to properly tell a wife that her husband will never come home again.

But a woman who has been called suddenly to the hospital knows that things are serious, and she needs to be told the truth as gently as possible.

Mrs. Woyshner had been there for the wives of other fallen officers and now was there on that cold day. Everyone's heart went out to her, together with admiration for her courage and her concern for those who came to pay their respects to a fine officer who had given his life for his city and its people.

The Detroit police widows are an exclusive, tightly knit sisterhood. There are none who seek membership.

But every policeman's wife has to live with the fear that someday her turn may come. I think all police officers' wives have a right to ask this much of the community: to respect their men.

Police officers are neither angels nor devils, but human beings who have assumed one of the most necessary but unpleasant chores in community life; being on the spot whenever there's trouble.

But they all wear the same uniform and share the same obligations and risks. They never know when they will have to put their lives on the line. Respect them at least for that.

It might help to console a policeman's widow just a little bit, to know that her sorrow was the community's sorrow.

Detroit's Image Needs Polishing

Dear Betty,

This column appeared on February 9, 1970. I decided to delve into what happens to the image and morale of a city when unsubstantiated charges of corruption are made against policemen.

Love, Dad

In 1968, when I was thinking about moving from New York to Detroit, I had little detailed knowledge of the city as a place to live. When I asked friends, their most frequent reactions were, "Not Detroit!"

I came anyway and found Detroit a splendid city with fine people. But the contrast between my personal experience and the negative impression held by so many outsiders has never ceased to disturb me.

Detroit's image is once again suffering and the morale of its citizens put under a new strain.

The reason, of course, is the charge by Lawrence Burns that three present and former Detroit police executives took bribes more than six years ago to protect an abortion racket.

Because one of those named had just been appointed police chief in another major city (and had to resign because of the charge), the allegations have received nationwide attention since the names of the three were printed in the *Detroit Free Press* on February 1. The result was to spotlight once again this city and its Police Department in a negative light.

Why is Detroit's image important? It is important, very important, because what other people think about a city has a tremendous effect on its future.

How many potential new residents decide not to move here? How many potential visitors never come here at all? How many groups hold their conventions elsewhere, despite the availability in Detroit of some of the nation's finest facilities?

A city where the emphasis is on the negative is a dying city. It needs some adrenalin, a good shot of "accentuating the positive." It's all too easy for the negatives to be overemphasized.

By accentuating the positive I don't mean artificial boosterism or glossing over real faults. I mean making an effort to do right in the first place, to correct faults, and consciously seek to put the city's best foot forward.

Everybody has a stake in the city and everyone has a contribution to make, including individuals, public or private organizations, and the news media.

The president of the homeowners association where I live describes how he took a taxi from the airport to his home. When the cabdriver started to badmouth Detroit, he allowed the driver to assume that he was a visitor from Chicago. For his $9.85 fare, he got both transportation and a steady diatribe on Detroit's deficiencies from the driver, a resident of the city.

It's bad enough when nonresidents find fault. We who live here have every reason to build Detroit up, not to tear it down. It's the people who live in Detroit today who will determine the city's future.

I couldn't help but contrast the cabdriver with a Detroit elevator operator named Charles Nusser who wrote me when I was police commissioner.

Nusser believes in his city and extols it to visitors. He believes it is important to "do his thing" well enough so that each hotel visitor will be able to take back home at least one recollection of extra friendliness and courtesy in Detroit.

Nusser "accentuates the positive."

The news media have special impact on a city's image and a special responsibility. Too often a city becomes stereotyped by reputation or events. When something happens that seems to dramatically reinforce the stereotype, it is spotlighted. Meanwhile less dramatic events that contradict the stereotype are ignored.

During my second week as police commissioner, a police sergeant was shot to death responding to "a family trouble call." He was white, the family involved happened to be black.

Before I knew it, a story was circulating on national news wires that Detroit might be off on another riot spree. I had to call a press conference late that night to set the matter straight.

Last October, a peace mobilization march was conducted in Detroit in a general atmosphere of calmness and coolness. I issued a well-deserved commendation to the entire department. But national television coverage gave a disturbing impression of the day in Detroit by focusing on one isolated 30-second jeering session between one speaker and a crowd that vigorously disagreed with his viewpoint.

Detroit again has attracted unfavorable national attention with the publication of Burns' allegations of a past police scandal.

I hope the accusations are unfounded. But even if any or all of them should eventually be proven true, they should not have been given such broad public circulation before they could be investigated and corroborated. Wasn't there a better road to justice both for the individuals involved and the city?

There is no denying that it would be a civic tragedy to permit public officials to violate public trust and escape detection and punishment. It is both a personal and a civic tragedy to punish without "due process."

If the facts eventually support the allegations, so be it. But by the time the facts are determined, if they ever are, the tarnish to city and individual reputations will be difficult to remove even if the verdict is complete innocence.

Color Your Valentine Blue

Dear Betty,

This article appeared on February 11, 1970. In the same newspaper was another article announcing that I took a job with the Oakland County prosecutor's office. This article was written because with Valentine's Day in the offing, I was reminded of when I called for a city-wide "love-in." Although it didn't accomplish what I hoped it would, the basic plan still offers a worthwhile guide for a city that is trying to "cool it." Here I am including only the last part of the article because it had something to do with you.

My article ran with a picture of the large Valentine's heart given to the police department by the St. Stanislaus School. You may recall that the valentine was signed by 212 students and said such things as "Our cops are tops!" "With luv to the fuzz!" and "Have a successful love-in!"

Love, Dad

> When I left office in January, I felt I could look back and see a gradual easing of community tensions; not to the point where we would like it, but at least steadily away from the boiling point.
>
> I think this has reflected a softening in some of the hardened attitudes that have caused concern in the past, and I like to think that some of it is due to the fact that a hare-brained ex-cop a year ago asked the people and the police of Detroit to try love for a while.
>
> One of the letters I got was from a Detroit woman who said: "You are the first public official who has mentioned love as a solution to world problems. You have the right idea that love will end the crime wave. Best wishes and may the Lord bless you for all you are trying so hard to accomplish."

I was glad to get such a response. But her hopes and mine, that "love" would have a noticeable effect on the rising crime trend, have not been borne out by the figures.

I still have faith, however, in the validity of what Paul told the Corinthians. The problem is that almost 2,000 years later, the message still has not reached enough of us.

Valentine's Day is a good occasion to remember and resolve that the kind of love that can end human troubles has to be an active force in all human hearts every day of the year.

This year my 11-year-old daughter Betty presented me with another of her handmade valentines. It says: "Love is a wonderful thing. Why not try it?"

Why not, indeed?

A Hot Pressure Cooker

Dear Betty:

This article appeared on February 22, 1970. My theme in this piece was to help citizens understand the problems they cause without even realizing it. It was a chance for them to sit in my seat for a minute.

Love, Dad

Years ago, a top police administrator in one of our major cities said he had to spend 90% of his time and concern on the investigation and control of gambling and only 10% on all other crimes.

In other words, he could only give one-tenth of his attention and concern to his major area of responsibility. He said the reason for this disproportionate emphasis was pressure; the pressure of political and other special interests.

Perhaps the 90-10 ratio is too extreme to apply to conditions today. But it has been my experience that any police commissioner has to operate inside a "pressure cooker" that distracts him and takes time away from the main goal of fighting crime.

So just as in that earlier day, crime still gets short shrift.

Today the pressures center less around which crime problems to attack first than they do around the ugly fact of tension between police and citizens, particularly black citizens.

To this the so-called "youth rebellion" has added another dimension.

Good police administrators understand these new facts of life in policing, recognize the seriousness of the dilemma, and have the background, training and dedication to resolve it, if anyone can.

However, one of the first "pressures" that a commissioner has to recognize and deal with is the pressure of the well meant but one-sided "solution" offered by individuals and groups whose concern is commendable, but whose objectivity and information are questionable.

More overt than the pressure of volunteered "solutions" is the pressure of conflicting "demands," not only from community elements, but also even from within the police department.

It is symptomatic of the times that most of the "demands" channeled into my office dealt with community tensions and very few with crime. The rising crime figures created their own pressure.

The first letters that crossed my desk when I became commissioner were from the Michigan Civil Rights Commission and the Mayor's Commission on Community Relations.

The third item was a stack of file folders; ten inches thick, on the "Poor People's March" incident at Cobo Hall. The incident occurred before I came to the city, but still required resolution.

I also received "demands" in my office in person from such diverse organizations as "Breakthrough," the Detroit Police Officers' Association, the Detectives' Association, and civic groups. Many of these were incompatible with each other, or with the general interest of the community or the Police Department.

A third type of pressure is common to administrators everywhere: the pressure of matching available resources in men, money and materials to the tasks at hand.

When the available resources are inadequate, which happens to be the case in Detroit and many other cities, the hard alternatives are either to secure resources equal to the tasks, find new methods to stretch what's available, or modify the tasks to fit the existing resources.

The fourth and overriding pressure is the pressure of events, the day-to-day incidence of crimes and "confrontations."

When events crowd too hard and fast, police and police executives have little opportunity to do more than respond. But prevention, not response, is the fundamental answer to the problems of crime and community tensions today.

If all four of these pressures are allowed to build up together to an excessive degree, it can wreck a police department and it can wreck a city.

Support Your Police: It's More Than a Slogan Now

Dear Betty,

This article appeared on March 5, 1970. As you will see, I wanted to encourage the community to support all officers, but black officers in particular.

Love, Dad

> A year ago, while I was Detroit police commissioner, I remarked that the police desperately needed greater support from the black community, especially in the recruitment of more black officers.
>
> I asked this question: "Why should a young black man want to put on a blue uniform when so many black voices call him 'fuzz' and 'pig' and 'Uncle Tom'?"
>
> I was trying to appeal to the "silent majority" of the black community over the strident voices of a minority.
>
> I would never have considered coming to Detroit as police commissioner without having faith in that vast preponderance of black people and their earnest craving for representative, responsive police protection.
>
> Subsequently, some black leaders have taken the position that such an idea was a misapprehension, that lack of support for police within the black community was a "myth."
>
> Since a year ago, public expression of support for good police work from responsible members of the black community has increased in frequency and intensity.
>
> But, in my opinion, it was no "myth" that qualified black prospects were discouraged from seeking a police career because of the vehement antagonism of some of their peers.

In that same speech a year ago, I said the Police Department could not expect community support as a matter of course; it had to be earned, by performing the police function fairly, professionally, and without discrimination.

I think the growing expressions of community support for police, especially from the black community, reflect two things.

One is the positive effort by the Police Department and most police officers to earn total community backing.

The other is the growing recognition on the part of both black and white citizens that black people are the ones who suffer most when crime gets out of hand.

Some blacks now have called for an organized community effort to halt the growing trend of "blacks killing blacks."

It's a sound approach. To fight crime effectively, you have to start with the people themselves. Community attitude, alertness, and moral concern are the first lines of defense against crime.

But white as well as black citizens need the same kind of rallying cry. Crime hurts everybody, and it takes a community effort to deal with poverty, social injustice, drug addiction, permissive gun-control policies, apathy and all other elements that make the crime problem what it is today.

It should be clear that the vast majority of all citizens, black and white, are willing, even yearning to support law enforcement that is fair, understanding and responsive; that respects and protects the decent man and his home.

Yet in American police work, we still have not provided this service to the black community. It is part of the reason why policing has become a thorny issue. Even with respect to the white community, police departments and their personnel over the years have tended to drift away from close familiarity with neighborhoods and individuals to the status of a somewhat aloof and impersonal presence.

The answers aren't in more technology, equipment and research, valuable as these are. The principal answer rests in the quality of the individual police officer and the opportunity afforded him to do a proper job.

Then it will be up to that vast majority of citizens, black and white, to keep showing their support of a truly professional police effort.

Can a "Pig" Laugh?

Dear Betty,

This piece appeared on March 8, 1970. I wanted to get across to the public that they could help make a better police force. Many people don't know how important they are to making a policeman good at his job.

Love, Dad

> Police administrators and citizens recognize that in too many cases throughout the nation, police themselves have been part of today's problem of community tension and crime, instead of part of the solution.
>
> What police are trying to do about it is to build complete and total "professionalism" into the practice of police work.
>
> The substance of what is meant by police "professionalism" is this:
>
> - Understanding the "what" and "why" of your professional role
> - Knowing the "how" of police work thoroughly and executing it proficiently
> - Putting service before self
> - Being better informed and alert to group and individual sensitivities
> - Keeping your "cool" always
> - Performing to satisfy yourself and to stand scrutiny of the public stare

Professional performance comes first from good example and good leadership; it is assisted by training, and made easier by recruiting the best type of men in the first place.

It needs to be fed by community confidence and respect. All these factors interact, and are interdependent.

The true professional cop is color blind, except when it comes to traffic lights. He knows when to use a handshake instead of a hand-cuff. He recognizes the difference between a nuisance complaint and a genuine call for help.

He knows how to laugh when he is called a "pig." He knows when to hold his fire, when that shadowy shape he's pursuing might be a boy, instead of a bandit.

He understands when force is necessary and he knows how to protect himself and the citizen who needs his help. But he also knows when he is being baited and how to ignore the bait. And he knows how to correct a dangerous traffic violation without making the violator resentful.

A professional who can do all these things has to be a paragon. But he can't get that way by accident, or through community neglect, or without sufficient education, training and incentive, or without a good mind, good body and firmness of character to begin with.

The making of a professional may start with the police but the process isn't complete until the total community has had a hand in the craftsmanship.

Bless Those Irish Cops

Dear Betty,

This article came out on March 15, 1970, near St. Patrick's Day. I kind of took off in several directions and I hope people enjoyed it.

Love, Dad

Few policemen ever had as great a reputation for rapport with citizens as the old Irish cops of New York, Boston and other cities.

These men were first or second generation Irish who once swarmed into the police ranks in such numbers that they created a lasting stereotype.

There was a time when you couldn't say "policeman" without conjuring up a picture of a red-faced man in blue with a brogue a mile thick who was friendly, tough when he had to be, but also ready with blarney.

Historian Thomas J. Fleming, writing in "American Heritage" points out that in the early days of the New York Police Department, as many as two-thirds of the officers appointed in a single year were Irish. A few years ago, about 30% of the force was of Irish descent.

According to Fleming, the basis of their rapport was that the Irish cop was of the same immigrant stock as most of the citizenry, and served as an ideal buffer between "old" and "new" Americans.

He tended to be tolerant of some infractions of the law, those that victimized no one and were enjoyed by many, and he concentrated on making the streets safe.

Toleration of this sort often was excessive and produced scandal, and a policeman could become too closely involved with some of the citizens for efficient law enforcement.

But there was much to be said for the friendly magnetism of a big man in blue who could charm a middle-aged lady out of her shoes.

My wife was raised a Fallon, and her father was one of New York's "finest," so there'll be plenty of green showing at the Spreen household March 17.

Reminiscing about the Irish influence in policing raises the subject of history of our city police departments. Where they came from and how they got started is an interesting story.

What happened when citizens decided to stop policing themselves, and to pay some of their number to become specialists in the function? Is there a real or only an imaginary conflict between keeping the peace and fighting crime? What is crime? Is it the same as "sin?" If both are distinct, should police be required to deal with both?

A peek into past history should provide us with some useful insights...and some intriguing sidelights, too.

Such as the relationship between the modern policeman and a "walker through puddles"; a town constable and a stable attendant; county police and the king's local administrators, and how the entire Anglo-American criminal justice system got a big assist from a "juvenile delinquent."

"The Man" Needs His Badge and Gun

Dear Betty,

You know I taught part-time college courses for police officers. One day I learned that other students were somewhat sensitive to what they felt was a "conspicuous display" of badges and uniforms in classrooms. They were even more sensitive about the presence of the guns that all the officers carried, even those in civilian clothes. A bulge revealed the guns sometimes, and sometimes when an officer opened his coat. So I did this piece, which appeared March 22, 1970, to explain police policies.

Love, Dad

Here's the problem about the wearing of guns. Let me start with an example from my own experience.

I was a young New York City patrolman and I was preparing to go to work on the 4 p.m. shift. We had no private home phone at that time.

I had to make a call, so I dashed out to the corner drugstore where there was a phone booth near the entrance. I was in civilian clothes, and I never thought about putting on my service revolver.

I made my call about 3:15, went home, put on my uniform and reported for duty. At 4:15, in my radio car, I got a report that the same corner drugstore had just been robbed at gunpoint.

In the first place, I was in technical violation of department rules, which require police to carry their guns at all times, on or off duty. This rule is in effect in Detroit today, as it was in New York then, and it's a strict regulation of every police department I know anything about.

The reason for the rule was demonstrated by what happened at the drugstore. Suppose the robber had entered an hour earlier when I was in the phone booth. The drugstore people saw me, and knew I was a police officer.

I would have been bound under my oath as a police officer to take action against a felony committed in my presence.

Whether I was technically "on" or "off" duty was irrelevant. How would I have dealt with that armed robber without my gun?

Any good citizen will do what he can in a crime situation. The police officer has more than his conscience to guide him. He cannot allow concern for his personal safety to keep him from intervening.

Detroit and New York police regulations say quite sternly and clearly that a policeman, whether in uniform or out of uniform, whether on duty or on his day off, who shirks duty in time of danger is guilty of cowardice. He is subject to immediate dismissal. A policeman is never really "off duty."

I am sorry that police uniforms and weapons can have a disturbing effect on conscientious citizens. I think police officers should make every effort to keep their weapons out of sight and to wear them as inconspicuously as possible, particularly in off-duty situations.

No good policeman wears a gun because he likes to, or flaunts it for purposes of intimidation. It's a burden and a problem to him, more often than not. The officers in my class are dedicated men and women. They are taking a positive step toward making themselves better and more understanding professionals by going to school, so that students and other citizens will have more reason to look up to them, not down on them.

Yet the gun and the badge keep getting in the way.

How a Panther Fray Was Averted

Dear Betty,

This article ran on March 25, 1970. A reader wrote in questioning whether police or Black Panthers were responsible for confrontations between each other after he read something that black Congressman John Conyers said. I took the opportunity to try to defuse tension rather than let it build between the races. Another reader, a young black man, asked about being a policeman.

Love, Dad

> Answer: I do think it is significant that Congressman Conyers' home city of Detroit has had no such "confrontations," in spite of the fact that a national magazine in its Febrary 6 issue ran a full page picture that included Detroit in the magazine's coverage of the "confrontation" story.
>
> The caption on the photo, which shows a young black man holding a revolver, peering out of a window beneath a drawn shade, says this:
>
> "At right, a Panther in Detroit kept a trigger-ready vigil in December following a report that a police raid was imminent."
>
> I think it's time Detroit got some credit for the intelligent, affirmative initiative undertaken by police, and the cooperation by black citizens, including of the so-called "Black Panthers," that has so far avoided this kind of confrontation.
>
> No such "police raid" was "imminent" on any known Black Panther location in Detroit, nor was I aware of any evidence in the possession of the Detroit Police Department to even suggest such a possibility.
>
> Here's what did happen in Detroit.

At 1:17 p.m. on Thursday, Dec. 11, a week after the shooting in Chicago in which two Black Panthers died, Detroit police received a phone call from an anonymous male voice, reporting a fight and a stabbing at an address in north central Detroit.

The address was recognized as a "sensitive" one, and an experienced sergeant headed the team sent to handle the call.

The sergeant visited the address and was told by an occupant that there was no need for police service. He saw no outward signs of a disturbance and left.

Very shortly afterward, the Police Department began receiving numerous calls from alarmed citizens asking if there was any trouble between police and the Panthers.

Key members of the department, predominantly black, were alerted to deal with the situation.

At 11:47 that night, a different male voice called to report a shooting at the same "sensitive" address.

A Police Department representative contacted the address by telephone, and got a negative response. No police were dispatched.

This was the start of a new "fail-safe" system by which selected Police Department representatives and members of the so-called "Black Panther" group can check each other out against false alarms, whether from cranks or groups motivated by deliberate malice.

The system is still in force, and obviously has been working. I think it's a major plus-mark for Detroit.

It provides striking evidence of this city's capacity to reduce tensions, as long as a kernel of mutual trust can be established, and coolness and common sense are allowed to prevail.

Question: I am 21 years old and black. I would like to join the Police Department, but my mother is dead set against it. Is there something you can say to make her feel differently?

Answer: I can understand a mother's or a wife's concern. Once, at a Detroit Police Academy graduation, I met the mother of one of the new graduates, who said she had tried to talk her son out of becoming a policeman.

Of course, her son already had won the family debate, but I felt she wanted some reassurance from me.

I couldn't tell her there was nothing to worry about. But I did tell her that everybody needed police, and that police departments in general were in trouble, partly because they didn't have enough good black officers.

I told her it was an honorable profession that could be kept that way only if honorable men were willing to keep joining its ranks.

I told her the profession would always be hazardous, but the hazards would be less if police were fully accepted, respected and aided by all segments of the community. I also told her this could never come to pass if young men, who were willing and able to face the challenges and dangers involved, were turned aside by the fears and concerns of their loved ones.

Police Should Respond Faster

Dear Betty:

So many people have wondered about the question that this reader posed, I thought it well worth a column. The column appeared April 8, 1970.

Love, Dad

Question: A friend of mine recently made a call to the police to report a suspicious car on his block, and they took over 10 minutes to respond. Shouldn't police response be faster than this?

Answer: Immediate response is the goal that all police departments aspire to. The quicker the response in crime situations, the better the chance of capturing the criminals.

Improvement in police vehicles, communications and supervision can do much to speed up police response. But we have seen a relatively slight increase in the number of police officers available in recent years.

Meanwhile, the number of calls for assistance and service has risen astronomically. You can shift manpower from one emergency to another, but there is just not enough total manpower to meet every community need satisfactorily.

Shortly after I became police commissioner in 1968 I instituted some strict guidelines on car-response that were made necessary by the increasing demands for police service. The increase had reached the level of 50,000 additional calls each year above the previous year's total.

Our first concern had to be the citizen in immediate danger because of a crime in progress, just completed, or about to be committed. The "Impact" telephone number was created just for this kind of emergency.

Minor crimes, discovered long after the fact of commission, and minor accidents where no personal injury was involved, could be reported, we felt, to police at the citizen's local precinct station.

A policeman cannot be in two places at once. Should he be more concerned about a brutal assault, or a rape, or a fender-bender (minor traffic accident)? Obviously, the personal harm is more important than the property damage.

Until there are adequate numbers of police, such guidelines will be necessary in the interest of providing essential police services where they are needed most.

Police History and the Garden of Eden

Dear Betty:

It seemed to me that citizens were more interested in their police than at any time in our history. I wanted to give them some perspective about where current policing practices came from. This article came out in 1970.

Love, Dad

Policing can be called one of the oldest professions. When God put Adam and Even out of the Garden of Eden, and put cherubim on watch to make sure they stayed out, our first social order was established.

Historians can trace police institutions back to the Code of Hammurabi, the Babylonian ruler, more than 2,000 years before Christ.

The Spartans in ancient Greece had "ephors" who performed some policing and other law enforcement functions. Rome under Emperor Augustus was served by thousands of men called "vigils", literally the "watchful ones." Their job was to keep the peace and look out for fires.

After the fall of the Roman Empire, the dark ages descended on Europe. The Asiatic horsemen known as "Huns" put pressure on the tribes of central Europe. Some tribes sailed to the British Isles from what are now Denmark and Germany.

As these people struggled and then mingled with the native Britons, and began to take primitive steps to provide local security, the earliest traces of our modern police principles began to appear. Under Alfred the Great, who was of Saxon descent, the beginnings of an army, a navy and a code of law occurred. The first major phase in the evolution of today's police role had begun.

This was the social determination that the maintenance of local "law and order" was the responsibility of the people themselves, not the ruler.

The people served as their own police, acted as judge and jury, and saw to it that any penalties or punishment were exacted.

The second phase in policing followed the Norman Conquest of England in 1066. Specialists emerged to handle some of the duties of the law enforcement system. The most prominent of these were "justices of the peace."

The third and present phase is the establishment of paid professional police to provide protection and assure "law and order."

Paid professionals began to appear in England as early as the reign of Queen Elizabeth I, but the fully organized publicly maintained city police force is less than 150 years old.

Is there a fourth stage in the evolution of policing on the horizon? Will we, or can we, learn from history?

Death Penalty Not a Crime Deterrent

Dear Betty,

This column came from a question I was asked about the death penalty. It gave me a chance to discuss my views on that very important subject and appeared on April 15, 1970. I've always thought gun control would be a more successful deterrent than the death penalty.

Love, Dad

Question: Some state legislators recommend the death penalty for criminals guilty of murdering police and firemen on duty. What about the murderers who kill doctors or storekeepers or people living quietly in their homes? There would be less killing if we had the death penalty in Michigan.

Answer: Is the purpose of a sentence to punish the criminal in retaliation for his offense, to rehabilitate him or to deter commission of crimes in the future?

It seems to me that all three considerations are involved in modern society's attitude toward criminal penalties.

Your question stresses the idea of prevention; that the death penalty would reduce killing.

Most law enforcement researchers believe a prospective criminal is more apt to be deterred by the certainty of being caught and punished, than by the severity of the penalty.

The President's Commission on Law Enforcement and Administration of Justice completed a massive and penetrating study of crime and the criminal justice system in 1967.

In its consideration of the death penalty, it made these points:

1. The death penalty is applied less frequently than in the 1930s.
2. There has been a decline in support for the death penalty.
3. Because of its awesome finality, authorities are reluctant to use it.
4. Cases with the death penalty take longer to try and result in more appeals.
5. Some evidence shows that the poor are more apt to get the death sentence.
6. There is no evidence that the death penalty is a crime deterrent.

In Elizabethan England, picking pockets was a capital offense. Yet, when the people came out to watch the public hangings, the pickpockets working the crowd had a field day. Hanging certainly was no deterrent.

The commission recommended that the form of capital punishment should continue to be determined by the states, and that where used, it should apply only to limited types of offenses.

My own feeling is that retaliation by means of the death penalty does little to help past or future victims. During 1960-1968, 475 police officers in the United States were killed by criminal action; 96% of them by firearms. A better approach to gun control would do far more than the death penalty, in my opinion.

We Needed Bucking Up

Dear Betty,

People used to ask me what I enjoyed the most as Detroit's police commissioner. I used to tell them the "Buck Up Your Police" project. So I did an article on that which appeared on April 19, 1970.

Love, Dad

> I made a speech to the Detroit Jaycees about a year ago. It mushroomed into an unprecedented demonstration of community involvement with police.
>
> Money was hard to come by, Common Council was looking askance at the police budget request, police morale was sagging and the whole department needed "bucking up." That's when the idea struck me: how about asking concerned citizens to send in just a "buck" to let the department know they were behind it, and to help pay for some badly needed equipment.
>
> The Jaycees, a fine bunch of young men, jumped in to manage the drive. When it ended six months later, 49,513 citizens had sent in a dollar apiece.
>
> The money provided extra scooters for neighborhood patrol, extra radio-transmitter-receivers for patrolmen, scuba equipment for a new underwater rescue team, TV equipment for better on-the-job training, books on policing and literature containing information for citizens.
>
> The first purchase after we received the Council's not-too-gracious permission to accept the money was 50 rolls of videotape. The largest single purchase was a shipment of 99 Honda motor scooters at $152 apiece, or $15,048. We eventually bought 120 with "Buck Up" funds. The money and the things it bought were wonderful. But even more wonderful was the sense of moral support the endeavor gave the policemen in the streets, and the out-

pouring of heartwarming support that reached me in the mails. Seven hundred letters arrived in one two-week period. I think the total reached the thousands.

Some signed their names, some didn't. Many were from blacks, even one from a young man who had been an unsuccessful applicant for officer.

The story was carried in newspapers across the nation, and letters and donations came in from other states and even the Bahamas.

St. Rita's School sent in a scrapbook filled with coins as well as drawings. Pupils from St. Agnes School donated a "pot of gold" filled with coins. Gov. Milliken saw it on a visit to Police Headquarters, and added his and aides' contributions. High school seniors turned over funds, which usually went for a gift for their school.

It was a wonderful experience and one I will never forget.

The Old and Young Must Shut the Gap

Dear Betty,

I wrote this article on October 28, 1970 after reading about a rash of young people who were committing suicide in dramatic fashion or slow motion through their lifestyle. It seems like it could still apply today.

Love, Dad

Young people with apparently high intelligence and a fierce but twisted idealism blow themselves and others up.

Famous rock and roll personalities destroy their bodies through drug abuse.

Black and white teenagers, instead of learning from the mistakes of their elders, revive the same old passions, with undiminished bitterness.

One of the consolations of maturity is to be able to look backward and take comfort from the lessons of the past.

The Roman poet-philosopher Cicero exclaimed about the times and the morals in ancient Rome. Aristotle and Socrates deplored the foolishness of undisciplined youth in ancient Greece.

Yet the young people matured, the world survived and very slowly mankind learned a little more and improved a little more in spite of constant backsliding.

So I continue to have faith in our young people, their energy, resiliency, recuperative powers and fundamental idealism. I continue to have faith that today's troubles and worries too will pass. But I sure would like to see the improvement process speeded up.

I think there's an opportunity to do so if we can stop overemphasizing the chronological and other differences that distinguish young from old.

Young and old have complementary abilities and skills that, put together, can make up for each other's deficiencies, if we can put them together. But this is going to require more mutual respect, of old for young as well as young for old, than seems to be the case today.

Part of this is due to a quirk of human nature, to which some news media tend to cater, that pays more curious attention to the abnormal than the normal.

When somebody wants to make a big splash in the world, either to make money or win public attention, it just doesn't pay, apparently, to be quiet, to reflect, to weigh all the issues and act in moderation. It's the big disturbance and the loud noise that catches the headline, the camera and the microphone.

PART IV

Oakland County Sheriff

o o o o o o o o o o o o o o o o o o o o o o o o o o o

"I do the very best I know how, the very best I can; and mean to keep doing so until the end. If the end brings me out all right, what is said against me won't amount to anything. If the end brings me out wrong, ten angels swearing I was right would make no difference."

—*Abraham Lincoln*

How I Become Sheriff

Dear Betty,

Now I'm going to write about my tough twelve years as a sheriff (the only Democrat at the county level) in a predominantly Republican county. These twelve years were filled with joy, sadness, triumph, tragedy, turmoil, trouble, treachery, and much more.

I had to overcome law suits, political pot shots, internal difficulty in the sheriff's office, battling with the media, suing the *Detroit News*, and never really overcoming the damage done by the *Oakland Press* in my relations with the 43 county police chiefs and their political bosses. There were problems in New York when I was there and there were problems in Detroit but there were more problems when I was sheriff. But I also am proud of my many accomplishments in all these areas.

I have regrets regarding Oakland County. One of my biggest regrets is that I could not accomplish many things I believed in for better law enforcement just because I was seen as a Democrat in the predominantly Republican county. I ran and won three times during those years during the Nixon and Reagan landslides.

I had never considered running for office as sheriff. It all started, I guess, with my success and public approval during my 17½ months as Police Commissioner of Detroit. (I also served for six months as consultant to Thomas Plunkett.) I did enjoy the Detroit challenge. To me, that was important. I do feel I could have done much to help the fine city of Detroit, a Detroit that was a beacon of hope, an admired city, until those fateful days of July 1967. Those were fateful days that Detroit has never really recovered from.

I could have stayed as Police Commissioner, but again, politics. Bah, humbug! Mayor Cavanagh chose not to run even though he had told me he would. Two polls commissioned by him had me included and had me leading for Mayor. I was told about this a couple of years ago. That was a job I did not aspire to. Richard Austin named me as Police Commissioner. Yes, I believe I could have been important to the city, that the 17½ months I served would have been a catalyst for proper law enforcement, police improvement in methods, personnel and practice. But then alas, dreams all dashed.

I do fault Roman Gribbs who became Mayor, an erstwhile so-called friend who did not give me the courtesy and consideration expected.

I then, out of consideration for my wife Elinor and you, Betty, removed myself from being considered or evaluated by Roman Gribbs, a weak mayor. He paved the way for Coleman Young, a strong mayor but with racist tendencies, which caused "white flight." He turned Detroit into an almost black city. Now it's 85% black.

I feel that many good white people would have stayed in Detroit with safe, secure neighborhoods and proper, professional law enforcement.

Mayor Gribbs weak leadership and Coleman Young's "eight-mile road comments" and his constant racial talk using black language helped cause the demise of a once great city. I hope it can rise from the ashes!

But after writing columns for the *Detroit News* and feuding with the *Detroit Free Press*, I ran for sheriff.

As I mentioned, I had never considered running for sheriff. It started with a surprise call from Thomas Plunkett, the Prosecutor of Oakland County, and the only Democrat at the county level at that time. He asked me to run with him as the candidate for sheriff. We met and talked though I knew him from my experience as his consultant. At the same time, the Republicans met with me four or five times to get me to run as a Republican. Brooks Patterson, now a Republican County executive, also asked me to run with him. I told them "If I run as a Democrat, Brooks, I know you are all for law enforcement and I know you and I can work together."

I found out differently. Brooks was all for Brooks. After a couple of weeks of so-called cooperation, he and the Republicans, resentful of my victory as the only Democrat at the County level, a victory they had not anticipated, gave me nothing but trouble. And that continued for the entire twelve years I was in office.

When the Chief Republican leader, Chairman of the Party in Oakland County, spoke to me on the phone and asked me to run as a Republican, he warned me if I ran as a Democrat I would not be funded for my programs. I was dumbfounded. This is what I said: "I feel that if I present my ideas and programs properly, and substantiate them with proper facts and figures, the county commissioners will vote objectively."

He said, "You are certainly naive." I guess I was. At that time there was no county executive. Dan Murphy was later elected over Gene Kuthy by only ½% margin. There is another story about how I was cajoled into endorsing Kuthy and that cost me my relation with Dan Murphy.

Frankly I found politics in Oakland County to be "piss poor," an old Army term, and that was true of the national as well as the state level. Because I had run as a Democrat against their wishes and won, I received little Republican support. Some Republicans were sympathetic but the majority rules.

When they had pleaded with me to run as a Republican, I had asked for their endorsement. They said their policy was against endorsing before the primary election.

I said, "But you endorsed Lenore Romney (George's wife) for Senator."

They said, "Yes, but we made a mistake. We can't endorse you." But they would see that their candidate, Leo Hazen, the current under sheriff, would not run if I ran as a Republican. Such power!

I asked for something less than the official party endorsement. A non-partisan organization called Civic Searchlight did rate candidates for office using terms such as Preferred and Well Qualified, Well Qualified, Qualified, or Not Qualified. I asked the Republicans to give me a Well Qualified if they could not give me a Preferred and Well Qualified.

In effect, I did not wish to be obligated to 20 or 30 big Republicans who said they would support me and would raise funds for my election. I'd rather be obligated to an amorphous group, the people, than to 20 or 30 "fat cats" that I felt I would be beholden to.

Guess I was naive, wasn't I? I did not understand politics then. I understand more now and I don't like it. And that's one of our problems in America today, that two party system. Democrats and Republicans are constantly battling with each other.

In my case, the Republicans, after rejecting their offer and blandishments, and after my election, their battle cry seemed to be "Let's get that bastard out of office."

Still I feel, if the tables were reversed, the Democrats would echo that same battle cry. Ah yes, "piss poor politics" to say the least. Is there a better system? Is a third party better? Probably not! But???

Politics to me is a constant battle against the other side, a constant battle for election with promises, promises not kept, and a constant battle for the funds to get and keep being elected.

I abhorred the chore of requesting monetary support from people. To me, big donors would demand big favors. In law enforcement that is tantamount to being unprofessional.

Even though I won three times and was in office twelve years, I never did raise much money. The good will of people who knew me as Police Commissioner of Detroit and who realized what I was attempting to do as Sheriff really put me in office, I believe.

One day, when I was thinking of what might have been, I asked my wife Elinor, "Should I have run as a Republican? We would not have all this storm and turmoil."

She said, "Yes, John, but you are still your own man, aren't you?"

Yes, but it comes at a price! A price not only I had to pay but also what the community and the county pay for things unfulfilled. Politics; bah humbug!

I think I understand why George Washington warned the country in his Farewell Address about parties. He urged countrymen to foreswear excessive party spirit and geographical distinction. In 1796 he said, "One of the expedients of Party to acquire influence, within particular districts, is to misrepresent the opinions and aims of other Districts. You cannot shield yourselves too much against the jealousies and heart burnings, which spring from these misrepresentations. They tend to render alien to each other those who ought to be bound together by fraternal affections."

Elinor used to say to me that my song was, "I did it my way," from Frank Sinatra's song. He was a friend of mine and helped Elinor. "Regrets, I have a few, but too few to mention!" As for me, my tenure of twelve years will also be a major regret. Oh, what could have been! I know I could have done more as Sheriff with proper support. Omar Khayyam wrote,

> *"The moving finger writes; and having writ,*
> *Moves on: nor all your piety nor wit*
> *Shall lure it back to cancel half a line,*
> *Nor all your tears wash out a word of it."*

But going back to Detroit, I was much happier as Police Commissioner of Detroit than I was as the elected Sheriff of Oakland County. My greatest disappointment as Commissioner was New Detroit, created to make Detroit a better city after the riots. They did little to help a new Police Commissioner.

Thank you, dear, for letting me get some of this off my chest.
Love, Dad

Gun Control

Dear Betty,

After I left my position as Detroit Police Commissioner, I was an associate professor for John Jay College for a couple more years. Then when I became Sheriff of Oakland County, I also taught law enforcement part-time for the Mercy College from 1971 to 1981. I still wrote columns in the *Detroit News* and this article ran on June 24, 1971 under the title "Gun ownership doesn't halt crime." The gist of the article was that I thought that we must do something about handgun control.

I will never forget the day that three shots rang out and a five-year old girl was killed by a bullet in her brain. There were so many stories of innocent people and police being sent to their deaths or a life of pain and suffering because of accidental or deliberate discharge of firearms.

I mentioned that although there seemed to be a correlation between rising gun ownership and rising violent crime, it couldn't be proven which was the cause and which the effect. Statistics suggested that during the past five years, as crime increased, gun ownership increased more rapidly. I assumed that the gun purchases were made not by criminals but by ordinary citizens in stores that kept statistics, because criminals usually obtained guns in methods that were not tracked. Instead of preventing crime or deterring killing, the rise in gun ownership was paralleled by an even sharper rise in crimes committed with guns.

Here were the statistics:

All Crimes Reported	***Year***	***Handgun Permits***	***Gun Homicides***	***Gun Robberies***
Up 39%	1966	Up 25%	Up 58%	Up 103%
Up 64%	1967	Up 107%	Up 121%	Up 162%
Up 65%	1968	Up 236%	Up 407%	Up 278%
Up 82%	1969	Up 151%	Up 498%	Up 398%
Up 105%	1970	Up 124%	Up 574%	Up 656%

If citizens rushed to buy guns for protection because of rising crime, obviously the increased possession of weapons did not protect or reduce the crime trend. I thought it was reasonable to conclude that each helped to escalate the other. Far from being the answer to the crime problem, citizen self-armament had merely helped to accelerate the amount of violent crime with guns. So I tried to go another direction to stem violence: disarm the criminal. I'll talk more about that later.

Love, Dad

Look on the Bright Side

Dear Betty,

I addressed the graduating class of your Mercy High School on June 4, 1972. This was, of course, before you graduated and I was thinking of you as I prepared my talk. Here are some of the highlights that I told those young high school graduates.

> Today is a day of great expectations. It is much more of a look ahead than a look backward. You, your teachers and your parents, we're all looking forward to a future that we know will be brighter because of you and what we know you are capable of doing to make it so.
>
> Here's my formula. It has three simple parts.
>
> First, look on the bright side of things. Be an optimist.
>
> Second, discipline yourselves so that you'll have the strength and purpose to accomplish great things.
>
> Third, never forget how to smile.
>
> First, let's think about optimism. When I suggest that we should look on the bright side of things, I don't mean we should be blind to faults, either in society or ourselves. We should examine faults and correct them. The point is that if you want to improve things, you build progress on hope, not despair. You can't expect to act positively if you're thinking negatively. Looking for the good in life rather than the evil is what turns people on, and helps society to achieve.
>
> International suspicion has reached a crescendo since the day of the atom bomb dawned. The Iron Curtain of suspicion came down in Europe. The Bamboo Curtain came down in the Far East. But now an American President in the space of a few months has pierced both curtains. Hopefully we are witnessing a new birth of more open communication that can lead us down the long road to

genuine friendship with those who used to be our enemies, and to international peace.

I think we can find things to be optimistic about in our long drawn-out war against crime. Stimulated by the rising crime trend, and the riots of the 1960s, our nation is in the midst of the most massive effort in history to mobilize local, state and federal resources. We're trying to find out what's wrong with our courts, our prosecution, our penal institutions and our police, and to do something about it.

So there is good reason for optimism and accentuating the positive in all these areas. But high hopes alone don't get things done. To make a dream come true you have to work at it. And you have to start with yourself and develop your own capacity to achieve. Your teachers and parents know this.

We all recognize that young people in every generation carry the burden of hope and accomplishment toward building a better world. That is why many older people are so distressed when they see some young people whose whole approach is destructive rather than constructive.

This is part of what some people call the "generation gap." It's perfectly normal to have a generation "gap" based on difference in age, and differences in environment and experience. But there is no reason, because of a difference in age, for a "gap" in understanding, love and compassion.

I believe that most young people and older people of good conscience are equally concerned about righting the wrongs of this world.

Shakespeare counts seven ages of man, from infancy to senility. In any one lifetime, I count four "generations." Up to about 20 years old, you're concerned primarily with yourself, learning your identity as some like to put it. It's a period of idealism, combined with inexperience and uncertainty, and a yearning for a better world. Like frisky colts, you youngsters are long on energy and wild oats and short on stability and prudence.

From age 20 to 40, the wild horses are in the corral so to speak. This is the period of family raising, and trying to make it in the world of work. You're in the system now, and have all the burdens of others, or so it will seem.

Then, as some of us know, life truly begins again at about 40. A lot of your family and career problems will have been settled, one way or another. You'll be able to look around again at how the rest of the world is making out. Your sense of personal responsibility turns outward toward others.

Finally, when you've done your thing well at each stage of life, by about 60 you should have earned the right to be respected by the younger generation, not just for gray hairs and longevity but also for having used your years well.

Building a better life for yourself and building a better world for all of us takes more than ambition, dreams and wishful thinking. It takes brains and you have to use them. It also takes physical and moral stamina, a combination of endurance and courage, as well as strength. It takes a good conscience and a sense of right and wrong, which is informed and strengthened by learning, example and experience. And it takes desire and will, having the determination to take the steps that are necessary to achieve those goals.

Self-indulgence is a trap and an invitation to weakness. We need moral and psychological muscles as well as physical muscles.

Now the last element in my prescription is to remember how to smile. The smile is important because it is an outward sign of the greatest of virtues, love. I hope your teachers have included love in their curriculum. It's easy to love what we're attracted to by instinct or taste or appetite. But the greatest religious teaching is that we should love our enemies. Imagine that, even our enemies!

Love is not just sticking two fingers in the air and saying "peace." People have been pointing fingers in the air for centuries and for all kinds of reasons having nothing to do with love. The best sign I know of that one human being can give to another to express love and sympathy and understanding is the smile. Cooperation involves winning people over and that means turning them on with something as simple as a smile.

And that's my prescription. From looking at the bright side, we get hope. From self-discipline, we develop the ability and confidence to accomplish what we set out to do. From love and our smile we get the incentive to act and pull people together.

You graduates of 1972 can have a beautiful future as long as you work to make it beautiful.

That's what I told those graduates at the time you were still in your early teens. What would you have thought?
Love, Dad

Could I Professionalize the Sheriff's Department?

Dear Betty,

When I became Sheriff in 1972, I brought many ideas from my former careers as police officer and police commissioner. Some Oakland County citizens had expressed doubt about the value of a countywide Sheriff's Department. They told me that the sheriff's role isn't visible or significant, that the performance by the Oakland County Sheriff's Department was inadequate, and that they felt better served by city or state police.

I wanted to explain that the sheriff's office was responsible for administering the jail and providing for the security of county prisons. It also provides police protection to citizens who have no local police of their own. I thought the sheriff's office commanded less respect than it deserved because it had not been providing overall countywide support to local agencies as an umbrella support.

I thought a strong and modern sheriff needed to build support by better communication with the people, better liaison with local police agencies, improving the quality of department service, and by broadening the scope of services.

I proposed the following programs:

- introduction of sound administration practice in management
- improved training and recruitment of personnel
- increased advancement incentives for personnel
- strengthening of supervision through training

- more effective use of available resources
- review and revision of organizational structure
- review of jail operations and personnel for upgrades
- guidelines for separation of prisoners by offense, age, recidivism
- humane standards of treatment, food, clothing, cleanliness
- high school and college level education for prisoners
- establishment of a well-supplied prison library
- seeking federal assistance grants for research and services

You will see as you track my career that I was unable to accomplish as much as I wanted in these areas and you will see why.
Love, Dad

Let's Disarm the Criminal!

Dear Betty,

As you know, I served as the Sheriff of Oakland County in Michigan for 12 years, from 1972 to 1985. When I was Sheriff, I testified in May 1975 before the Senate Judiciary Committee about Senate Bill #127, Use of Handgun in the Commission of a Crime. The bill proposed that a mandatory minimum two-year sentence be given to those who carry a firearm during an attempt or actual commission of a felony. You might be interested in what I told them about handguns.

> Citizens are being murdered daily in their own homes and businesses and on the streets. Police who respond to aid them are laying their lives on the line constantly.
>
> I have seen the distressing toll in robberies, burglaries, rapes, citizens frightened and killed, and policemen hurt and shot. I have had the heart-breaking experience over and over again of attending their funerals. In the past ten years alone, a thousand law enforcement officers have been killed and 70% by individuals using handguns. There is no reason why this massacre should continue.
>
> Four years ago, I wrote a newspaper column calling for an additional jail sentence for the carrying of a gun when it was used in the commission of certain crimes. I recommended five years mandated by law with no probation, no parole, no early release and no good time.
>
> We must do something about handgun control but we are not going to accomplish anything by trying to ban all handguns, since gun prohibition will not get the gun away from the criminal. We know that police cannot protect every person in his own home. We do not have the money or the manpower. We are losing the battle in the streets. Yet, we must do something, something better than we have done in the past.

Let us start by getting at the real problem. Let us get at the criminal who brings and uses a gun when he commits a crime. This is gun control. Later, we can address the problem of too many handguns possessed by too many citizens. That problem may alleviate itself, if we solve the other problem first.

The bum who uses a gun should not be allowed to thumb his nose at society. Let us remove these potential killers from the scene. If a five-year term went into effect, they would go to prison and know that they would not be out again until five years later. And if these hoodlums are convicted a second time of using a gun in the commission of a crime, the mandatory sentence should be doubled or tripled. The third time we should throw away the key!

Just recently several state legislators proposed a two-year mandatory sentence for the use of a gun in a felony. While I still would like to see a stiffer sentence (five years), I definitely support their proposal.

The criminals, no doubt, always will be able to get a gun, and of course, the bullets for it. But if this legislation is passed, they will think twice before bringing a loaded gun with them when they go out to rob, burgle and rape.

The "professional" burglar of old would never have brought a gun with him. He had a "certain pride in his craft." He wasn't a mean killer. But who do we have committing these crimes today? About 75% are recidivists, a small core who are committing the majority of the crimes over and over again. And kids commit half of all serious crimes. Far more than half are drug addicts who are hopped up. A gun should not be in the hands of people who could care less, are immature or crazed, and hopped up by drugs.

The smart criminal is one who is "jail smart." He wheels and deals, delaying and adjourning the trial, using and abusing our criminal justice system, while the victim lies in the hospital or the morgue. We citizens must get smart now, so that we leave our children a better day years from now.

Let's send out a strong message to the bums and punks, and potential killers everywhere, and put some fear into their hearts. Let us save our good citizens and save our police.

I believe that there is not a police chief or a sheriff in this country who would not agree that something must be done about the

> use of guns while committing a crime. Let us leave the gun-carrying burglar, robber, and rapist to his "peers" on the jury. Let him know that if he "does the crime," he'll "do the time."

Betty, as you know, it was made more difficult to buy guns after 1981 when John Hinckley shot President Reagan and three others with a handgun. But I cannot imagine that this country will ever reach the level of Canadian gun prohibition.
Love, Dad

The Money Farces of Oakland County

Dear Betty,

You'll notice a very discouraged tone as I tell you about a report I made to the people after being sheriff for three years. In fact, I called my report "The Money Farces of Oakland County." I tried to describe these "farces."

I started off by telling them that I felt as if there had been a deliberate, planned, calculated effort to render the sheriff powerless and ineffective in what had become a tale of politics, red tape and bureaucratic morass. In my 2-½ years as sheriff, millions of dollars had been funneled into Michigan under the Law Enforcement Assistance Administration arm of the federal government but not one cent had gone to the Sheriff's Department except a continuation of the Narcotics Enforcement Team started several years ago and supervised by State Police.

I told the people that crime was up 23% last year in Oakland County so the ultimate losers were them, the people.

I told them the story of nine grant attempts by my department and gave details of some of them. There was a Cadet Grant to encourage young people to apply for criminal justice intern jobs. Another was a request for a traffic grant. Another was a crime prevention grant. A communications grant was hopefully still alive which could provide portable radios for our officers.

I assured the people that even though our department had not received help, I would continue to fight for a strong sheriff's organization but I would not waste time with further applications for federal grants.

I promised the people that I would ask state and congressional representatives to look into the system of disbursement of U.S. funds in Oakland County. I promised to ask President Gerald Ford to look into the present system for a better way to share monies contributed by our citizens for law enforcement agencies.

I vowed to make requests for needs to the Commissioners of Oakland County for direct funding rather than go through a process that was "politically contaminated" as I called it. I suggested a new way of distributing law enforcement monies similar to the English system. For example, the total law enforcement dollars for a community law enforcement effort could be ¼ local, ¼ state funds, and ½ federal funds or it could be 1/3 across the board. I said that such a plan might stop much of the political ploys, jockeying, and nonsense, which seemed so prevalent in Oakland County.

Little did you know that I made that presentation only two days before your high school graduation ceremony.

Love, Dad

My Commencement Address at Your Graduation

Dear Betty,

I was very fortunate to be able to address Mercy High School on the day you graduated, June 6, 1976. I was lucky enough to do the same when you graduated from Mercy College, where I was a professor at the time. I'll never forget that Cardinal Dearden gave me your diploma so I could personally hand it to you on stage. Just in case you can't remember what I said to your class on that beautiful day in 1976, here are some of the highlights.

I told your class that we were celebrating the 200th anniversary of the country and moving into the third century of our country's existence. I told your class the importance of education, college and used my own career rise as an example. After describing the importance of various careers and contributions to child rearing, I described that old formula that you have heard me describe before.

First, look on the bright side of things and be an optimist. Second, discipline yourselves so you'll have the strength and purpose to accomplish great things. Third, be aware. Fourth, communicate. And fifth, never forget how to smile.

I went into those four ages of man that I described in another high school commencement, and the physical and moral stamina needed to achieve high goals and build a better world. I then ended with the message that love, as reflected in our smiles, helps people pull together to accomplish the great things in life that they cannot accomplish alone.

Little did I know what lay ahead for me in the next few years. But you'll soon see.
Love, Dad

I Had to Beg For Help

Dear Betty,

On April 7, 1977, I addressed the Oakland County Board of Commissioners for only the second time since I became sheriff. I told them we had not been funded to add a single new position since I had taken the job despite the continued growth of crime and population increase.

I told them of my new plan to create three teams, each having one sergeant and six patrol officers. Each team should also have four paraprofessionals, a training sergeant, a statistical analyst and a records specialist. With such teams, not only crime deterrence but also immediate response could help prevent crimes, especially those involving children. I called this plan a "Crime and Accident Prevention Unit".

I described how each of the six patrol officers on each team would be trained in a specialty such as evidence technician, narcotics, juveniles, accident prevention, preliminary investigation and crime-scene investigation, as well as being cross-trained. The paraprofessionals would be assigned to headquarters to assist in compiling statistics, assisting with public education programs, and riding in patrol cars for specific purposes and for training.

"Can we afford to place a dollar value on any human life?" I asked them. I reminded them that because of the recent child murders we were getting national attention. I estimated that the program I proposed would cost each person in the county 60 cents. Summer was near and I suggested that children soon out of school would place additional strain on all 43 police departments in Oakland County.

Before the year was over, I would be in the press a lot more than I wanted to be.

Love, Dad

My Rebuttal to Criticism

Dear Betty,

On August 4, 1977, I issued a rebuttal to criticisms made by Prosecutor L. Brooks Patterson and the Southfield Police Chief. The Chief, Milton Sackett, had told the press that I had spoken to the press criticizing the investigation of a child's murder without being properly informed. I had criticized the fact that the body was moved from its original position before pictures were taken which distorted the pathologist's report. Then I criticized the fact that the body was taken to the police department and clothes were removed there before the body arrived at the morgue, which was a violation of procedures.

The Oakland County Prosecutor accused me of wanting to create a county police force and that I wanted to run that agency. My rebuttal stated that I have never advocated a county police force and wouldn't want to be head of such if some politician appoints the chief.

I explained that some law enforcement services can be performed at a centralized level more economically and effectively. The prosecutor was therefore favoring the proliferation of 43 crime labs, 43 traffic units, 43 surveillance units, 43 records systems and 43 crime prevention units with 43 police departments in Oakland County. This was costly for our citizens. My rebuttal ended as I said that Prosecutor Patterson was so motivated by ambition that he assumed everyone else was similarly motivated.

I just hated getting into these name-calling situations with politicians. I never asked more than to be able to do my job effectively and protect the citizens whom I had sworn to protect. But you know that, don't you, dear?

Love, Dad

I'd Rather Be Right Than Free

Dear Betty,

I'm really glad you were 19 years old and grown at the time I went to jail or it might have been very hard for you to understand. I knew I had your staunch support and that of your mother. But even so, I'm going to try to tell you in my own words why that happened.

I was the Oakland County Sheriff, top cop in the state's second most populous county. I was arrested and jailed for refusing to obey a court order to reinstate a sheriff's deputy whom I had fired the year before. You see, on March 11, 1976, I fired Detective Sergeant Keith Lester, 33, after he was charged with larceny by conversion for failing to turn over $200 a court gave him to pay a crime victim. He had pocketed $200 of a $750 restitution payment made by three youths in a larceny case in which they stole a trailer. The restitution was to be collected by Lester and given to the victims.

The charge against Lester was dismissed in February, however, and he sued for reinstatement of his job and back pay of $20,000. Judge Thorburn had dismissed the case because he said Lester should have been charged with embezzlement, not with larceny by conversion. Judge Beer granted the request to dismiss the case.

My view was that the charge against Lester had been improperly dismissed and that Lester was guilty. If I reinstated Lester, it would have lowered morale in the department. Besides that, Lester should have followed normal channels of appeal through the county employee appeal process to regain his job before he went to court.

The Oakland County Circuit Judge William Beer ordered me to be jailed indefinitely on contempt charges. He said I would stay in jail until I changed my mind and intended to lodge me in my own county in a local jail. Sheriff John O'Brien of Genesee County heard the news and sent his administrative assistant to suggest to Judge Beer that I be taken to the Genesee County jail in Flint, Michigan. I was grateful.

The judge's order came late after a day of legal haggling. I had appeared at a press conference with a toothbrush in my pocket, saying that I was ready to be locked up for my principles. I told the reporters, "I never thought I would see such a day when I myself would be charged with a crime. But I'd rather be right than free." The Oakland County deputies later presented me with a plaque with those lines.

Judge Beer, 67, who had been a judge for 20 years, said that I had violated the separation of powers doctrine by refusing to obey his order. The judge told reporters, "Judges' orders, even if distasteful, must be obeyed."

Judge Beer denied my request to delay the jailing from Friday to Monday so that I could make arrangements to take care of your mother, who was by that time an invalid, suffering with multiple sclerosis and curvature of the spine. She had undergone six operations during the last year and I wanted to spend Mother's Day with her instead of in jail.

When he denied the request, he said, "That has already been fully discussed."

Just before being sentenced by Judge Beer, there was a graduation ceremony in my jail for inmates who had attained their G.E.D. We had the Pontiac School system in our jail, teaching inmates so they could acquire the G.E.D. and pursue a better life. I had been scheduled to give the graduation address.

I had felt that a motivational type speech was in order. The inmates did not know that I was myself going to be jailed that very afternoon. I praised their efforts, told them they were started on a better road, and to keep going.

I then related the story of my life starting as a little immigrant lad from Germany who could not speak the English language. I wound up telling them about growing up in a Depression, gathering old newspapers to sell for a few cents, shoveling snow, lugging boxes of wood to make a little money because we were so poor. I described how I helped my father make cigars by stripping tobacco, how my parents didn't speak English very well, and that I never went to college until I was 35 years old. I congratulated ones getting their GEDs and added, "If I can do it, you can do it."

I told them to keep on and said, "When you get out, I don't want to see you back. Go out. Be a success. You can do it."

At the conclusion of my remarks, I informed them that I would immediately become an inmate like them. I was very touched when they all stood and gave me applause that continued until I left the room.

Before going to the jail, I called your mother and told her that if she felt she needed me, I would acquiesce to Judge Beer's order.

She said very crisply, "Stick to your guns, Sheriff. We're all right." I'll never forget that remark. She really would be all right. A contingent of officers from the Sheriff's Office was already at our home to offer assistance to you and your mother.

I turned my gun over to my undersheriff, John Nichols, and was taken into custody by Kenneth McArdle, administrative assistant to the Genesee County Sheriff, John O'Brien. O'Brien, a fellow Democrat, arranged for an attorney for me. I wasn't handcuffed, but the Judge had cautioned McArdle that I was to be treated "just as any other prisoner in jail."

When I arrived at the jail, Sheriff O'Brien welcomed me and we chatted for fifteen minutes before I was taken to the booking area and fingerprinted.

A deputy checked my personal property, which included a wallet with $54, an uncashed paycheck, sheriff's badge, checkbook, tie, tiepin and shoes. I said, "I never violated a court order before. To me, this is kind of like a comedy, but it's a tragedy. All I know is my 35 years in law enforcement seem to be going up in smoke."

Your mother had packed clothes into a small suitcase, which I was not able to take along. You were 19 at the time and the newspapers quoted you and mother saying that you "stand behind him 100 percent. They think he is right."

My attorney, Robert White of Grand Rapids, began working on an emergency appeal of Beer's order. White told reporters that I might be released the next day if he could get the appellate judges to hear the case.

They let me keep my civilian clothes rather than wearing a prison uniform. I was placed in a cell apart from other prisoners, a 10-foot square room. The room had a bed, a desk, two barred windows, and was usually used for intake. I was in "solitary confinement for my own protection." The idea was that some of the 303 prisoners serving time for murder or robbery might like to show a sheriff or a policeman what jail is like.

Prisoners on the floor above me called officers with shotguns to control a disturbance during the 24 hours I served in jail. A group of inmates had overpowered a guard and stole his keys but they returned to their cells after they found that the guard's keys did not fit doors that would let them out. I was thinking, suppose they can't contain it? Suppose it gets down here? Would I be considered friend or foe?

I slept from about 1 a.m. to 4 a.m. and then decided that was no good way to spend time. So I got up and made some notes. I thought a lot about freedom while I was deprived of it. I'd never been in jail before where I couldn't get out. It kind of gives you a feeling of standing in the other guy's shoes. Being behind bars yourself, you maybe develop a little bit of understanding, a little bit of empathy. Here's what I wrote at 4:00 a.m. on May 7th, 1977.

> You do a lot of thinking in jail. You think about how long you may be in, how long you will stay behind bars. You realize the importance of freedom. You think of your loved ones, particularly when they are dependent upon you and you cannot be there to help.

> In my case, you think of why you are here. How can you as a sworn servant of the law possibly be in jail for violating that law? You wonder at the strange turn of events, this strange paradox that has led me down this particular road ending up behind bars. Have I really flouted the law of my country? I guess I have but that was never my intention. And I would not say I flouted, I respectfully differed.
>
> How strange, I hear the sounds of people and traffic passing by and yet I cannot leave and join it. Why? My thoughts were on the protection and service of the people, under the law of our land. To do so with the best possible service under my constitutional obligation as the chief peace officer of the county.
>
> Yet this has led me into a collision course where principle met principle head on. Where I as an officer of the court had to object to its ministrations. I felt for the public good and the people I serve.
>
> Yet I am sure those same motives were in the mind of the judge who put me here. How odd; we are both attempting to do our job. Is there a greater morality over the legal letter of the law?
>
> I do not feel I really violated a law violently. I wanted to pursue another road but that was apparently impossible. I do not feel unclean inside. I do not feel wrong. I did what I felt was right.
>
> It is unusual that my 35 years in law enforcement and my earnest belief in proper and professional law enforcement has led me tonight to a barred cell in the Genesee County jail.

I also kept thinking about my decision. It was the first time in my 35-year career as a policeman that I had not lived by the law. I thought, "Did I flout the law?" I guess I did but I only meant to respectfully disagree with it.

When Mayor LaGuardia gave me the oath of office in 1941, he said there would be rough times ahead. He said I'd be looking down the barrel of a gun. But he never said I'd be looking through cell bars as a prisoner.

Supporters and well-wishers sent some 30 telegrams and made 74 calls on my behalf while I was in jail. One telegram from my own department read, "We are proud of you. Hang in there. The department stands taller because of your action."

Another telegram sent by the administrator of the Criminal Justice Institute in Detroit said, "All professional law enforcement personnel salute you as an administrator and as a man." That was very gratifying. I put myself out there on a limb, and it could have been cut off.

I arrived after supper had been served so they got me a hamburger from a nearby Burger King. Saturday I ate the normal prisoner fare of cereal for breakfast and hot dogs and beans for lunch. I talked with several of the inmates at meals. One, who was in for non-payment of child-support, told me he would be perfectly willing to pay if his wife would use the money for the child and not for herself and her boyfriend. I thought it odd that we put a man in jail where he could not earn any money for child support. There has to be a better way.

Through the night, a 30-page appeal was delivered to a court clerk Saturday morning. By early afternoon, a three-judge panel of the state Court of Appeals freed me on personal bond. They met Saturday and granted my motion to postpone the Circuit Court order pending appeal after I served 23 ½ hours. The judges set no date for the appeal hearing.

I told a couple of the jail trustees who befriended me that they ought to continue their education. I said that if I could overcome hardship, so could they. The reporters who covered this said that I was often accused of being more of an educator than a police administrator.

I was 57 at the time but I did what I felt was important and necessary. I believed I had an obligation to law enforcement to try to upgrade the profession. I felt that Keith Lester had violated a trust and to restore him would be wrong. We would have no confidence in him. The public would have no trust in him.

I'll never forget that when I came home, you had draped yellow ribbons across the bushes and a large sign on the garage declaring "Way to go, Pa." As you recall, I was able to spend Mothers' Day with you and your mother after all.

I was vindicated two months later by the Michigan Court of Appeals, which ruled that I should not have been jailed for refusing to rehire a fired deputy. At the press conference after the ruling, I told reporters that the judge made a number of mistakes but it sure was nice to be right and to be free. Especially when I learned that Deputy Lester was not only fighting his dismissal but was arrested on another criminal charge of willful neglect of duty.

The brief tenure in jail sort of rounded out my education. You may recall that I told some of those who greeted me that I hoped I never had to take advantage of Sheriff O'Brien's hospitality again, or reciprocate.

Part of my fervor against rehiring Lester came from previous orders from the appeals board and the courts forcing me to rehire four other deputies. I couldn't have that because after awhile, half the department would be less than satisfactory.

Later we found out a very interesting thing about the Judge who had sentenced me. Judge Beer was discovered to have had nine kids in all, three by his first wife and six by his secretary. He led a double life for years until it was discovered after one of his children died. One of his kids (by the secretary) wrote a kind of gossip column in the *Detroit News.* Judge Beer, to his credit, later appeared as a party held in Mona's restaurant for a fundraiser saying to all that Johannes Spreen was a decent, honorable man, in effect that he had been wrong.

Love, Dad

Unions, Management and the Sheriff

Dear Betty,

After I was released from jail, I gave an address to the National Sheriff's Convention on June 20, 1977. I discussed some knotty problems and thought you might be interested in what I said. I began my address rather humorously, don't you think? Here's what I said.

> I don't know if I should speak to you today as Sheriff of Oakland County, Michigan, or as Prisoner #7702276, Genesee County Jail. I will have more on this later, as it has much to do with labor unions. First let's take a look at law enforcement.
>
> Law enforcement does not work in these United States. It probably never has and it probably never will. The big cities and their police chief executives are embattled, the suburbs and their myriad of small independent departments are being buffeted by tidal waves of crime and even rural areas are not as pastoral as before.
>
> Certain constructive changes could be made in groups that affect law enforcement, such as the politicians, the press, and the people they serve and represent. But in the direct provision of law enforcement services, the two main principals clearly concerned are management and the labor organization (the police unions or associations).
>
> Can management and police organizations travel the same track in the interest of law enforcement services and protection? Frankly, I am pessimistic. Why not? Because of the "bread and butter" narrowed viewpoints and positions of our many organizations representing law enforcement personnel.
>
> Before we go on, however, let us remember some of the benefits of unions to their members. They protect employee's job security

and guard against unfair labor practices. They obtain higher wages, fringe benefits and safer equipment. They enable employees to collectively exercise political strength through the bargaining process and endorse prospective elected officials. They provide legal assistance to members. Lastly, unions have the force to change the status quo and to redefine the police role.

Some of the problems police unions present are resistance to change in organizational procedures and policies, lack of consideration of ability to pay their higher wage demands, strikes and work slow-downs, challenges of administrators which curtails flexibility and innovation, political involvement which polarizes communities, refuge and protection of lazy employees and those unwilling to upgrade themselves, insistence on senior rather than the most qualified personnel for job assignments, and protection or legal assistance for those that are below professional standards.

At the bargaining table today are three interests: the union, with their economic and non-economic demands; the political subdivision such as the city or county; and the law enforcement chief executive such as the chief or sheriff. As Police Commissioner in Detroit, I watched and felt the rise in power and influence of the unions.

The crippling malady afflicting police management today is that management cannot effectively achieve its legitimate goals. In some departments, management has allowed employees to virtually determine their own working conditions and the level of services to be delivered to the public. Other agencies have failed to understand the nature of collective bargaining and surrendered basic management rights. And then there are those departments that have attempted to fend off some of labor's illegitimate demands only to find themselves manacled and shackled by either the courts or labor arbitrators.

May I suggest some reasons why law enforcement simply does not work? You are not alone. You are not alone sitting in your seat of department leadership. The police unions are trying to sit there too. The important question is who really controls law enforcement today? Is it law enforcement management? I don't think so. Money talks. We in management don't have dues paying members but unions do. Management must somehow strive to attain at least equal rights and be a proper balance wheel for working constructively with police unions for a better law enforcement function for all of us.

Speaking of union power, let me tell you about the "Lester case" in Oakland County and how I became a number in the system. I went to jail to uphold the standards of the law enforcement profession. I have now spent 36 years in law enforcement. I have had an unblemished record, and yet I wound up in jail with a number, was searched, my property was removed, and I was incarcerated like a common criminal. Why? I refused to return a man to duty as a sergeant, whom we had dismissed on charges of thievery. A sergeant should guide, supervise, instruct and set an example for those under his charge.

In court the trial judge said he was a thief but the prosecutor had presented the wrong charge. It should have been larceny by embezzlement, not larceny by conversion. And so he dismissed the case because of this legal technicality. A second judge then ordered him restored to duty and be paid $20,000 in back pay one week before the County Personnel Appeals Board was to hear his case.

The prosecutor is appealing the dismissal of criminal charges. I have not yet returned the man to duty. The case is still in process. I am presently out on $50 personal bond by the Court of Appeals of the State of Michigan, and may have to go to jail again in order to uphold the standards, ethics and honor of law enforcement.

In addition to the emotional trauma of going to jail, there was some family trauma. My wife is ill and confined to a wheelchair yet the judge denied my request to make arrangements for my wife's care before commencing to serve my jail sentence and sent me directly to jail. I now also stand to be financially indebted to the attorneys I had to hire to represent me in my appeal. Yet, I would do the same thing again. If I had to choose one or the other, I would rather be right than free.

In the "Lester case" I had inadequate representation on my behalf from the county attorneys. The Civil Counsel of the County admitted that they were not on a par with the experience and expertise of the sharp lawyer for the union who specializes in such matters. The union has almost unlimited funding to hire attorneys.

We played with cap guns while the union was manning heavy artillery.

Of course we at the top must become better managers, be fair and square. Some cooperation between unions and management is most essential. There should be a working together for each other in the people's interest.

Management needs rights too, and management needs professional help to allow us to respond to the unions on more equal terms. In our department, only the sheriff, the under sheriff and the secretary are not union members. Kind of unequal odds!

To cure the malady I spoke of, we must believe in and retain our right to manage while recognizing our fundamental accountability to the public we serve. Let us be the managers of our enterprise and be the main man in that seat with our hands firmly on the throttle. We can certainly ride together with unions on the same track that leads to professional status of law enforcement, but we must control the train.

My dear, the talk was so well received that they asked me to make it the following week to the Michigan Sheriff's Convention on June 28, 1977. Much as I hate to admit it, the problem is just as bad today as it was then.

Love, Dad

The Child Killer Investigation

Dear Betty,

I gave an address to the Southern Police Institute Alumni Association in Atlanta, Georgia on July 29, 1977, about the "Child Killer" investigation. They had been wrestling with three Atlanta "Lover's Lane" killings. On January 16, 1977, a killer shot LaBrian Lovette and Veronica Hill. Lovette drove from the scene but crashed into a vehicle and also died. On February 12, a killer injured a couple and they described their assailant as a large black male. On March 12, a stalker approached another car and killed Dianne Collins and wounded her boyfriend. The killer or killers were never caught but at that time they wanted to explore every avenue to solve their murders and thought they might have a serial murderer.

I told them about the two-year Michigan investigation of seven Ann Arbor college coeds which led to the conviction of John Norman Collins in 1969. On August 7, 1967, farm workers found the naked and mutilated body of 19 year-old Mary Fleszar, an accounting major, who had been stabbed repeatedly in the chest. Her feet were severed at the ankles. In March 1968, Jane Louise Mixer, a law student at the University of Michigan, had posted a request for a ride and after leaving with an unknown man, was found dead. She had been shot twice in the head and strangled, and her body laid out on a gravesite. On June 30, 1968, another murder of coed Jane Schell was reported. She had been beaten, stabbed, raped, her throat cut and her naked body dumped. Next 13 year-old Dawn Basom was found stabbed and strangled on April 15, 1969. In June, another Ann Arbor student, Alice Kalom was shot and stabbed. In July, Karen Sue Beineman, freshman, was found strangled and beaten in a ravine in Ann Arbor.

John Collins left the area for Salinas, California, and was charged with the death of 17 year-old Ann Phillips whose body was found July 13, 1969. All of Collin's victims were found nude, sexually mutilated and had one of their earrings missing.

John Norman Collins was arrested for murder and convicted. He claimed to be innocent although Karen's underwear and hair was found in a house he often visited. (He is still imprisoned in 2001, despite having appealed his life sentence and once tried to escape by tunneling out.)

Our Michigan county of Oakland thought, "It can't happen here." They thought that even though Jimmy Hoffa was kidnapped from a posh Detroit restaurant on July 30, 1975. But in 1976 and 1977, it did happen here. So I was invited to discuss the child slayings that we investigated.

I began by describing how fragmented law enforcement was in Oakland County. Coordination of police efforts was virtually impossible when two sheriff's departments, the state police, the F.B.I. and eight local police departments were directly involved. It even involved two medical examiner's offices, three crime labs and two prosecutor's offices.

Then I told them about the "Child Killer" and the problems we had during the investigations. On February 15, 1976, 12 year-old Mark Stebbins was reported missing. Four officers handled it as a runaway until the next day when circumstances made them suspect foul play. Four days later, his body was found next to a dumpster.

The state police and county crime labs were not called to process the scene. By the time the county medical examiner's office arrived, the body had been moved. It was transported to the police department rather than to the county morgue. The police took clothes off the body and it arrived at the morgue nude. The killer had not tried to conceal the body. It did not immediately appear that Mark was sexually abused. Later post-mortem disclosed that he was. To this day, the crime is unsolved. No one knows what might have been found at the scene had proper crime scene procedures been followed and a crime lab been involved.

On December 22, 1976, 12 year-old Jill Robinson left her home after an argument with her mother. It was believed that she rode her bicycle to her father's home a few miles away. When she did not arrive, she was reported missing by her mother. A friend saw her riding her bicycle on a main corridor according to investigation. The day after Christmas, her body was found 200 yards from a police station.

She had died from a shotgun blast to the head. Again, no crime lab was called to process the scene. Again, there were no attempts to conceal the body and no apparent evidence that she was sexually abused. The head and face were blown off. The condition of her clothes and body made it appear as if she had just walked out of her home and was murdered.

Noting the similarities of the two cases, it was suggested that a coordinated effort involving state police, sheriff and local authorities be implemented, but the offer was declined by the local agencies. I had welcomed the suggestion because coordination had always been my belief.

Less than a week passed before 10 year-old Kristine Mihelich left her home January 2, 1977, to go to the store three blocks away. She was reported missing after a short time. Fearing the worst, two detectives initiated a search. The news media broadcast similarities to the two previous murders and our office and the state police offered assistance but it was refused.

The body of the girl was deposited in a very small community with only a five-man department. Many problems in protecting the crime scene arose at the outset. Traffic, onlookers, response of many local departments, media, etc. created confusion. The chief of the five-man department, having no personal experience in homicide investigation, turned the matter over to the State Police who then requested assistance from area departments. That afternoon, 30 investigators committed themselves to finding the girl's murderer. The Oakland Task Force had been implemented.

The Sheriff's Department crime lab processed the girl's room for evidence that would hopefully be used later. Some 20 days after her disappearance, her body was found. She had been suffocated and gently placed next to a street. She was fully clothed and still wearing her backpack. Again, there was no positive indication of sexual abuse.

As hundreds of leads came in, investigators began the tedious task of checking each piece of information. By the first of March, the sensationalism had diminished and only 11 investigators were sorting the 800 remaining tips and solving the crime.

The work of the Task Force was hampered from the start by each jurisdiction's different procedures. The press allowed the politically ambitious prosecutor to use this opportunity to assume the role of coordinator and spokesman. He summoned a Canadian crime expert to handle fingerprints when our department could have handled that task.

On March 16, 1977, 11 year-old Timothy King left his home to go to a corner drugstore. He was reported missing that evening. The next morning, Task Force members were sent to coordinate the investigation. The news media put the public into a state of fear saying that a maniac child killer was on the loose!

The Task Force recognized the strong possibility that they had a minimum of four days to find Timothy alive. That evening 300 investigators converged to find Timmy. They stopped suspicious vehicles and searched for the missing boy. A witness furnished a composite of a man she saw talking to a boy believed to be Timmy, as well as a suspected vehicle. This information was given to the media in hopes a citizen might recognize the subject.

Six days after Timmy disappeared, his suffocated body was found along a main street in Wayne County. The killer had broken his pattern and dumped Timmy outside of the county. The state police crime lab division had processed the scene and the body apparently revealed no sexual abuse. An autopsy later revealed that he had been molested.

Several concerned groups posted rewards totaling $70,000 for the arrest of the child killer. The Task Force was flooded with tips. Parents turned in sons, brothers turned in brothers and church members turned in their pastors. Over 12,000 tips were turned in. Realizing that police agencies could not bear the financial responsibilities of immense investigations, the Task Force was awarded $700,000 to fund and equip 21 investigators for six months to identify and capture the killer.

A computer system was installed to assist the Task Force. Before the computer, several tips concerning the same individual would be investigated by several investigators resulting in a loss of time and duplication of effort. The computer system allowed names of suspects in any of the four homicides to be entered and checked. The victimization file revealed that over 1,100 cases of attempted abductions were never reported to the police.

Although admirable efforts were made at supervision, coordination was nearly impossible. It was a case of "too much, too late." Some departments were virtually using the Task Force as a training experience for their personnel. The mere fact that some of the investigators were inexperienced led to the improper elimination of some suspects.

I think that the problems encountered here exemplified problems in law enforcement in general. Law enforcement is fragmented, uncoordinated, ineffective and costly. What is the answer? One county police agency may be the answer. Crime knows no jurisdictional boundaries. I urged police administrators and political leaders to ignore political differences and to put an emphasis on service to the citizens.

I told them how the 1967 report of the President's Commission in Law Enforcement and Criminal Justice showed the fragmentation of urban police in the Detroit Metropolitan Region. This problem, pointed out a decade ago, is still with us and so is our unapprehended child killer and others like him.

These cases haunt me to this day. They have never been solved and in 2002, the mothers of the four victims provided blood samples to compare DNA in hair found on or near the bodies. The purpose was to determine if samples found near the bodies belonged to the children or to a suspect. The killer, sometimes dubbed "Babysitter" has never been caught.
Love, Dad

Law Enforcement Life Is Hard

Dear Betty,

I was fortunate enough to be asked to address national and international business leaders in Detroit on February 27, 1980. I thought you might be interested in some excerpts from this talk.

I began by saying that 90% of police budgets was wages and pensions. Thus the quality of work life is extremely important for police officers. Their goals are the same as business people; i.e. more employee involvement in decision making, improved relations between supervisors and those reporting to them, better cooperation between union and management, effective job designs and improved integration of people and technology.

Some differences from business are that law enforcement is dangerous and the mental stress of facing unknown danger day after day builds up protective barriers. Police officers are no longer just guardians of peace but must be sociologists, psychologists, lawyers, physicians, marriage counselors, educators and babysitters. The public's attitude has changed and their disrespect has caused frustration, hostility and apathy.

Marital problems can affect the work environment because work hours and rotating shifts play havoc with his home life. Additionally, police officers can't just forget about work when they are done for the day. They are on duty 24 hours a day. They may be going out to dinner with the family when they pass an emergency and are obliged to respond immediately. And they must be pleasant and tactful when doing this, no matter the disruption to their lives.

Manpower, equipment and training vary in each police department depending upon available funding. As a result, the officers in one department may get more training than those in another. The community suffers when the technical competence of individual officers is not consistent. While that is not unlike the business world, incompetent employees make less profit for the owners but incompetent police work hurts everyone.

One of the biggest problems for law enforcement management is to maintain the motivating drive that makes a police officer excel in his work. Without a feeling of self worth and personal accomplishment, many police officers regard their job as just a job and nothing more. Many basically good officers have had their attitudes shaped negatively because they feel they have no say in problem-solving or management operations.

To overcome this, my department is operating with team policing. Each team member is a specialist and the members work together as a unit. Cross-fertilization occurs as each trains the other in his unique specialty. Traditional communication lines through rank are eliminated and direct communication between top management and team members occurs weekly. I am actively involved with the three teams that have been established.

These new teams are not only concentrating on crime and accident problems but are dealing with interpersonal relationships to improve their relationships in the community. Police officers generally have been reticent to show their emotions and permit people to see that they too are human. They are concerned that it will be taken for a sign of weakness.

Our department is now using contract law enforcement services to help small communities or large townships. Under this agreement we assign a specific number of officers to patrol the community, and provide the back-up investigators, crime lab, aviation and marine division and administrative staff services. Most officers serve in those communities in which they reside and this gives them pride in their contribution to their own neighbors.

Substations have been established in communities under contract, which give officers a centralized location at which they can report for work. We also try to honor shift preference and work closely with the officers' union representatives, to improve the family home life of the officer. Shift rotation turned out to be highly disruptive so that was stabilized.

Many times officers were afraid their spouses wouldn't or couldn't understand their problems. Our department developed an awareness program for wives so they can walk beats and improve their understanding of each other. Technological changes require continual in-service training as we try to keep officers aware of crucial changes.

Our youth will be tomorrow's leaders. They must be involved with law enforcement at an early age but our money seems to be mostly spent on juvenile delinquents. We must begin concentrating on the winners, not the losers in society. We are reaching out to teachers, students, community leaders and we have created a new program for this purpose. We call it ESCAPE, which is an acronym for "Enlisted in the Sheriff's Crime and Accident Prevention Education."

We are lucky to have U.S. Senator Donald Riegle joining with us in developing a demonstration project to improve the quality of work life of officers in Oakland County. We hope it will become a model for the nation. While our system has imperfections, our programs are aimed towards bringing the community and law enforcement agencies together in true teamwork to improve the quality of life for the officer who serves that community.

That was the gist of my address. I described ESCAPE to the Sheriff's Reserve Academy in 1982, and other groups. I'm glad to tell you that the program raised over $36,000 and involved hundreds of volunteer hours.

Love, Dad

My Third Wife

Dear Betty,

In the midst of criticism and turmoil, it's very valuable to have someone to come home to who loves you. So I thought I'd tell you about another part of my life. How did I meet Mona? That's very interesting. It's funny how twists and turns occur in our life's path.

I was dating Jackie Gordon. You remember Jackie. She was the widow of Lou Gordon, who was host of the syndicated *Lou Gordon Show*. He also published *Scope* magazine.

Lou took public officials to task at times including Detroit Mayor Jerry Cavanagh. Some people referred to him as a "muckraker." He was good!

When Lou died, Jackie asked me to provide protection for her house. I was glad to. Jackie had taken my side and gently reproached Lou when he blasted me for not appearing on his show after I became Police Commissioner. I was willing but high police officials advised me not to. Lou had a vendetta with Mayor Cavanagh and was always taking pot shots at him, even accusing him of being in bed with some in organized crime. I didn't want to get involved with that as the new Police Commissioner. I had enough to do with the aftermath of the Detroit Riot, racial tensions and crime.

Jackie called me one day and wanted me to come to a party for her upcoming radio interview show. The party would be held at the Butchers' Inn Restaurant at the famous Eastern Market of Detroit. I really did not want to go that Friday night but I did.

Mona was the owner of the restaurant along with another lady. When I walked in, she was standing back wearing a white Western cowgirl hat. (There's that hat again.) Mona was shapely, tall and good-looking. Her hair was sort of platinum blond (dyed, I found out later.)

I think we were mutually taken with each other. I was wearing my Sheriff's Stetson hat for the party. Mona later told me that when she saw me walk in the door she said to her female business partner, "That's the man I'm going to marry!"

Mona Hemmerling had been divorced from an unsavory man that I later found out had been in trouble with the police for allegedly fixing horse races and doping horses. They had a 10-year-old daughter from their marriage. There was dancing at the party. Mona asked me to dance. We danced a few numbers. Jackie Gordon got very upset.

After a couple of hours, I left to go home. Jackie stayed there; it was her party. She kissed me quite soulfully as I left, maybe because I'd been dancing with Mona.

After I arrived home in Farmington Hills, a call from my office awakened me. "Sheriff, Jackie Gordon called and said you have the keys to her car and she can't get home."

Jackie had asked me to move her car that evening. The keys were still in my pocket. So about 3 a.m., I drove back to the Butchers' Inn to give Jackie her keys. A fateful trip!

After Jackie left, Mona asked me if I'd like a hamburger and coffee. I said, "Yes, thank you."

Guess I was interested in Mona and she in me. We made a date. The date was around Valentine's Day, February 1980. I brought her a vase of flowers.

We were married November 15, 1980 at Holy Trinity Lutheran Church in Detroit. We had a big reception. My good friend Lyle Smith whom you know was my best man.

November 15th was the start of the deer season in Michigan. I got a "dear." For a while, everything was great.

Mona sold her home and came, with her 10-year-old daughter Kelly, to live at my house in Farmington Hills. She was an excellent worker who had two loads of wash in by 7:00 a.m., a gourmet cook, and kept the house in great shape. She was very happy to be a housewife I thought.

She did one thing in the beginning of our marriage that really irked me. She had wanted to go roller-skating. As she had not roller-skated since she was a youngster I asked her not to go until I could go with her. I was a good roller skater dancer.

I said, "Mona, wait till I can go with you and Kelly. Let's do it as a family. I'll teach you. If you go alone, and since you haven't skated since you were young, you can fall on your back and hurt yourself." I made her promise she would wait for me to go with her.

A few days later, I came home to find Mona and her girlfriend at home. She was sitting half on a chair, looking kind of sheepish. I then found out she and her friend and Kelly had gone skating and she fell on her back and broke her tailbone. Mind you, now we've just been married a few weeks. This put a great dent in our relationship because she had promised to wait until I could teach her.

Mona was great in many ways. In other ways she was mysterious such as when I decided to run again for governor. I had run for governor of Michigan when Elinor was alive.

I was on the printed ballot but removed before the election. It seems the Democratic candidate needed over 18,000 signatures statewide to be certified, the Republican candidate only 9,000 or so. The Election Board said I was 108 signatures short. I took them to court and won. Then they did something else to deny me being on the ballot. Again I sued but this time the Michigan Court of Appeals ruled against me with lots of media attention. To go to the Michigan Supreme Court would have been very costly and would have left no time for a real campaign. So I gave it up. It was 1977, I believe.

Two years later, Elinor was still alive. She surprised me immensely when she said, "I think you should run for governor again, John."

I was shocked. I said, "Honey, you are in a wheelchair. I'd have to go all over Michigan...."

She said, "Yes, but John, you would make an excellent governor."

I was taken aback but very pleased and proud. Elinor was always very proud of me. But then April 19, 1979, Elinor passed away after 11 days in the intensive care unit of Mercy Mt. Carmel Hospital, a victim of multiple sclerosis. My love for her reminds me of Tennyson's wonderful line, "Tis better to have loved and lost, than never to have loved at all."

After I married Mona, I told her about Elinor's encouragement to be governor. She and her friend immediately started a Johannes Spreen for Governor campaign, formed a committee, etc.

But shortly thereafter, I found that Mona (who had lost 35 pounds of weight and looked bad) finally had to tell me that she had borrowed $15,000 from a bookmaker friend of hers. She had been under so much stress that she had lost weight worrying about me finding out. The bookmaker had died. His wife, who had a promissory note, was demanding the money. I said Mona was mysterious. There were other things that upset our marriage, especially regarding politics and the sheriff's office.

Needless to say when she finally told me about the bookmaker's wife and the $15,000 she owed, I removed myself from even attempting to run for governor again. I feel Mona had her heart in the right place but there were many problems in our marriage. I finally sued for divorce after a political and otherwise fracas. Five years later, the divorce was final.

What happened was that on September 27th, Mona and I had another argument. She threw a heavy article at me and punched me in the mouth. She also called the police.

When the police came, apparently she thought better of it and told them everything was okay. I came around the other side of the house. The Farmington Hills Police Department had sent a Captain with two officers to the Sheriff's house. I guess it was a big deal to them.

I said to them, "Look, she has no marks on her. I do." My lips were cut and bloody. The next day I called a lawyer and filed suit for divorce. As you can see, I've had some problems in my love life, dear.
Love, Dad

Overcrowded Understaffed Jail

Dear Betty,

I presented a paper on our jail conditions called "Enough Is Enough!" on August 23, 1982. You will be able to see how fed up I was becoming.

I told them everyone was talking about the jail and very little was being done to alleviate a damnable situation. Prisoners and attorneys had more influence than the sheriff. What disturbed me was that we spent more time fighting politicians than fighting criminals, because there is no room left in the jail. I told them things like this.

> We have a revolving door policy where the criminal is back on the street faster than the officer booking him. Our counts were 580 prisoners Saturday, 581 Sunday, and that is 130 and 131 over the mandated 450 figure set by the Federal Court!
>
> The sheriff and the department can do nothing that requires bricks, mortar and money. That is the job of the executive board. The Oakland County Commissioners and the Administration have been and still are unresponsive to the economic climate and the ever-increasing crime rate.
>
> The criminal justice system is a complete failure. It provides protection for the criminal, not the citizen. I will not be a party to it! If they do the crime, they should do the time. When the police and courts do their job, the sheriff should have proper means and facilities to hold those charged with crimes.
>
> Some Oakland County Commissioners and the Administration had more important priorities such as:
>
> - A six million dollar office building for the County Executive
> - Waste and mismanagement in untold millions

- Not taking the lowest bidders
- Increased salaries and perks for officials
- Unauthorized second police agency in the County costing taxpayers over $1.5 million per year with fragmentation, duplication and waste
- New non-functioning divisions and departments.

Because Oakland County operates in the black, no one cares. This county is one of the wealthiest in the U.S. Yet requests to resolve the jail-overcrowding problem are ignored by the Commissioners and executives. For nine years, I have not been able to get a crime prevention officer or youth officer or administrative assistant, even part time. The County Executive has a dozen. Not one cent is provided for crime prevention and working with citizens in providing for their safety.
Sad, isn't it?

Well, dear, it wasn't often that I let out so many angry feelings but I was reaching the end of my rope. I was receiving much criticism. I guess it reminded of some words by Theodore Roosevelt that I very much admire. "It is not the critic who counts, nor the one who points out how the strongman stumbled or how the doer of deeds might have done them better. The credit belongs to the man who is actually in the arena, whose face is marred with sweat and dust and blood, who strives valiantly, who errs and comes up short again and again; who knows the great enthusiasms, the great devotions, and spends himself in a worthy cause; and who, if he fails, at least fails while daring greatly, so that his place shall never be with those cold and timid souls who know neither victory nor defeat."
Love, Dad

Personnel Problems

Dear Betty,

On February 1, 1984, I addressed the Personnel Committee of the Board of Commissions of Oakland County.

I began by describing the inmates' lawsuit against the sheriff's department because of the overcrowded jails. I next described the reduction of our staff by 27 patrol officers. Then I went into the present problems with overcrowding, lack of training, jail escapes and ineffective supervision.

I outlined that our 200 staff members were responsible for the supervision of over 700 inmates. At issue was whether detention officers should be deputized or should be non-police status officers. I recommended the creation of a totally new non-police classification to replace the current detention officer class. Then I urged them to establish professional career development programs within the sheriff's department for police and non-police personnel.

I recommended that we reclassify detention officer class to non-police class and establish entrance level non-sworn civilian positions at lower salary levels to save taxpayers money. In return, this would allow us to restore road patrol personnel from the jail to countywide road patrol services to help our funding situation.

Six weeks later I reported that our supportive and back-up personnel were at a minimum and asked for 15 of the 27 job deletions to be reversed. By this time, I felt the department was so stripped that it could not perform adequately. I had just about had it.

Love, Dad

My Fourth and Current Wife

Dear Betty,

My work life was rough enough that I guess I was looking for relief in some personal direction.

About the time Mona and I were having marital difficulties, I was driving by Oakland Community College near where I lived in Farmington Hills. Looking to my right as I passed the college entrance road, a large sign struck my eye. "Michigan Senior Olympics."

Knowing very little about the Olympics and curious, I drove in and saw a lot of seniors (over age 55) running, walking, swimming, playing tennis and doing other sports events. I spoke to the one in charge, Marye Miller, saying that I lived only ¼ mile away and could I participate. She said, "Sorry, you have to register in advance."

Just about to leave, I heard music coming from the cafeteria. Seeing a group of ladies together with T-shirts labeled "Senior Street Walkers" amazed and intrigued me, especially the one who was quite a bit younger and very pretty.

She wore no hat, so I had to look elsewhere and liked what I saw. She not only had a very nice face but also was well endowed in the upper body.

I went over to those leaders and said, "I'm the Sheriff of the County and I ought to run you girls in for wearing shirts like that" with a broad smile. "But as the jail is full I'll let you go if I can have a picture taken with you."

They made me show my badge. I asked the good-looking one, Sallie Highstreet, to please send the picture to my office.

We had an amusing dialogue, asking where they were from. Sallie said, "Cherry Beach."

With a start, I retorted, "You're pulling my leg."

You see, I'm from New York. Out on Long Island by the Atlantic Ocean is a place called "Fire Island." I had a friend, Rudy Blaum, who built a home by the ocean at Fire Island Pines. But next to Fire Island Pines was Cherry Beach. Cherry Beach is known far and wide for being an almost completely gay community. I remember unusual names on cottages where Rudy and I walked through Cherry Beach. Two names were: "A womb with a view" and "Sinerama."

So when Sallie said they were from Cherry Beach I was non-plussed, taken aback. Only visions of the gay community on Fire Island raced through my mind.

I did find out that Cherry Beach is a Senior Center in Marine City, yes, with friendly and "gay" people in the old sense of the word.

Sallie sent the picture to me at the Sheriff's Office. That was 1984 and I was still married to Mona. I never acknowledged the picture.

The following year, 1985, I entered the mile race walk event for the Senior Olympics. I won, but didn't expect to.

There were about 60 competitors who started. I started slowly, most of the pack ahead of me. I had good endurance and after about 100 yards I passed a group of 15 or so. I must have liked Sallie. She was there that day with her "Senior Street Walkers" from Cherry Beach. It was a walking group. As I race-walked I kept thinking about her. As I passed a few more I felt maybe I could do it. Then as I saw only 10 or 12 ahead of me I thought I might make a medal. What drove me faster and faster that day was repeating and repeating "Sallie Highstreet, Sallie Highstreet," picturing a locomotive while gaining speed.

Finally there were only five ahead. If I could pass two, I'd have a Bronze medal. I did that. Then there were two ahead. Fast, faster, "Sallie Highstreet, Sallie Highstreet." I passed one and now I'd have a Silver medal. The man ahead was approaching the bottom of a hill (probably called Heartbreak Hill by these aging seniors.) He was about ten yards ahead of me. Increasing my "Sallie Highstreet" chant, I caught up to him at the hill bottom. There was a four foot wide paved walk up the hill. Surprised to see me, the other guy lunged to his right to force me off the path. But I doggedly pushed on and at the crest of the hill was a couple of steps ahead. Down the hill—a winner! First place: Gold medal.

At the bottom of the hill, Sallie was there with some of the others waiting at the finish line. Not knowing, I asked her, "What does your husband think of you wearing a T-shirt like that?" She had it on.

She replied, "I don't have a husband!"

My next statement was, "Would you like to have dinner with me?" She said yes!

Now Sallie was very smart. She suggested we meet for dinner at a restaurant in Anchorville called Surf North alongside Anchor Bay. They had a wonderful three-piece band playing music from our era mostly. Naturally I was obligated to ask her to dance after dinner, don't you agree?

Sallie had divorced her husband, George Highstreet. I was still married to Mona but was filing for divorce.

Sallie, who was Program Coordinator for the Cherry Beach Senior Center, had conducted a late life divorce seminar and other counseling programs. I told her I might need that, citing the problems of my marriage to Mona.

Sallie and I were just friends at the beginning. She listened to me, helped me even knowing that if Mona had met me half way I would have stayed married to her. But I had filed for divorce from Mona.

Sallie and I met almost every week. We lived 67 miles apart; she in Marine City and me in Farmington Hills. We met always at Surf North. We enjoyed discussions over dinner and dancing afterward. There was nothing else, dinner, then we went our separate ways. Still hoping to save the marriage to Mona, Sallie said I was a "sad sack."

Six months passed. We had never kissed although I kept dancing closer and closer to her. The three-man band noticed and watched as the romance grew.

Her eldest son, Steve, asked her "Mom, you say you meet the guy every week, he buys a bottle of wine, dinner, and you dance. And he never tries anything. What is he, a faggot?"

Sallie and I stayed friends. My divorce finally came through May 26, 1987. We were married December 28, 1988. You might say Sallie was my first wife that started with a friendship connection rather than with a love or lust connection. Guess that's the best way! We are still happily married 14 years later.

As Sallie was Program Director for the Cherry Beach Senior Center, she had a coping group. She asked me to address the group about coping. She felt in my lifetime, coming from Germany, entering the police world, serving the country in the Air Corps, back to police work, becoming Chief of Operations in the New York City Police, then Police Commissioner of Detroit under very tense conditions, then a three times elected Sheriff (Democrat) in a very Republican County, that I had coped with a lot and taking care of a wife through years of sickness.

As I said, she's very smart, and crafty too. She got me to do a personal coping session for seniors. Then she got me for four more weeks teaching about the physical body, positive thinking, how to make life interesting, and making the most of your time. And we're still doing it. Now we do a seminar called "practical memory" and "aging positively." We were on local television several times recently on memory improvement and aging.

Well, my dear, that brings you up to date on "all the wives I've loved before" and where I am in my love life now. But I want to return to some other issues.

Love, Dad

My Dog Brewster

Dear Betty,

I know you remember when we had to put Brewster to sleep. It was tough, very tough for me when you took him away for that last time. The tears flowed when I had to say goodbye. All good dogs should go to Heaven!

I'm not sure you ever understood how much that dog meant to me and I just want to tell you. We got Brewster way back in 1978. He was a German shepherd and he knew my three wives: Elinor, your mother, Mona and Sallie.

Elinor and I were married for 31 years when she died of multiple sclerosis and other complications on April 19th, 1979, a day you remember too well. The year before, a deputy sheriff brought Brewster to our home. We didn't expect him to come that night. I had to leave in 15 minutes to make a speech.

When she saw Brewster, all Elinor could say was, "My, he's big." Brewster was then two years old. I knew she was apprehensive but the deputy had to leave and so did I.

All that night I worried. I had visions of coming home to a house in disarray, even to scary thoughts like your mother and you being attacked or bitten by this huge dog. The deputy did say he "felt" he was a good dog.

When I finally arrived back home, I was not ready for the sight that met my eyes. There was your mother in her chair, Brewster at her side, lying contentedly as she stroked and petted him. You were lying on the floor, also giving him alternate strokes. Talk about a "dog's life," Brewster had found a home.

Your mother and Brewster formed a loving partnership. He became her friend when I was at work, her protector. After Elinor's death, you comforted me because you were still at home while attending college, and so did Brewster.

Brewster and I played a lot of ball together. I'd throw a tennis ball on the lawn so it would bounce high, Brewster would catch it in his mouth with one great leap. He made fewer errors than Joe DiMaggio.

Near the end of 1979 I started dating. I had mixed emotional feelings. At first, I felt guilty and then even guiltier as I started to enjoy the company of other women. Later as I dated more frequently, and with several women, I had to ask you to answer all phone calls as I was not always sure which lady was calling just by her voice.

In February 1980, I started dating Mona. I told you how we met, earlier. Mona sold her home and came to live with me. Brewster and I were still pals and played ball. But Mona asked that we get a kennel for him, feeling that such a big dog would be better off outside. So I went along and had a large kennel with a doghouse put on the property.

Poor Brewster. For over five years, he was out in the weather, hot, cold, rain, snow, lightning, and thunder. I felt very sorry for him. Mona's ten-year-old daughter didn't particularly like Brewster or me. When she had occasion to feed him, she'd demand he "sit up" in a harsh, strident tone before the poor dog could get a bite. Often his bowl of water was empty, dirty or frozen.

There was trouble in the marriage, as you know. I sued for divorce and after 1-½ years, was awarded a divorce decree. After Mona left, it took Brewster only a few hours to get back in the house. Did he sense she was gone? A moving van pulled up in front of his kennel that day. He was a smart dog! Could he read?

I dated Sallie after meeting her at the Michigan Senior Olympics. On the phone, I told Sallie I felt sorry for Brewster and that I would allow him in the kitchen for a while. (She snickered, she later told me.)

Then, another day, I told her I'd let him in the laundry room to sleep. Then I allowed him to be in the living room when I was there.

Sallie continued to snicker. Finally, it wasn't long before Brewster allowed me to be in *his* house. He had the run of it, downstairs and upstairs.

Good old faithful Brewster. Asleep at the side of his master's bed! I think I was the master. He was good company for a divorced man now all alone.

Then Sallie and I were married, December 28th, 1988. She came to live with me. I don't know how worried Brewster got with another woman in the house. Did he remember being put out when Mona came?

Brewster took to Sallie. Sallie, not being too fond of animals and a little fearful, grew to like Brewster also. Brewster assumed his role as protector for Sallie too. I guess he thought, "If she's not putting me back in the kennel, I'd better be nice to her."

Wherever Sallie sat, Brewster sat alongside. One day, while I was out, Sallie was typing, sitting on one of those secretary chairs with roller casters. Brewster was lying right behind her. She inadvertently leaned back against the chair. The chair rolled over Brewster's tail. He let out a great scream, howl, yipe, etc. Sallie apologized profusely to poor Brewster. He seemed to be pacified.

About an hour later Sallie had to go outside. The kitchen door had a locking device on it. Brewster locked the door with his paw and now Sallie was on the outside and couldn't get back in. Smart dog, eh? Sallie later realized how funny that was.

But Brewster liked Sallie and protected her when I was not around.

One day the mailman had a package so he came around to the back of the house to deliver it at the kitchen door. Sallie opened the door. The mailman reached in over the threshold to hand her the package. Brewster lunged forward, opened his jaws and held the shocked mailman's thigh in a tight grip. Sallie was concerned that Brewster had bitten the nice mailman. The mailman said he was all right. Sallie was insistent. She made the mailman take down his pants to check. (I'm only kidding.) She did, however, make him roll up his trouser leg to see if the skin was broken.

Yes, Brewster was a beautiful dog. A smart dog! A proud dog! A loyal dog! Sallie, you and I lost a good friend when Brewster was no more. I do hope all good dogs go to Heaven.
Love, Dad

My Gal Sal

Dear Betty,

Sallie will be 72 on January 30, this year of 2003. In making speeches, she often refers to "moments of ecstasy," particularly when she remembers a double such moment.

When I proposed to Sallie, on my knees of course, (she now says she heard the creaking sounds) I knew she was a chocoholic. I presented her with a box of her favorite chocolates. As she opened it, there in the center of a most luscious chocolate was imbedded a "diamond" ring (K-Mart's) but she didn't know it then. Later I let her pick out the real ring.

She always said she had two moments of ecstasy that day. She didn't know whether to go for the chocolate first or the ring since her two great loves were chocolates and diamonds.

That night was a "blue moon," (twice a full moon within the same month.) Now our favorite song and song request is "Blue Moon." And listening to it we remark often how touching and appropriate those words were for us.

We were married seven months later, December 28, 1988, at the Prince of Peace Lutheran Church in Farmington Hills by Pastor T. Richard Marcis.

The church was beautiful, all decorated for Christmas with a huge lovely Christmas tree. Sallie's three sons all gave her away and you, Betty, gave me away.

I got a kick out of Sallie when the opening notes of the wedding march, "Here Comes the Bride" began. Sallie did not come slowly down the aisle. She rushed. (She thought she was late and I guess didn't want to miss it.)

A fly in the ointment that night was unbelievably the pastor. I had felt we should have a commercial photographer do the pictures but Pastor Marcis said, "What do you think I did before being ordained? I was a photographer! That will be my gift to you."

Unfortunately when we came back from our honeymoon on the Holland-American ship we were chagrined to find that he had not tested his batteries. No pictures at all and everything and everyone were so beautiful. Thank goodness our friends Lois and Don Overton were there. Don took video pictures. The pastor did have a stationary video going of the ceremony. So you see, we have proof we were really married.

There was another fly in the ointment that night at the reception, which was held at the Elks in Farmington Hills. We had a great dinner and the best wedding cake ever, said all the guests, from the German bakery in Farmington Hills.

Sallie's son Scott's boy, Brad, seven years old, was taking Karate lessons and showing some moves to Sallie's son Steve's boy, Jay. With a swift kick Brad shattered the glass door. They never told me. I first learned it writing this just now. Scott paid for the door. No one wanted the lovely occasion to be marred as we married.

Then it was off on the cruise. We and other honeymooners were treated special. One night at show time there was a contest in "Leading the Band" with the baton. They put me up. I waved the baton. You never heard such a cacophony of squeals and utter noise. Then they grabbed Sallie. She raised her baton and the band went into a great harmony version of "The Stripper." Then I realized how great she could dance and gyrate and kick. She received great applause. Many guests asked later if she was part of the show.

Yes, Betty, 1988 was great and we are still going strong 14 years later.

Love, Dad

PART V
Opinions

o o o o o o o o o o o o o o o o o o o o o o o o o o o

"Those who cannot remember the past are condemned to repeat it."

—*George Santayana*

Police Use of Deadly Force

Dear Betty,

I don't know if you read recently about Detroit Police Officer Brown and his use of deadly force. I just wanted to give you my take on police use of deadly force.

Most police officers in American cities go through their entire careers without firing a shot at anyone. So when the officer got involved in nine shootings within six years, killing three people and wounding another, questions arose. It has pained me recently to see the police departments like Detroit so under the gun over the deadly force controversies.

The decision to use deadly force is unquestionably the most difficult choice a police officer must make. As the Detroit Police Commissioner in 1968 and 1969, this aspect of policing was a concern to me. As Sheriff of Oakland County, I was part of a task force on the Police Use of Deadly Force, in cooperation with the Michigan Civil Rights Commission, and spokesman at their hearing.

Earlier in my 25-year tenure with the New York City Police Department, there were occasions where public clamor and outcry arose at some police shootings. During my five years of instructing at the New York Police Academy, I taught recruit training for two years, promotion training for two years and firearms instruction for one year. So I understood that police officers are in the unfortunate position of being "Damned if we do and damned if we don't."

It must be realized that police officers respond to incidents where firearms, knives and other deadly instruments confront them, and they must size up the situation and take appropriate action within seconds or sometimes split seconds.

Lawyers, prosecutors, and judges can take days, weeks or months in the comfort of their easy chairs discussing the officers' actions. Frankly, in today's world, I would not relish the calling to be a police officer as I once did, and I never fired a shot at anyone.

It is in the apprehension of suspects that police officers run into great difficulty. Self-defense or preventing imminent danger to others is definitely acknowledged as a police responsibility by all.

The fleeing felon is another matter. As instructor at the Police Academy, this was my maxim to the classes. "A fleeing felon does not present an immediate danger to the officer. All possible alternatives should be explored. Besides the moral question, which the officer should weigh very highly in his decision-making, there should exist almost virtual certainty that the suspect is in fact the real felon. If in doubt, *do not shoot.* The possibility may exist that the person running in front of you may not be the perpetrator, but another police officer or a concerned citizen attempting the capture of a third party, the real felon."

In the case of Officer Brown, I do not know all the facts, only what the media described. There is some discrepancy between the prosecutor's office and the Detroit Police. Chief Benny Napoleon, who was an A+student of mine at Mercy College, has his hands full.

One particular Detroit City Council member always seems to be against law enforcement. When I was Police Commissioner, she implored the Archdiocesan Development Fund for video cameras ostensibly to film police doing illegal acts. Yet I could not get video cameras to film demonstrators and rowdies throwing stinky liquids and garbage and waste at police. Training and equipment are important for police to do a professional job and that is what council members should be espousing.

I will always believe that it is important to have proper screening for law enforcement positions to exclude anyone with bias, bigotry or brutal tendencies. I also believe there must be adequate and proper training in firearms procedures and proficiency including not only how to shoot but when to shoot, with the moral factor emphasized. Finally, the training, proper equipment, sound policies considering the rights of suspects and the rights of police are a must.

Well, at least you know where I stand on the police use of deadly force.

Love, Dad

A Policeman's Lot Is Not a Happy One

Dear Betty,

I wrote an Opinion article for the *Times Herald* in Port Huron, Michigan about the difficulty of being a police officer. I used the phrase from Gilbert and Sullivan's operetta, "A policeman's lot is not a happy one."

In Marine City, Michigan, police officers want to get rid of their new review board but some citizens still want it. (It failed by one vote.) The Port Huron police chief started a police academy for interested citizens to learn more about their police, a wise move.

I have long thought that the public expects too much of police officers. Maybe I've told you this before but they expect the wisdom of Solomon, the courage of David, the strength of Samson, the patience of Job, the leadership of Moses, the kindness of the Good Samaritan, the strategic planning of Alexander the Great, the faith of Daniel, the diplomacy of Lincoln, the tolerance of the carpenter of Nazareth, and an intimate knowledge of every branch of the sciences.

If a police officer had all these qualities, he or she *might* be a good cop but not necessarily.

The public has interesting ideas about cops, a term that not everybody embraces. They think that a neat cop is conceited, a careless cop is a bum, a pleasant cop is a flirt, a brief cop is a grouch, a cop who hurries overlooks things, a cop who takes their time is lazy, a cop who arrests you has it in for you, a cop who passes you up is easy, a cop who doesn't hit back an attacker is a coward, a cop who does hit back is a bully, a cop who outwits you is a sneak, a cop who lets their presence be known is a bonehead, a cop who gets promoted has pull, and on and on with unfair stereotypes.

Now you understand why I had a "Wall of Honor" in my office, honoring good, professional police, real "Protectors of Liberty." As I've always said, God bless our cops! They are your protection, dear.
Love, Dad

Senior Issues

Dear Betty,

I must warn you about how seniors must beware and take care. It is sad at our age, when you trust someone and find out that trust was misplaced. It is sadder still when trusting seniors are taken advantage of.

Telemarketers are notorious and one must be careful against their blandishments. Sallie and I had one unfortunate experience. I will relate this experience with an auctioneer and appraiser, namely the Frank Boos Gallery, located in Bloomfield Hills, Michigan.

Many years ago I had a beautiful wedding ring made for your mother on our 25th wedding anniversary. When she died, I kept her beautiful ring, made in New York by a very good friend of mine, jeweler George Andrew. The ring had diamonds all around a platinum band, 62 full cut diamonds and 26 marquis diamonds.

Stephen Till, gemologist and appraiser, appraised it at $12,300. I kept it in a safe deposit box for you for 22 years since you were my only child. You probably recall that you suggested several times that I sell and use the money for something special for Sallie and me, like a vacation or travel. That's why we went to the Frank Boos Gallery.

At the Gallery, Boos and a woman, either his wife or an assistant, said it was a beautiful ring and that he knew the appraiser, Stephen Till. They were nice to us, marveled at the ring, and gave us a letter indicating a $4,000 low and $5,000 high estimate. This we understood was their estimate of the money we could realize after the auction.

We were then shocked to receive a call that the ring had been sold for $2,000 and after a 15% commission, we would receive $1,700 (this, for a ring valued at $12,300.) That day we received a check for

$1,680. We asked how could this be? The caller said they always start at one half of the low figure. This was never told to us nor is it to be found in the Auction Consignment terms I signed.

I would never have given the ring to him under those terms. I contacted Boos by phone twice and visited his gallery office. He was very curt and brusque, and said, "Read your contract."

Prior to our meeting with Boos, I had shown the ring to the reputable Blue Water Jewelers in Port Huron, Michigan. The owner, Jim Morosco, said they did not sell previously owned jewelry. He would have to take it apart to use the diamonds. He offered $3,500, but said it would be a shame to take apart such a beautiful ring, that I could get more. He mentioned the DuMouchelle Gallery in Detroit and I probably should have gone there.

I feel that Frank Boos took advantage of us. I now caution senior citizens to be aware and to be careful. I feel this should be looked into, because I do not feel Boos is an honorable man.

I have many questions such as why weren't we told the bidding would start at one half the low figure, why wasn't that mentioned in the contract or the letter we received prior to the auction. We told Mr. Boos that we wouldn't accept less than $4,000 but it wasn't written on the contract; we just trusted that it would be done. Our ring wasn't pictured in their brochure yet another lady's diamond ring was. Was ours sold at auction or sold privately? Who got this exquisite ring for $2,000 and was there any relationship to someone at the Boos Gallery? Was the auction handled properly and fairly? Why were there no other bidders over $2,000 for the ring? The contract said the auctioneer could return the item to the consignor if he felt a fair price had not been offered so why wasn't that done?

When I spoke to Mr. Boos, I told him we would try to follow this up with the proper authorities, and he said, "Do whatever you will." So I will, as long as there is life in me!

So I urge senior citizens to beware, take care, read the fine print, ask questions, get answers and do not be taken advantage of. Turn the phrase "Caveat emptor" around to let the Seller Beware, particular at the Frank Boos Gallery.

You know that I am not asking you to feel sorry for us, dear, but we have discovered that some of us become too trusting as we age.

Love, Dad

Crime and the Elderly

Dear Betty,

I was frequently asked to address the problems of crime and the elderly in police work and as sheriff. I have also been asked to speak on the subject since I retired. I thought you might be interested in some highlights of what I tell people.

> Nearly one out of every five persons in the United States is 55 years or older. That's 20% of the population, a percentage that's increasing every year. Like other population groups in our society, older persons have special needs that all of us must understand.
>
> Many older persons have adequate financial resources, possess good health, live happy and productive lives, and experience no crime problems. Some older persons, however, do become victims of crime and suffer economic, physical or psychological hardship resulting from a crime experience.
>
> National surveys indicate that seniors have lower victimization rates for the violent crimes of murder, rape, and aggravated assaults. However, they are frequently the target of fraud and swindles by con artists, and have a higher-than-average victimization rate for strong-arm robbers such as purse-snatchers and pickpockets.
>
> Many older persons must live on fixed incomes; the arrival of monthly pension or social security checks. While direct deposit is helping this, some seniors are afraid to trust such mechanical means and want the check in their hands. This makes them especially vulnerable to theft of mail and at check-cashing locations.
>
> Physical injuries suffered during a criminal attack can seriously impair an older person's health and mobility for a long time. Moreover, the fear of crime can increase their isolation, not only affecting the quality of their lives but also increasing their vulnerability.

Seniors are often the victims of con artists. Their susceptibility is influenced by loneliness, isolation, and impairments in seeing and hearing. Preoccupied with physical disabilities, a senior may exert such concentration in stepping from a curb, for example, that he becomes unaware of what is happening around him or her. Thus they are frequently the targets of bunco schemes involving hurry-up transactions and immediate payments of money. They also may become victims of younger people and may even fear reprisals should they report a crime.

In a nationwide trend, more seniors live alone from other members of their families. This trend has been increasing since the early 1960s. Widows may spend many years alone. Crime intensifies fear and can prevent loners from making essential trips to the grocery, doctor, dentist, church, senior citizen centers and other places. Additionally, those who must live in lower cost housing are even more vulnerable to the baser elements of our society.

Elderly victims often react with intense aversion to the home after burglary. The home that was once their shelter now entraps them, making them fearful to remain alone.

Elderly blacks are more fearful of crime than elderly whites and 69% fear walking their neighborhoods alone at night compared to 47% of white seniors. Some studies have found that as many as 75% of seniors do not go out at night for any reason, and 1/3 are afraid to go out alone at any time.

Seniors often feel less worthwhile and may be lured into spending money foolishly to rebuild their image. Their desire for communication to relieve loneliness may make them more vulnerable to criminals who talk and spend time with them. However, when an elderly person loses their life's savings, this trauma leads to isolation, poverty, shame, and depression.

Some schemes used by criminals are the following. The bank examiner scheme usually involves three people. The team pinpoints bank locations on a map in certain target areas. They go through the phone book underlining women's names and single out those who live alone and are not likely to discuss their scheme with someone else. The first team member calls the victim, verifies the identity of the victim's bank and informs her that a bank official will be calling shortly. The second con artist, impersonating a bank official, telephones to obtain the victim's correct bank balance, to advise her of suspicious withdrawals, and to persuade her to withdraw money to help trap a suspected dishonest employee. The third member, the bagman, displays forged credentials, and collects the money withdrawn from the bank by the victim.

A second fraud scheme is the "pigeon drop." One team member approaches an elderly person and as they talk, the second member joins them and asked whether or not some money belongs to either of them. A note is pulled from the package of money and shown to the intended victim. The note induces the victim to think that the money has been gained illegally or will be used for illegal purposes, and that the finders should not keep the money. Then the con artist offers to consult his boss or attorney to see what to do with the money. He reports back that the three can split the money. However, they will have to withdraw money from the bank to show good faith and to prove that they will not spend the money found until the bank boss has worked out some legal procedures. Then the accomplice, pretending not to know the finder, produces money and urges the victim to do the same. The victim withdraws savings and shows it to the con artists. They place it in an envelope, and in a fast switch, give the victim an envelope stuffed with nothing but paper.

A third fraud scheme is the home repair con game in which an elderly homeowner is shown a part of his home that needs repair. The con artists confide that they have just finished a job nearby and have some material left over and thus can save the homeowner money. For a small fee, the victim allows the con artists to do the job but shortly finds that the material and workmanship were inferior and repairs have started to fall apart.

A fourth type of fraud involves a phony building inspector who mysteriously appears at the victim's home on a "routine" inspection. After the inspection, he finds some kind of very dangerous situation like faulty wiring that demands immediate attention. Fortunately for the victim, the inspector has a friend who can do the job quickly and reasonably. The reasonable rate is usually several times higher than the normal service call and may not even be needed.

> Another type of fraud is the phony sales demonstration. After the demonstration, a slick-talking salesman asks for a signature to award a prize or gift. The piece of paper is a sales contract that costs the victim hundreds of dollars for something they never wanted.
>
> Seniors often suffer from medical disabilities. Fraudulent medical or quick cure schemes, fake laboratory tests, miracle cures, and offers of free medical diagnosis often trap them into expensive, long-term and useless treatments.
>
> Con artists prey upon the victim's charity or the victim's greed in most of their schemes. One sign of this is a deal that involves a hurry-up transaction or payment. Other signs are free or spectacular offers, stolen goods, leftover material from a nearby job, hurry up deals, signing a contract as a mere formality, pay for the material now and labor costs at the end of a job, new company selling at sacrifice prices to establish a product, phone calls from "officials" inquiring about financial status or requesting money, groups having a similar name to a well-known group, and surveys seeking salary, age, marital status, etc.

I usually end by suggesting that seniors don't go to a bank alone when planning to cash a check or withdraw a large amount of money, don't carry a lot of money in their purse or wallet, don't fight or confront the criminal, and don't go to a bank on a set schedule.
Love, Dad

Fountain of Youth

Dear Betty,

You know how important physical conditioning has been to me throughout my life. If I had not been in good shape, I would not have been selected to join the New York City Police Department. If I had not been in good shape, I would not have been able to withstand the rigors of a police officer, police commissioner and sheriff careers. If I had not been in good shape, I would never have been able to enter the Senior Olympics where I met my wonderful current wife, Sallie.

Let me tell you about the fountain of youth, long ago sought by Ponce de Leon, which many say is located in St. Augustine, Florida. But let me tell you where the *real* fountain of youth is!

The *real* fountain of youth is located in Levagood Park in Dearborn, Michigan. You must learn the closely guarded secret of how to drink from it, and it must be done only that way or else no way, Jose!

Now that I have your interest, this special fountain is located along the perimeter of a one-kilometer track in the park. As you approach it, you should be in proper apparel, namely, lightweight clothing and tennis or walking shoes. Then with a bend at the waist, keeping your stomach muscles firm and holding everything in at the beltline, take one swallow. Only one, mind you, or it will not work.

Then you, with your tennis or walking shoes, must walk as briskly as possible around this one-kilometer track. No cheating or else no go! After one kilometer, you then approach this special fountain again and you are entitled to take another swallow. Note this carefully, only one (two will not do) then around the track once again and return for a third swallow.

When enough swallows have been taken, you will begin to feel better, look better, perhaps lose a chin, and bounce with energy once more. You will then have discovered the *real* fountain of youth.

Now that I have shared my secret with you, I can tell you that I have discovered two more real fountains of youth in these intervening years. One is located in Arizona at the Lakeview Recreation Center in Sun City. The other is at Algonac State Park located between Algonac and Marine City in Michigan. Some friends tell me that they have discovered a *real* fountain of youth in Sun City West, Arizona; Dallas, Texas; Santa Fe, New Mexico; etc. If you find one, will you let us in on your secret? I imagine these special techniques of drinking and walking will be similar to those my original walking friends still follow at Levagood Park.

I know you will discover your own fountain of youth but I wanted to tell you about my own discoveries.
Love, Dad

Always Learning, Always Growing

Dear Betty,

In 1994, a reporter named Barb Pert Templeton interviewed me for an article about senior citizens in Cherry Beach. I thought you might enjoy my answers to some of her questions, which were printed in the newspaper. By the way, did you know that I took a memory course in New York with Dr. Bruno Furst? I was even on television with him.

"You seem so dedicated to senior fitness. Did that come with your retirement?"

No, I have always been pretty active, always been a tennis player and I used to run a lot. But I never was a swimmer. Now I'm winning medals for the backstroke in the senior Olympics. And I do walk three miles every morning.

"At what point did you start teaching the aging courses?"

That was after I met Sallie. She was program coordinator for the St. Clair Council on Aging and started many of the programs at Cherry Beach Center. I teach the Body Recall class there three times a week in the summer.

"Is Body Recall an exercise course?"

Yes. We usually exercise for 30 minutes and then do a routine that I designed. It's to the music from the show "Cats." Body Recall is good for me. The body is a movement machine and you have to keep working at it and walking and swimming.

"What kind of classes do you teach in Arizona?"

We embrace a curriculum called Positive Attitudes for Positive Aging. Beyond the fitness, we teach coping skills and memory improvement courses. This October we will be teaching round dancing and I hope to teach conversational German.

"The memory course sounds interesting. What's it all about?"

I read a lot of self-help books and I've read a lot on the brain and memory. The books talk about how everything we do and hope to ever do is right up there. And I really enjoy teaching the memory course even more than the criminal justice classes I used to teach. It's the criminals who are winning, not the cops. It gets discouraging when we're saying what can we do and we're not really getting anywhere.

"Your career in law enforcement goes back a long way. What made you pursue it?"

A buddy of mine asked me to go and take the test to be on the New York Police Department. It was during the Depression and it turned out that I made it but he didn't. The police were respected at that time and well regarded, not like today.

"What prompted your move to Detroit?"

It was just after the riots in the city and Mayor Jerome Cavanagh asked if I was interested in coming to Detroit to be police commissioner. It was a challenge and it was a job that was important. I remember so many people saying to me, 'not Detroit, not Detroit,' and I made a speech later on and said 'why not Detroit?' When Mayor Cavanagh decided not to run for reelection, I resigned after 17 months in the job.

"Did you enjoy heading up the Detroit police department?"

Yes. I think I did a lot even though I was only there a short time. I put the scooter cops on the streets. I started that program in New York, too. The idea was to get the police out on the streets where they could meet people in the neighborhoods. I don't think it's working that way in Detroit now, though.

"What was it like to be the Oakland County Sheriff?"

The politics of the sheriff's post made it very tough. I ran as a Democrat in a Republican county. I don't think the sheriff should have to carry a political label on his back and have to run in a presidential election year. All the attention goes to the top of the ticket and it becomes who cares who's running at the bottom. Yet I was reelected and held three terms there. I was the only Democrat who ever lasted 12 years there.

(At a reception in Washington, D.C., I spoke with Ed Meese, former Attorney General of President Ronald Reagan. I told him some of my political problems. I said, "I ran as a Democrat. I talk like a Republican. I act like an Independent.")

"Do you feel you got things done in spite of the politics?"

Well, 19 of the 27 commissioners were Republican and so was the county executive. I helped to professionalize that county but I still think I accomplished more in Detroit in a year and a half than I could accomplish in 12 years in Oakland County.

"Would you want to be a cop on the beat today?"

I wish I could have stayed on as police commissioner in Detroit. But, no, I wouldn't want to be a cop today. I wouldn't want to be a young person either with AIDS and drugs and the sexual revolution. So many kids can't even read or write anymore.

"Do you miss being in uniform at all?"

I miss it in a way but I'm too old now.

"You sound to be in pretty good shape."

Well, I'm alive and enjoying life. We aren't going to let old age hamper us and we're getting a chance to help others.

Betty, dear, I thought it was a pretty interesting summation of my life up to the present time. I'm convinced that people never stop learning and growing.

Love, Dad

Toastmasters Changed My Life

Dear Betty,

I wish I had joined Toastmasters years ago. It would have been a great help to me as a police officer, instructor in the Academy, police executive, sheriff and professor. Those positions all required good communication with people.

When I joined, I learned that all great, world-shaking events had been brought about by the spoken word. Words are very important, written yes, but most importantly how and when they are spoken. Jesus Christ did not write anything. Nor did Socrates.

Consider the effect of these sentences by Roosevelt, Churchill, Kennedy and Reagan: "The only thing we have to fear is fear itself." "We shall fight on the land; we shall fight on the beaches; we shall never surrender." "Ask not what your country can do for you; ask what you can do for your country!" "Mr. Gorbachev, tear down this wall."

Sallie reluctantly joined Toastmasters at my prodding. Then she made her second speech entitled, "Old Is Not Bad." She later cut this 6 ½ minute award-winning address to 2 minutes, 45 seconds to become Ms. Senior Michigan 1999. She also placed in the top 10 for Ms. Senior America. Speaking, as she discovered, was her talent.

As an area governor for Toastmasters International, I have a dream and hope that my fellow Toastmasters will help make it come true. My dream is to reach out and interest senior citizens in the advantages and benefits of joining Toastmasters; to bridge the generation gap by bringing older and younger people together in a mutually-supportive and enjoyable, communicative relationship.

I even look for chances to help others and enjoy being a substitute teacher that students like and respect. I want to help motivate them as they enter their real life.

I would so much like to see more seniors taking this step. I like to tell people "To locate a nearby club, call 1-800-9WeSpeak. It may be the best call you ever make."

Love, Dad

What I've Learned About Public Speaking

Dear Betty,

I've done a lot of public speaking over the years and am doing lots of it with Sallie now. I thought I'd share with you some things I've learned.

Listeners will be more impressed with stories than statistics. They like to hear about what happens or happened to other people. We settle down to listen to a human-interest story. Like one person relating an interesting story to another. An audience likes that.

Stories should be relevant and not just dragged in for the sake of the story. You can always use old stories (golden oldies), but make a new angle to make your point. Personalize jokes or stories whenever possible. Make it yours. Localizing a story or joke will increase its effect. Bob Hope was very good at that.

Humor is the hottest spice of all. Add humor when sharing personal stories but humor must be relevant to the presentation. Natural humor, directly related to the subject you are presenting will greatly enhance the material, its understanding and its retention.

Don't tell jokes if it's not comfortable or natural for you. Don't tell long, drawn-out, awkward jokes. Don't poke fun at your audience, poke fun at yourself.

Opening your speech may be difficult but it's very important. Your first two minutes are probably the most difficult part of your speech. This is where you must grab your audience. You can do that by relating a human-interest story, arousing curiosity, asking a question, opening with a striking quotation or starting with a shocking fact.

Stories that tell of struggles, of things fought for, or of victories won are great stories. If you can touch their hearts, their minds will follow! You should depend on knowledge of your subject. Your belief in it and eagerness to tell about it make the audience want to be informed, persuaded, entertained and understood.

A good rule is to never tell a story or a joke during the first two minutes of your speech, unless it is a blockbuster. Use funny stories sparingly, and if it doesn't relate or sell your idea, don't use it. Self-deprecating jokes are easily enjoyed.

Use words to create pictures to make it interesting. Sprinkle pictures throughout your speech. Words that can set images flowing before your listener's eyes are excellent.

Think back in your past to situations or events that may have been embarrassing, stupid, humiliating, etc. Telling stories on yourself enhances your listeners' positive perception of you. Be sure they are not the boastful kind.

A major danger in telling stories is that many speakers stretch them out with far too many details. Remember to be entertaining, but not too long, or people will not really pay attention to what you are saying.

Glorified gossip and stories of interesting people will almost always hold attention.

Soar to a conclusion that reinforces your presentation in an uplifting way. Enjoy yourself, be enthusiastic, but give them something to grow with. Challenge them to be as good as they might be at whatever they attempt.

A good technique is to close with an appropriate quotation from a great leader or another sharp wit, such as Churchill. Generally avoid concluding with a joke or humorous story. It can trivialize your presentation when it should be most compelling.

The real inside story of any person's life can be interesting and entertaining. If one has struggled and fought, and who hasn't, his story if correctly told will appeal. Remember, Jesus did not write anything. He told stories and parables and changed the world!
Love, Dad

The Drawn Curtain

Dear Betty,

This is a wonderful world full of wonder. And I wonder a lot. I guess I am an Agnostic or one who believes that any ultimate reality (such as God) is unknown and probably unknowable. But this belief in only the rational and credible is not a comfortable position for me. I am envious of those who have faith. I wish I had that comfort. I wish I had the faith my wife and you have.

I recently met a minister whom I like and admire, and I would like to talk further with him. He mentioned, "Yes, there is a little agnosticism in all of us."

I often pray for understanding. Yes, I often wonder about the wonders of the world we live in. There must be someone or something behind it all. There have been three incidents that have caused me to wonder even more.

Driving home from Arizona in April 1996, we were routed through Gary, Indiana. The sun was setting as we approached Gary. I was apprehensive. Gary, a steel town, was burdened with a high rate of serious crime. I knew the former chief of police of Gary and he had his problems there.

Not Gary! I had been told in the past, as you will recall, "Not Detroit!" I was not looking forward to driving through Gary as darkness was approaching. Well, I didn't drive through. We had a complete tire blowout!

Darkness was closing in. Speeding cars and monster trucks whizzed by. There was no phone or C.B. radio in the car and no store or gas station in sight. It meant a long walk for help.

I was concerned about leaving Sallie alone in the car. Then a car stopped. It was a fairly old car but a young couple and the man offered to help. Our back seat was full and our trunk was loaded. That little donut tire was under it all but his jack did not fit our car. They drove me to several tire shops and gas stations looking for a tire. No luck or they were closed. But I did call AAA. They drove me back to our car. We said goodbye and thanks and waited for AAA.

They didn't show up and I began to think that AAA stood for apathy, abandonment and alas or absence. Then another car came by. It was now completely dark. A young man and his girlfriend showed concern and he helped greatly. We took all the stuff out of the trunk and shoved some in the back seat and put the rest on top of the car. He got the donut tire out and put it on. Then he warned us not to stop in Gary but to continue about ten miles further where it would be safer. We thanked him profusely and felt we just couldn't thank him enough.

But alas, a couple of miles down the road in Gary, where it was pitch dark and cars and trucks were speeding by, we hit a pothole and the donut came off its rim. Now we had only three wheels, a blown tire, no donut and we were stuck. We locked the doors and decided to stay in the car until daybreak.

Then lights pulled up behind us. It was a pick-up truck driven by another young man. He said he knew of an all night truck repair shop that could help. Was he okay? I went with him and left Sallie alone and hoped.

At this strange repair shop in a strange area, the man said he had to leave for a while but would return. Oh, sure!! Now all kinds of apprehension overwhelmed me. Why was he going? Where was he going? Sallie was alone!

But he did return. He had a big jack in his pick-up truck. A new tire had been found. He took me back to my car and put the tire on. He said, "Don't stop anywhere in Gary."

We finally arrived at a motel. Five hours had passed since the blowout. We were safe! Not one of the three angels would accept any money. We decided that Gary was a city with a bad reputation but some very good people.

The next day we tried to look in the area phone books for names they had given us. They were not to be found. Sallie swears they were real angels. I wonder?

And then I recollected a happening that really caused me to wonder. It was 1980 and the forthcoming election for sheriff of Oakland County, Michigan was approaching. I had served two terms and we needed to get brochures and flyers ready, arrange for radio and newspaper ads, and everything that goes with an election for a third term.

Little did I know that a man would try to kill me! My secretary did not like the pictures that had been taken. She had another photographer come to my office to take new pictures. It was a warm and sunny day. The photographer said it was much too light in my office to take good pictures. He drew the drapes of a large picture window tightly closed. He went on to take his pictures. As several shots had to be taken, it took about ten minutes.

All of a sudden, a deputy breathlessly burst into my office. "Sheriff, there's a man outside your window with a rifle. Two deputies are out there now!"

While those drapes were closed, quite a scenario had taken place. The man who serviced the coke machines had come running to alert our deputies. At the same time, County Judge Hilda Gage had also come running in to relay the same news. Two deputies had quickly gone to the scene, about 50 yards south of my picture window, and overpowered the man with the rifle. The man was Lewis Grusnick. Not only did he have the rifle with a scope on it, he had purchased four boxes with 50 rounds of shells that very day. He had put the rounds in a paper sack.

After he was captured, he said he was going to shoot the sheriff, the prosecutor (Brooks Patterson) and the judge of the circuit court (Judge

Thorburn). Later I facetiously asked, "Why necessarily in that order?" And remember, at that time there was a song being played on the radio, *I Shot the Sheriff!*

Well, he didn't shoot this sheriff! Why? Because those drapes were closed! Now, those drapes had never been drawn closed in the previous eight years I had been sheriff. They were only drawn for about ten minutes in eight years! Someone up there?

This occurred in early 1980. Your mother, Elinor, a victim of multiple sclerosis, had died a year earlier on April 19, 1979. As I said, I am not very religious but I wondered. I'd like to think there is a heaven and that Elinor is there and somehow helped to save my life that day. After all, ten minutes in eight years?

Only recently I was struck by recalling the doctor's name that night in the hospital in 1979. I had slept in the emergency care room for ten of the last eleven days. There was a shift change and the doctor was there. He told me that he had to perform an emergency operation to remove fluid or something from the lung. I think it was called a pneumothorax. It was to no avail. She passed away that night. It was terrible to see her go. I held her hand and said, "I love you." And you, Betty, were at the side of the bed, too.

The doctor was Dr. Freivogel, which means "free bird" in German. Was he the instrument of freeing Elinor from her debilitating, incapacitating multiple sclerosis? Her death allowed her soul to escape her weakened and tortured body and fly away. All this together with our experiences have made me wonder and wonder, and you know, Betty, it's getting harder and harder to be an Agnostic.

Love, Dad

Terrorists and the Press

Dear Betty,

I sent an article in to the newspaper on October 7, 2002, a year after the horrible 9/11/01 attack on our country. My article related to an ongoing manhunt for two snipers who were eventually arrested. My article was not printed but here it is:

> Six people died, unexpectedly, without apparent reason. Killed by a sniper or snipers.
>
> Five died on the streets of Maryland, one in Washington, D.C., a possible victim in Virginia.
>
> Who the assailant or assailants are, using a high-powered rifle or rifles, is still unknown. Police are searching for a white box truck seen by a witness to one of the shootings.
>
> Fear is now, understandably, widespread in the surrounding communities.
>
> Was this the work of terrorists? Maybe. Maybe not.
>
> I wondered if I should write this column. Would it give ideas to terrorists? I thought about that a lot. But I realized terrorists read our newspapers also. If this thought came to me, certainly it could come to them.
>
> Our nation, all of us, received a tremendous shock last year with that terrible attack, September 11th.
>
> Then we had the anthrax scares and some deaths. Perpetrator or perpetrators still unknown.
>
> We have received warnings from our government that there may be other attacks, nature unknown.
>
> Consider this! Suppose the enemies of our country decide to do similar indiscriminate random shootings in many other states and communities all over America.
>
> *What shock! What fear! What panic!*

Yes, it could be easily done. Nineteen enemies of our country hit our financial and business complex, our defense complex and apparently were on the way to strike at our government complex in Washington, D.C. that September 11th.

One, possibly two men did Maryland and Washington, D.C. shootings from a distance.

Twenty men scattered throughout our nation, using sniper, long-range rifles, could create tremendous fear, turmoil and tie up America.

There are, of course, many dastardly ways enemies of our country could use against us to promote fear, disorder and anxiety.

What can we do? As President Bush has said, we must carry on, go about our business, work, shop, eat, go on with our daily lives, but be alert.

One solid answer is for us good citizens to work closely with our law enforcement and protection people, local, state, and federal.

We must all realize police are our friends, our protectors, and protectors of our liberties, our freedoms.

Get to know your police, and police must also get to know us good people, and provide service and protection to the highest professional degree.

And police must clean ranks of the unfit, the corrupt and the criminals who wear that badge! It must remain a Badge of Honor.

Now the Detroit Police Department, working with the U.S. Justice Department, has indicted eight current and former employees on the Detroit Police Department regarding drugs (cocaine) stolen from the evidence property room, replaced with flour, and are apparently getting these drugs back on the streets through "associates" for their mutual profit. *This clouds all law enforcement!*

There should be no more blue curtains coming down, cops closing ranks, no "ratting" on rats. Not in these days!

We are all Americans! We must work together as Americans. We are all in this together; not as Afro-Americans, Irish-Americans, Polish-Americans, Italian-Americans, or Hispanic Americans.

I was born in Germany but I don't say I'm German-American. I am an American. We are all Americans and must realize that terrorists make no such distinctions.

> When we Americans see something unusual, something out of the ordinary, something that seems suspicious, we should take note, make notes, and make that call. Be prepared to cooperate with your police. Be prepared to testify.
>
> Again I repeat what I have said for years. "Apathy of the people plus apathy of police will equal anarchy."
>
> America responded to World War II after the attack on Pearl Harbor. I was one of them as a lieutenant in the U.S. Army Air Corps.
>
> Americans will respond now! Americans will respond to whatever from those who hate us.
>
> Let's all think as Americans, not as hyphenated Americans!"

Betty, I started writing that article in late October after six people died. The count is now 13 people shot, ten dead, a 13-year-old child shot.

The communities involved are shaken to the core. This systematic killing causes all of us real concern.

Last year's devastating strikes at our Twin Towers in New York and our Pentagon Defense complex shocked and saddened our entire nation, and many countries worldwide. Many rushed to help physically and financially.

Other communities in our country were impacted emotionally but not physically. Now everyone in America is uneasy.

The release of the chilling statement by the elusive sniper, "Your children are not safe anywhere at anytime," is debatable. The sniper, in effect, is holding our nation hostage. America is in danger. Copycats may appear. Enemy terrorists may get ideas.

I've only just learned, like everyone else, that two black men (one only 17-years-old) have caused all this panic and destruction.

When I sent in the article, I was not told why they chose to omit it. I can only guess that the press feared it would give terrorists ideas and thought they were doing some good by not stimulating the minds of predators. But I fear that the publicity generated by the snipers played a part in creating their pleasure in terrifying thousands of people. Yet publicity also aided in their capture. Once again, the press is a two-edged sword.

Love, Dad

P.S. I will add that two black men were arrested as the snipers. The car was rigged up so that one would shoot through a hole drilled in the trunk lid.

My 83rd Birthday

Dear Betty,

Yesterday I was young, only 82. Today at 83, I don't feel any different. The body may not respond as before. But the mind still goes on, thank God!

In fact yesterday, 9/27/02 Sallie and I did our program of "Practical Memory Improvement" in the morning and our "Aging Positively" program in the afternoon, after a wonderful lunch.

This was at "Council on Aging" in Port Huron. It was a fund-raiser for the Council. The cost for people attending (24 of them) was $10 and we performed gratis.

For the morning segment I covered:

- The importance of memory, our brain is who we are!
- Typical memory problems
- Why we forget
- Fun devices for better memory (acronyms, verbal elaborations)
- The number problem, how to remember names/faces
- 21 practical memory tips
- Two mnemonic systems: visual and auditory
- Visual system: What a number looks like
- Auditory system: What a number sounds like

Memory retention is facilitation by attaching or hooking things, words, objects we want to remember (the unknown) to the known.

The depicters on these systems would be the known, once you master them.

Really, Betty, you can remember almost anything, especially isolated facts, with these systems.

I also explained about the "Curve of Forgetting." Experience shows us that people forget about 60% within a day or two. The key here is to quickly re-read what you studied the day before, before going on to new works.

This is how I achieved the highest mental marks in the New York Police Sergeants Exam in about 1948. The only man who beat me, I'll always remember his name, was Valentine Pfaffman. Over 7,000 men took the exam; no women. At that time women, while allowed to take entrance exams, were not allowed to take promotional exams. That has been changed, and rightly so. "We've come a long way, Baby, eh?"

After lunch, Sallie and I did "Aging Positively." We used to call it "Positively Aging." All of us are Positively Aging. Tomorrow we'll be a day older. But are we "Aging Positively?" There is a difference.

I started this off by stating we would cover the mind, the body and the spirit. The mind works on the body and vice versa. If the mind and body are in harmony, you'll have good spirit, joy, and enthusiasm. Life will be really worth living.

Sallie then gave a great presentation regarding the mind and attitude. She described where she was after her traumatic and life-changing divorce, depressed, disillusioned, not really caring about living. Then she succinctly explained how she got out of this funk, by changing her attitudes, etc.

For the Body part, Sallie and I have both taught "Body Recall." This involves exercises designed for mature people, although any age can benefit. We explain that the body is a "movement machine" and requires exercises to keep in shape.

If a car is not up to par, the auto companies issue a recall notice and fix the car problem. If the body is not in shape, similarly, it's time to recall and fix it up.

I've often kidded that I might design my own program called "Body Recoil." If you look at the mirror and "recoil," it's time to get into action and do something to better the image.

One thing I stress is that poor posture "ages," while proper tall posture, head high, makes one "younger."

So on my 83rd birthday today, I will from time to time do a "Posture Check" on myself.

By the way, Betty, you know I just came back from "Body Recall" headquarters in Berea, Kentucky. Dorothy Chrisman designed the program years ago. Body Recall instructors are required to undergo a week of re-training to be re-certified every three years. I now have my 5th re-certification certificate. Good until 2005!

Of course, in addition to exercises like "Body Recall" people should walk, swim, play sports, dance, whatever to keep the body moving and in shape.

Sallie and I ended the "Spirit-Joy Session" with an emphasis on Humor. We did the skit we created where "W. C. Fields Meets Mae West." They really enjoyed the 4 minutes.

Then we did Dr. Krankheit (means sickness in German). I heard this in burlesque in New York when I was young. We've done it with different jokes each year at the Macomb Center of the Performing Arts. This time I (Dr. Krankheit) had 7 "sick" patients. When I walk on stage at the Macomb Center, my nurse (Miss Gotalot) comes in from the other way and the audience starts to applaud. They love it. I'm glad I went to the Oxford Theater, the Eltinge and Minsky's in New York. Guess you felt I went just to see the strippers, eh?

I did "fall in love" with one particular stripper. I remember her name, June St. Clair. She was beautiful with a very great body and beautiful long auburn hair. Wonder where she is and what she looks like now. It's funny now because I live on the St. Clair River with my wife Sallie, whom I love very much, and she had a great body and real long auburn hair, also. But that "poor bloke," George, her ex-husband, did not appreciate what he had. I do!

I ended our seminar yesterday with a monologue from Sid Caesar's book "Where Have I Been?"

It was of great help to him. The seniors in our audience really enjoyed it. I call it a "Philosophy To Live By." It struck a chord with them as it has with me.

Love, Dad

The Now (from Sid Caesar)

Dear Betty,

Here's how the Sid Caesar routine goes. In his book, *Where Have I Been?* he described creating the *Now* philosophy when he was on the road with Ginger Rogers in *Anything Goes.* He said he was reading a line by Albert Einstein's physics teacher in Switzerland, and Hermann Minkowski said, "If you want to put Einstein's theory of Relativity in one sentence, it would be: 'One man's now is another man's then.'"

So many people keep waiting for something big to happen in their lives. And while they're waiting and waiting the *now* is passing them by.

A *now* is the most precious thing you can have. But a *now* goes by almost with the speed of light.

No matter how much you might love and enjoy a particular *now,* that's how fast it goes, and it becomes a *was.*

That *now* is never coming back. No matter how much you want to hold on to it. It's going to be a *was.*

And that *was* ties into some going-to-be's.

So if you don't learn from the *was's* you will have bad *going-to-be's.*

It's like a cycle and it will complete the cycle and bring in new bad *nows,* and that's bad news.

The only time you can switch from a negative to a positive is in the *now.*

But you have to do it *now.* You can't just *think* of doing it now because it's rapidly going to be a *was* and it's too late.

And then those *was's* get heavy and start to decay into *should-coulda-woulda's.*

And you never have time for the new *now.*

Many people say we're *going to*. Yes *going-to-be* is you *may* do it and you *may not.*

But if you do it *now* you know it's *done* and you *got* it.

So where you have a good *now* you'll have a good *was* and that leads to a good *going to be.*

So you see you should take advantage of a *now now,* not then.

Maybe you can even change a *bad* now into a *good* now and have a good *was.*

From which you can learn and change your whole life.

So don't let the *"nows"* go by anymore. And don't ever say *"if"* because an *if* is a *never was.*

Betty, we add a few more words when we do a show sort of like this.

"So, folks, grab the *now* and make it work for you. We have a really good show for you. At the end, we hope you will all say, '*It was a good was.*'

Love, Dad

PART VI
Solutions

o o o o o o o o o o o o o o o o o o o o o o o o o o o o o o o o o

"Men should be taught as if you taught them not
And things unknown proposed as things forgot."

—*Ben Franklin*

Oakland Police Merger Urged

Dear Betty,

I thought you might be interested in my proposal to merge Oakland County police departments, which I thought would help to solve many problems. Paul Gainor for the *Detroit News* wrote about it on October 22, 1970.

Love, Dad

> Consolidation of Oakland County police departments has been urged by former Detroit Police Commissioner Johannes F. Spreen.
>
> Spreen, a consultant to the Oakland County prosecutor's office for six months this year, said the county's present law enforcement structure is not adequate to meet increasing demands.
>
> 'What we have today is not the answer,' Spreen said.
>
> 'Many young people are dissatisfied with things the way they are, and young policemen are dissatisfied and have a tremendous yearning for professionalism.'
>
> Spreen made his remarks in a talk last night before the Big Brothers of Oakland County in Royal Oak.
>
> He said his suggestions are contained in a report he has given Prosecutor Thomas G. Plunkett.
>
> He called for a 'task force' of federal, state and local police to deal with rising crime rates and street confrontations.
>
> 'What we need is coordination, consolidation of efforts and a working toward eventual consolidation of police departments because no department can do it alone,' Spreen said.
>
> Also, Spreen said, a law enforcement and justice implementation team should be formed by police, the courts, prosecutors, youth and adults to 'get out there with the community and turn it on' to law enforcement. He said: 'What I propose doesn't take

much money. We've got a start with very capable people who are now available.'

Spreen, a *Detroit News* columnist, said he has arranged to buy a home in Quakertown, an Oakland suburb, but denied a report that he will run for Oakland sheriff in 1972.

Spreen said he has 'made a decision that Michigan is my home' and does not plan to move back to New York where he teaches part time at John Jay College, commuting to his once-a-week class."

Community Policing Cuts Crime in Flint

Dear Betty,

I was happy to report about how new policing ideas and helping officers become protectors were paying off in cities like Flint, Michigan. Here is my article of July 21, 1971.

Love, Dad

> Police operations in Flint began to receive some well-deserved statewide and nationwide attention last year, when a combination of imaginative leadership, additional funding and community support finally put a crimp in local crime.
>
> By year's end, Flint was one of the few cities in the nation to show a decline in the overall crime figures. Crimes of violence had been cut by nearly 12% from the 1969 level, and robbery, a major indicator of street crime, was down 30%.
>
> Earlier this summer I called on Flint Police Chief James W. Rutherford to find out how his department had been able to achieve such favorable results. The answers reinforced my faith in the ability of sound methods, police-citizen teamwork and good management to meet today's challenges.
>
> The introduction of motor scooters for the first time in Flint made a contribution, but it was the total approach, not just the adoption of some handy new equipment, that did the job.
>
> The essence of the new approach was to get the entire police department oriented to "community relations" as well as to "law enforcement."
>
> The department's community relations section was almost quadrupled in strength. Most patrolled on scooters, and their assignment was to emphasize service and visible police "presence."

District cruiser cars continued to handle the emergency runs. But as the emphasis on preventive patrols increased, the demands for cruiser runs tended to decrease.

The areas of the city selected for the added patrols were administered under three separate "projects."

One covered the Oak Park district on Flint's north side, considered a high-crime area. Another covered the "Model Cities" district on the fringe of the city. The third was in an area that included a mixture of public housing, town houses and individual residences.

The Oak Park project, financed as a six-month operation with federal funds, was unique. It used volunteer officers, who worked a normal week at other assignments, and covered the Oak Park area in addition, on overtime pay.

The overtime pay incentive helped to overcome the resistance of some officers to trying the new scooters, and generated additional man-hours without increasing the size of the force.

At the height of the operation, the Oak Park district was patrolled by 10 teams on scooters and five teams on foot. They "rapped" with citizens, dealt with street problems and prevented crime.

In the "Model Cities" area, scooter patrolmen and Flint police officers paired in cars, and a mobile city hall provided new services.

Community Service Officers, a concept suggested by the President's Crime Commission, were employed for the first time.

These officers were young men without complete police training or full police responsibility, uniformed but unarmed, who provided service and problem-referral functions.

In the public housing area, a single additional college-educated police officer was assigned to take charge of the neighborhood as his personal responsibility.

The officer not only patrolled and "rapped," but attended community meetings, spoke to school groups, and generally made himself the respected "neighborhood" cop.

This service has seemed to resolve neighborhood frictions, and applies another one of the President's Crime Commission concepts, that of the highly trained, completely professional "police agent."

A city-wide Police-Human Relations Committee, a "college cadet" program, a selective traffic enforcement project, and "cadette" programs in grade schools as well as high schools, are also part of Flint's all-round effort.

Citizen cooperation and citizen confidence in police operations have taken a significant upswing since the new approach has been instituted.

Students Studying Crime Get Frustrated

Dear Betty,

I discovered a disquieting fact about the secrecy of police and government agencies. This article of August 5, 1971, described one facet of that secrecy. I hoped it would open the eyes of police. Unfortunately, the competitive nature of agencies to get credit for their results blinds them to the value of research and cooperation.

Love, Dad

> Are some suburban communities "hiding" crime? Would Detroit's crime figures look quite so bad if all of Detroit's suburbs reported their crime total with equal frankness?
>
> These are questions three young Detroit-area students have been seeking to answer this summer, with the backing of the Detroit Central Business District Association.
>
> I have no idea what the figures will eventually show, but the wide variety of responses from the suburban departments has been interesting. Their research technique was to begin with individual phone calls. They identified themselves simply as students preparing a crime report on Michigan and asked for each community's 1970 crime figures.
>
> They followed with letters to about two-thirds of the departments called. After about six weeks, they received the figures they sought from 22 departments. The 22nd report, sent in a self-addressed envelope the students provided, arrived with no community identification on it. The researchers have no idea whose figures it contains. Of the others, seven have promised to send reports, 20 told the researchers they must appear at the police department in

person, two charged a nominal fee and two insisted on a formal written request.

Thirteen gave no definite response, while 13 others declined to provide the requested information for no reason or because they were "too busy" or because the figures were "not available."

For a telephone survey, I think the response provides a fairly representative sample. And I can understand that very small police departments might keep their crime records only in a ledger, and might truly be too busy or have too few men to prepare a report, especially for what they might interpret as a casual student inquiry.

Even larger departments are not always able to cover all the demands of patrol, response and clerical services with existing personnel.

However, 24 of the agencies contacted do make regular reports to the FBI, and 14 of the 24, for one reason or another, would not make copies of these existing reports available to the students.

To the young men having their first personal contact with police officialdom, the response from too many departments was either suspicion or discourtesy.

The students' premise is that crime figures are a matter of public record and should be freely available to citizens.

Word to the Wicked

Dear Betty,

This column came out on April 26, 1970. I know it sounds strange that I would use my column to try to communicate with criminals, but it was really to advise anyone, even youngsters, to do what police say or they could wind up dead.

Love, Dad

This is about the short, unhappy life of Randall Clark. His and other names in the story are fictitious, but the story is not.

Randall Clark was a career larcenist, and a part-time drug peddler. He had a record in three states, going back to when he was 15. He had spent time in three federal penitentiaries. He was arrested some 25 times in 25 years.

His first arrest was on suspicion and he was released.

At 18, he was arrested twice in three months, for theft. He was discharged the first time. The second time he was given a suspended sentence and put on probation.

At 20, he was released after another larceny arrest. Then he was caught in a narcotics violation.

This cost him his first prison term of 60 days.

In his 21st year, he spent 90 days in jail for larceny, 60 for a narcotics violation. He avoided trouble for two years, then served 30 days on a larceny conviction. The next year, he had another larceny conviction; four months.

The next year he was in worse trouble; grand larceny. He pleaded guilty to a lesser offense, but he was now a full adult at 25. With his record, he received a year's sentence.

A few months after his release, he was back in for pushing heroin. This got him five years. After his release he stayed clean for a year or two. Then he needed money again, got it the easy way and was re-confined for another year.

Free again, he committed a minor offense, driving without a license. He ignored the fine and a traffic warrant was issued for his arrest.

Two years later, he was arrested and found guilty on a charge of attempted larceny from a building. The sentence was 11 months.

He was barely out when he was caught driving without a license and fined $105 or 10 days. His next offense was carrying a knife: $115 or 11 days.

Months later, officers Evans and Moore were in their scout car and received a coded message to intercept an out-of-state car carrying a man suspected of drug peddling. He was believed to be armed.

The officers found the car and questioned the man, later identified as Randall Clark. After some interrogation, the man broke and ran. The officers shouted at him to stop. He kept running. They drew their guns.

Clark reached down in full stride, pulled something out of his sock, and threw away two small packages, which were later found to contain heroin. This motion caused him to stumble and fall, but he quickly jumped up and ran. He turned, moving his arm toward his clothing.

One officer yelled "gun!" His partner fired one shot. It was over in a split-second.

Randall Clark went down with finality. At the hospital he was pronounced dead on his arrival.

In his pocket was a knife. No gun.

The officers had been alerted to believe the man was armed. Would the officer have shot if his partner had not suddenly cried, "gun?" Who knows? All too often a split-second delay can mean, and has meant, death for an officer.

I have some advice for the suspects in cases like this; a "word to the wicked," you might call it.

When a police officer tells you to stop, you stop! Right then! Stand very still! Keep your hands away from your clothing! Do what he tells you! Then your life might be a little longer than Randall Clark's, if not happier.

What were Clark's thoughts as he ran away? Nobody knows, but one thought was to get rid of the evidence. Then perhaps a good defense lawyer could have created a "reasonable doubt" in a jury's mind about the fact of narcotics possession.

But why did Clark keep running? Did he think another trip to jail might be a fate worse than death?

By the People, For the People

Dear Betty,

This article appeared on April 27, 1970. I wrote it because a recent downtown Detroit anti-war demonstration had brought up the power of the police.

Love, Dad

On April 15, those who protest our continued involvement in the Vietnam War held another demonstration in Kennedy Square. The war issue is a matter for the individual conscience of every American. From the war issue spring other matters, the role of the police in protecting every American's right to dissent, and every American's right to the preservation of order in his city.

I have no special insight into the peace rally of April 15. What I know about it I learned from reading the papers and from friends who were there.

These sources indicate without qualification that the police played a protection role. They did not interfere with the public expression of legitimate opinions.

Detroit police should be congratulated. Their restraint contributed so much in making the day of protest largely peaceful.

There were some provocative incidents, but they were the exception and were disavowed by leaders of the rally.

But there was one newspaper headline that I disagree with. It touted a feature story by a reporter who walked with the marchers. The headline read: "For an Afternoon, the Streets Belong to the People."

This raises a question. Who are the "people" and who are entitled to use the streets? As thousands of office workers got into cars and buses to start homeward, there was considerable interference with their right to use the streets.

This interference was generated by a handful on the fringe, who took advantage of the large audience attracted by sincere peace protesters.

Still the police used restraint. A small group of troublemakers repeatedly rushed to block traffic. Police responded with disciplined spearheads to keep the streets open. The situation developed into a nuisance game to which the police responded admirably.

According to the press, the leaders of the peace march took strenuous steps to insure peace during the rally. The vast majority of participants exercised their right of dissent peacefully and sincerely.

Both the people and the police deserve commendation for acting responsibly, and rendering vain the provocations of the few.

Perhaps it is wrong to use the words "police" and "people" as if they were separate and distinct entities.

Actually the word "police" originally meant a special function or power of the people, exercised on their own behalf.

In fact, by derivation as well as by democratic practice, "police" stands for the basic power and right of the people to provide for their own general security.

This power must not be abused and the people should remain on constant alert so that this or any other aspect of government is not used against their interests.

But in theory as well as in practice, the people and the police are not adversaries. One is derived from the other.

Police, who perform at their professional best, truly serve as "protectors of liberty." They guard the people against the abuse of personal liberty when the extreme and distorted exercise of individual rights becomes a danger to the total community; a danger to the people.

The Future Shire Reeve (Sheriff)

Dear Betty,

I wrote a chapter in a book called *Crime and Justice in America* back in the 1970s. I called the chapter "The Future Shire Reeve: Tribune of the People." You might find it interesting as the ideal for future sheriffs.

First let me tell you where the word Sheriff comes from. In England during the 1200s and 1300s, the basic units of society were groups of ten families, which were called a "tithing." An elected leader known as a tithing man led this group. Each group of ten tithing men represented 100 families and had another elected official who held the title of "Reeve." These men had the powers of both the police and the judge.

The next unit up was the Shire or county. The Shire was headed by an appointee of the crown and was known as a "Shire-reeve" and that is where the word "Sheriff" comes from. Eventually the Shire-reeve was relieved of collecting taxes and had only to be concerned with maintaining law and order. When a crime was committed, a citizen was obliged to raise a "hue and cry" and others were compelled to assist in the pursuit of the fleeing felon. The Shire-reeve gave the group the position of "posse comitatus" (power of the county). These tithing men helped the Shire-reeve bring the felon to justice.

Now, let me give you the gist of the chapter that I wrote. I said that law enforcement doesn't work, at least not very well. The police system is archaic, fragmented, overlapping, confused and subject to bickering and jealousy over jurisdictional power. The court system is costly, time-consuming, ineffective, political, and a hollow mockery of what it should be. The corrections system is a shambles, a stepchild, and a growth area for the cancer of crime. And the personnel of the criminal justice system are not all professionally selected or trained, nor professionally dedicated. Unless vital changes are made, we will muddle into the future with problems we cannot even begin to anticipate.

The great dollar impact of crime as well as the psychic impact creates a serious economic drain on all of us. It is my firm opinion, after 37 years of study and practice of law enforcement, that more effective crime control can and should be the county sheriff. The future of law enforcement should be directed by a modern Shire-reeve, a tribune of the people, a sheriff who will champion people's rights with proper liaison between local agencies of county, state and national law enforcement agencies.

Thomas Jefferson pointed to the office of sheriff as being the most important of all the executive offices of the county. The sheriff has lasted over a thousand years, so there must be something there. The sheriff is the only office holder touching all the bases: law enforcement, court service and corrections, and having the power of posse comitatus!

A modern sheriff is a people's representative, the only elected peace officer in criminal justice. The modern sheriff can be the key and the hope for better law enforcement in the United States because he is a seasoned veteran who represents the people.

I tried to address why present-day law enforcement doesn't work. We have several federal law enforcement agencies, state police or state highway patrols, county police, sheriff and his deputies, local police, and constables. Administratively this kind of setup is chaos, especially when there is no cohesive cooperation among these agencies.

Tenure in office is a key problem in many of our major cities. Even J. Edgar Hoover, head of the F.B.I., undoubtedly stayed in office too long. But short tenure is also a problem and accounts for many problems of the City of New York and Detroit with police commissioners averaging two years more or less.

I referred to the problems associated with the Oakland County Child Killer investigation, which I described in another letter to you. What is the answer? I keep asking myself that question. In 1973, the National Advisory Commission on Goals and Standards recommended the elimination of very small police departments. In an issue of *Law Enforcement News,* Robert DeGrazia faulted the International Association of Chiefs of Police for being a social club that perpetuated the status quo in law enforcement. He further accused the I.A.C.P. of fearing consolidation.

I explained my views and told how I issued the following attestation and signed it before the media at a press conference.

1. I do not believe in a county police force.
2. I have never advocated a county police department in Oakland County.
3. I would never serve as the head of one Oakland County police department.
4. I do believe in local government and local rule.
5. I do believe in the consolidation of police services more than consolidation of police departments.
6. As Sheriff, representing all of the people in Oakland County, I do believe I should be a law enforcement service agent supporting and assisting local police departments, so they in turn can service their citizens more economically and effectively.

I ended the chapter saying that we must revamp the function of the sheriff, the oldest and most continuous law enforcement and justice office in the history of the English-speaking world. How should it be revamped? I'll describe that in another letter to you.
Love, Dad

Law Enforcement Coordination is Lacking

Dear Betty,

I was invited to give a talk on May 17, 1979, in Chicago to the meeting of the American Academy for Professional Law Enforcement. I was very excited over this opportunity and thought I would focus on the role that sheriffs could play in coordinating law enforcement.

I began by saying what I had said elsewhere, "Law enforcement doesn't work! At least not very well. The police system is archaic, fragmented, overlapping, confused and subject to bickering and jealousy over jurisdictional power."

I told them that with between 25,000-40,000 police agencies, there was no cohesive cooperation between them. Administratively, this kind of setup is pure chaos.

Big cities have the bigness problem, requiring a top-notch law enforcement administrator who can blend education, training, experience and managerial expertise. Long tenure is a problem because some administrators resist leaving. Short tenure is a problem because turnover at the top level cannot provide the sustained direction for programs and progress. Smallness isn't always good either because there is fragmentation of effort and jurisdictional difficulty.

State police are too distant and the "big brother" approach should not displace local police authorities. A national police is even more distant and abhorrent but could serve to support local police agencies. But investigative coordination at the countywide level through the sheriff's department may be a better alternative.

I told them how police consolidation has been discussed for over 80 years. In 1920, Raymond Fosdick in *American Police Systems* said, "The increase of crime in urban districts traceable in many cases to the isolation of small police departments in heavily populated sections would seem to make necessary some form of cooperation as yet untried."

In 1936, August Vollmer in *The Police in Modern Society* said, "There are more than 250 separate and distinct police units in the Chicago region. It is no wonder that men like John Dillinger and others were able to avoid the police in that section."

In 1940, Bruce Smith in *Police Systems in the United States* said, "If every local government, no matter how weak or how small, is to maintain its own police facilities, the latter become so numerous that their interrelationships are unduly complex and burdensome. When to sheer complexity is added the confusion and destructive rivalries arising out of overlapping enforcement powers, the discouragement that so often overtakes police administrators is readily understood."

In 1967, the *President's Commission on Law Enforcement and Administration of Justice* stated, "A fundamental problem confronting law enforcement today is that of fragmented crime repression efforts resulting from the large number of uncoordinated local government and law enforcement agencies."

In 1971, the *Advisory Commission on Intergovernmental Relations* stated, "Many metropolitan areas are faced with an almost hopeless proliferation of small and inefficient local police departments.... A ten-man force has difficulty providing full-time patrol and investigative services, not to mention the essential back-up services of communications, laboratory and records."

In 1973, the *National Advisory Commission on Criminal Justice Standards and Goals* stated, "Police agencies that employ fewer than ten sworn employees should consolidate for improved efficiency and effectiveness."

It is my strong opinion that small police departments should stay, but in effect they are not full service departments. Specialized and supportive services should be provided to them from the county and state through reasonable political and sensible mechanisms. I believe that the sheriff's position is the key to harmonizing and coordinating law enforcement. Of course, I'm talking about the position, not necessarily the person in it now.

The sheriff can be the effective pivotal wheel between ineffective local law enforcement and too much centralized government in law enforcement matters. The sheriff should be the Chief Peace Officer of his county, to be concerned with the peace, safety and welfare of its citizens and responsible for a just maintenance of law and order and to enlist responsible citizen participation in this effort, through the posse and other avenues.

The office of sheriff must bring within law enforcement togetherness, almost like in a marriage. In addition to this marriage within law enforcement, a marriage with the people can create a most effective crime control team. Yes, it will take a team, the concerned people of a county along with their police departments and their sheriff, bolstered by state, and where appropriate and needed, national support to bring the "blessings of liberty" and the "pursuit of happiness" back into this land.

Some thought my comments were self-serving but you know that I was not talking about myself but about the role of a sheriff in a county.
Love, Dad

Sheriffs and Police Chiefs: Partners

Dear Betty,

I was very excited when I was asked to give a talk to the first joint meeting between Michigan police chiefs and Michigan sheriffs on June 30, 1981. Here are some of the things I told them.

> We must examine that which we offer our public, service and protection, asking ourselves, "Can we do these things in a better way?"
>
> Service and protection involve the control of crime and the control of accidents. This attempt at control is costly, not controlling is even more costly. From a society who must ultimately pay the price comes our challenge. Is it not time for police and sheriffs to unite under the common task of meeting the challenge?
>
> Law enforcement in our state is fragmented, and nowhere is the problem more acute than the tri-county area that surrounds Detroit. There are 103 police departments that encircle Detroit in the counties of Wayne, Oakland and Macomb.
>
> This immense fragmentation is a delight to the criminal mind and a frustration to the sincere police officer and police executive.
>
> Most concerned police executives voluntarily cooperate in spite of the fragmentation. But there are islands of isolation where there should be bridges of understanding. Each of you represents one department but our similarities far outweigh our differences. I see before me a group all bound to the same common public trust of protection for the citizenry. But we are divided by our lack of trust in each other.
>
> This lack of trust is a natural defense that we have developed in a time of change and financial cutbacks. We become jealous of our positions and we see other chiefs and sheriffs as possible threats. We covet information, rather than share information. But citizens

see the police as one body of people, whether the uniform be brown or blue, cooperating to fight crime and prevent accidents.

The public does not understand overlapping and fragmented policing service. By remaining fragmented and competing, not cooperating, we are setting the stage for our own extinction.

I do not believe in one large county police department. As one county executive said, "Is there a way that we can get three, four or five of our cities together and decide that maybe they don't need individual police and fire departments?"

If we do not work together to free ourselves of the jurisdictional constraints that impede solving crimes, then do we not invite consolidation by another hand? We must not allow the erosion of trust between agencies to continue. We must share information and make the best use of our scarce manpower. We must complement each other's efforts.

The coed murders in Michigan some years ago, the child killer investigations, both in Oakland County and now in Atlanta, and the Jimmy Hoffa disappearance are striking examples of investigations that brought out police fragmentation at its worst.

Rather than a county police department, a shared-power concept is needed. We want our police to be close to the people they serve. Rapport between the police officer and the citizen is one of our chief defenses in curbing and preventing crime. But local police cannot do the whole ball game in today's sophisticated crime, brutal crime and terrorist crime.

I have asked the Michigan Sheriff's Association to pursue the possibility of non-partisan elections for sheriffs in order to have a better chance to remove politics, factionalism and favoritism that could hinder professional ethics. I strongly feel that a sheriff's role is that of specialized, scientific assistance to the community, usurping no department's authority, and threatening no department's sovereignty. A sheriff's role is to provide policing where there is no policing, and to provide supportive assistance to each department within the county.

Toward this end, we have instituted some programs that deal specifically with cooperation between local police departments and the sheriff's department. We call one program S.H.A.R.E. (Scientific Homicide, Arson and Rape Effort.) I had the pleasure recently of deputizing a number of local police officers that completed 40 hours of training in homicide investigation, and we now have a team prepared to investigate any major homicide in a participating jurisdiction in Oakland County.

Through the Oakland Community College Police Academy, there is a program whereby data is compiled comprehensively on all arsons that occur in the county. Members of the Sheriff's Department Arson Unit, members of the Southfield and Troy Police Departments and other agencies work together on major investigations and data sharing.

In the City of Southfield, the city and county have a contract whereby the city pays the salary of a staff of sheriff's detention officers, and the county pays the salaries of five sergeants for professional correction services provided to the city jail.

For the last six years, we have provided prisoner transport for all departments within Oakland County to and from the county jail. This takes the burden off the police departments, freeing manpower for protective patrol in their own communities.

Oakland County has shared resources for years in our N.E.T. (Narcotics Enforcement Team.)

These types of sharing concepts are only the beginning. Other services of a sheriff's department could and should provide local jurisdictions with specialized traffic programs, accident reconstruction, police driver training and other activities.

Other supportive services could include crime lab services, a comprehensive juvenile delinquency prevention program, marine program, canine, and various types of specialized training and aviation services.

We must realize our common dilemma is one that requires immediate action to succeed. Pull together for progress or continue on our divisive paths and fall victim to the consolidation efforts of the efficiency experts as they attempt to force us to do that which we should do on our own: cooperate.

Dear, surprisingly this speech was greeted with applause and a standing ovation. I think the audience agreed with these ideas.
Love, Dad

The Roles of American Law Enforcement Agencies

Dear Betty,

After I left the Sheriff's Department, I offered input from a lifetime in law enforcement through writing, public speaking, and other avenues.

I spoke to groups about the need to revamp the future sheriff's role and improve the professionalism and selection of police chiefs and sheriffs. I explained that law enforcement fragmentation was compounded by feelings of insecurity, petty piques, and jealousies engendered by widely different qualifications of police chief executives. I said things to groups and tried to offer solutions such as the following:

> As emphasis is increased on establishing the professional qualifications of our police chief executives and our sheriffs, we can begin to ascribe and define roles for each level of law enforcement where there is a multiplicity of agencies. This will do much to solve the overlapping jurisdictional and duplication-of-effort problems that impede the effective and economical delivery of law enforcement services to our citizens.
>
> Federal agencies must be on a national and international range in specifically prescribed areas so that there remains the division of powers that the framers of our Constitution so wisely provided for. For instance, the federal government should concentrate on such national and international areas as organized crime, white collar crime across interstate lines, the growing narcotics problem with its international aspects, terrorism, etc.
>
> State police forces generally should provide supportive services to county and local law enforcement. State police should concentrate on areas such as organized crime, narcotics control, and

white-collar crime from a state perspective, and leave the provision of local law enforcement to local and county authorities.

Sophisticated and costly services beyond the ability of local departments should be provided to local communities such as intelligence and investigative services, communications and records information networks, computerized criminal histories, major forensic laboratory services and statewide patrol of state freeways and expressways such as interstate and limited access highways. Mutual aid support should be provided as necessary upon the request of local communities.

The local law enforcement agency should provide local law enforcement and basic 24-hour police services in the nature of preventive patrol, immediate response to citizens' calls for assistance and emergency situations, initial investigation of crimes and accidents, and if needed, obtain additional supportive and investigative services from the county sheriff and through him, if necessary, from the state police.

The sheriff, as elected representative of the people of the county, has constitutional and statutory functions and should be concerned with county-wide law enforcement services involving multi-jurisdictional matters: modern, humane custody of offenders as per the laws of the state and the proper administration of the county jail; general preservation of the peace, security of the courts, patrol services for unincorporated areas either by agreement or contract; and general specialized scientific and supportive services that can be provided from the county level. If more assistance is needed, he should request it from the state and federal authorities on behalf of the local communities of his county.

Contract policing is provided by the sheriff's department through agreements with local agencies of government like townships in exchange for a pre-established annual, semi-annual or monthly fee.

Of course, all county residents already have the protection of the sheriff's departments but these services usually only include indirect technical assistance, jail services and supportive services, due to the existence of local police units in many areas and the limited manpower budget of the county force. However, through contract policing, the local governmental unit receives not only the above-mentioned general services, but also regularly assigned deputies to work directly within the local jurisdiction, often out of a local substation set up in headquarters of the village. The contract provides the necessary funds to hire qualified and trained deputies for local jurisdiction. This is at a cost savings to the contracted areas, since the sheriff's department does recruitment, testing, training, equipping, dispatching and has an established technical communications system.

In Oakland County, Michigan, where contract policing is operating effectively, there are 10 townships out of 25 contracting with the Sheriff's Department. The county also has some 42 local police and public safety units, particularly in the heavily populated areas, supported by local jurisdictions.

I believe that the sheriff can be the bridge between the law enforcement world and the people of society. He can, as the people's representative, talk to them about the need for involvement in crime prevention; about obtaining their assistance and support for the development of modern police administration; for scientific advances in criminalistics; for better crime detection; for improvement in the correctional process, and so on. Likewise, he can be a voice from the people to the law enforcement world when some within that aspiring profession fail to live up to its ethics and standards. He can operate within the governmental framework on a par with his peers, the other elected officeholders in county government.

The sheriff can be the balance wheel between ineffective local law enforcement and too much centralized government in law enforcement matters. The sheriff, as of old, should be the "keeper or chief of his county," concerned with the peace, safety and welfare of its citizens, and responsible for a just maintenance of law and order.

The future sheriff can be a modern "tribune" who can champion the people's rights. And that, my dear, was what I tried to be.

Love, Dad

An Idea for Youth from the Swiss

Dear Betty,

As I have explained to you before, the greatest preponderance of violent crimes and property crimes are directly traceable to our young people, ages 17 to 21. The cause may be idleness, ignorance, poverty, poor educational and health systems, peer pressures, drugs or just don't give a damn attitudes. I fear that we have created an undereducated, unemployed, listless, uncaring and resentful generation of youths.

I believe our solutions have not worked and we must try something different. Let's take a page from the Swiss, a proud people who live at peace amidst powerful neighbors. Their pride in country translates into great patriotism. It is my understanding that every man in Switzerland serves his country for a period of time. He is trained to defend his country, and proudly keeps his weapon at home ready to come to the aid of his country if needed, and to help each other in time of need.

Let's assume that we could start a program like the Swiss, say a National Service Corps. We rallied to defend our country and democracy in World War II. Many young men and women enlisted or were drafted into the Armed Services. The training they received, the discipline, the rubbing shoulders with those from other parts of the country, the indoctrination, instructions and work habits stood many in good stead. My three years in the Army Air Corps did not hurt me; rather the contrary, I believe.

We are closing many military installations now that could be used. Many trainers, teachers, retirees, experts in many fields, including those in the military, could be used in paid and unpaid capacities.

Look at the example of volunteers in many fields such as S.C.O.R.E., (retired executives who help people with small businesses), P.R.I.D.E. (the retirees who clean the streets of the Sun Cities in Arizona), and sheriff's posses in some communities (reserves of dedicated unpaid volunteers trained by the sheriff's department).

Many young people cannot find work after graduation from high school and many do not graduate. Idle, succumbing to improper peer pressures, temptations, broken families, wrong companions, the drug culture and the like are not conducive to a good future. We have a Peace Corps to assist underdeveloped countries. Why not an extensive peacetime Service Corps for our own country?

This would take many of our troublesome youth off the streets and put them in a responsible, mature shaping environment. It could diminish crime in our neighborhoods. It would remove much of the violence and relieve helpless victims. It would give the hard-pressed police of America a break.

Boot-camp type training with its discipline, along with other training and career orientation would benefit youth before they become societal misfits, to be warehoused in our prisons. We are spending our money on the wrong people. Let's spend our money on the right people. We build thousands of prison cells but money could more wisely be spent on our youth.

The young people in such a program could gain literacy improvement, good work habits, self-esteem, opportunities for education, exposure to various careers, including those in the Armed Services.

Half of their tenure could be either in a training program in one of our military branches or in some civilian enterprise enhancing our environment, helping in hospitals, assisting the needy and aged or reclaiming and preserving our land and neighborhood parks. They might fix and repair the vacant and vandalized homes in our inner cities. This could help many to own a home they could not otherwise afford.

Our youth can do much for their country and for themselves. Our country must do something for them such as providing a safe and secure environment, training, education and skills to cope with today and tomorrow. Subsistence and some wages comparable to what young people serving in wartime realized would seem only fair. Thus, we could defend ourselves from crime, violence and drug evils and, like the Swiss, be prepared to defend our country if needed.

Unfortunately, hours of community service required to circumvent going to prison appears to be the only use of this sort of program currently.

Love, Dad

One-Year Stint with Uncle Sam Needed

Dear Betty,

My idea about one year of service for youth got out. *Daily Tribune* writer John Basch did a story about my feelings on serving our country in 1983.

He began the article on Lincoln's birthday by saying that all our tax dollars had not cured drug abuse, improved education, or stamped out violence. But he told of my answer.

I told him there ought to be a one-year mandatory service to this great country. It doesn't have to be in the military service, although that could be one avenue. Our young people could plant trees, help out in old folks' homes or help clean up the pollution problem. There's lots of work that needs to be done and a one-year conscription into government service would solve nearly all the country's problems. It would solve the youth unemployment problem, the violence problem, the public education problem and would get at the root of the nation's crime problem.

It could be divided into six months for training (educational, physical, mental and moral training) for young people ages 17-19. The other six months could be for actual service in the military or non-military service.

I told him that the criminals were winning in our society. I tried for ten years to get the elected Oakland County commissioners to listen to this idea. But I didn't have much success.

The idea is still offered today by many politicians. I surely wish it would be considered seriously.
Love, Dad

The Voices of a Police Officer

Dear Betty,

Lon Chaney, Sr., a silent films actor, was before your time. He was known as the "Man of a Thousand Faces." Since there was no sound, his face had to convey feelings, threats, emotions and other expressions.

The professional police officer of today must be an actor too, using his body language, his voice, and his message to interact with others. When we speak of a professional police officer, it is important that he/she displays the attitude and demeanor of a professional.

His attitude must convey sincerity, friendliness when appropriate, confidence and a desire to be of assistance. His voice must impart the proper tone, volume and pitch appropriate to whatever situation confronts him. No dese, dem or dose guys are needed in policing. He must have the wisdom to know what manner of voice to choose to use.

These amusing little examples of situations can give people an idea of how many voices a policeman must have:

Voice of Comfort:

To a lost child: "Is your mommy lost? Don't worry, honey, we'll find her. Want an ice cream cone?"

Kids at school crossing: "How ya' doing? Pass your history test? Yes, Andrew Jackson was the 7th president."

Voice of Authority:

Accident or robbery scene: "Sir, you're all excited. Be calm. We've got to get a description of the car on the air. Which way did it go? What color car, year, make of car? Did you get the license number?"

Voice of Compassion:

Notification of injury or death: "Mrs. Jones, please sit down. I'm very sorry to inform you that your husband…."

Voice of Censure:

To a speeder: "Do you know how fast you were going? Let me have your license and registration, please. No, put your money away, sir!"

Informative Voice:

Directions: "Yes, ma'am. McMorran Auditorium is two blocks down and one short block to the left."

Voice of Meaning:

To gangs or toughs: "Okay, you bunch of wild asses, move your butts off this corner—NOW!"

Family fight: "Mr. Brown, if you do strike your wife, you're going to the slammer. Understand?"

Burglary suspect: "Okay, assume the position. You have the right to remain silent…."

Drawing Room Voice:

At functions or social situations: "Rembrandt tried to show his subjects exactly as they were while Gainsborough usually flattered his subjects, making them look more beautiful or handsome than they were. Don't care for the French Impressionist paintings. To me daVinci and Michelangelo have never been surpassed."

Psychological Voice:

To bad guy: "Okay, punk, we know you did it. Cut the bull…lies." Then leave the room while the other officer plays the good guy.

Good guy officer: "Son, we all got problems, I know. We all make mistakes at times. Would you like a coke? Cigarette?"

Witness Stand or Voice of Truth:

To the court: “No, I did not bring the bloody glove to O. J. Simpson’s house. I found it there, sir.”

Specialized Voices with Street Jargon:

Undercover work: “Honey, what will you do for $50?” “I need some crack bad, buddy. Got any?”

Crime Prevention Dog McGruff: “Take a bite out of crime.”

Voice of Command:

“Lieutenant, you take 20 men and space them along Fifth Avenue on the Park side, from 59th to 64th streets.” “Sergeant, you take ten men and cover the Review Stand.”

As you can see, professionals must look, act and talk like one. The voice and tone must fit the occasion and not inflame but inform or influence people. I always felt that the attitudes, actions and demeanor of one bad police officer affected all police officers.

Now, the voice I want to use with you is this. “I will always love you and do what I can to help you.”

Love, Dad

Our Killing Fields

Dear Betty,

I think what I am going to tell you will shock you.

Our country is now well over 200 years old. We have fought in many wars. Our American men and women have encountered enemy troops from various countries: British, Spanish, German, Italian, Japanese, North Korean, Vietnamese and others. There have been many Americans killed by enemy forces in the last two or more centuries. Yet all these casualties are far less than half of all Americans killed by the automobile. And cars have only been around for the last century.

From 1775 to 1982, 1,186,654 Americans died in all the U.S. wars up to then and that did not include Desert Storm or the war in Afghanistan. From 1900 to 1982, 2,442,865 Americans died in U.S. highway accidents. Another twenty years have passed and I assume that at 40,000 a year, almost 800,000 more have died or perhaps a million more. Thus about three times as many have died in the last century from the car than were killed by enemy soldiers in around two and a half centuries.

Our killing fields are our streets, roads and highways.

The car, fostered in Detroit, mass-produced by Henry Ford and others, has produced a death toll of 2 ½ million, at a rate of one every ten minutes.

I used to tell groups that the four main reasons for car accidents were drunk driving, dangerous driving, driving without seat belts, and driving while fatigued or medicated.

Drunk driving causes about 50% of all deaths in car accidents. Crash scenes are bloody. Cars are so crumpled that special tools called the "jaws of life" are used to pry drivers and passengers out.

"Mothers Against Drunk Drivers" or MADD has conducted one of the most effective campaigns against drunk driving. Their annual Candlelight Vigils feature the roll calls of the names of the deceased, and they are mourned by weeping spouses, relatives and friends.

Another successful campaign was the "Designated Driver." There is concern today that in many instances this does not work. It may only create a license for passengers to drink more.

Dangerous driving is the cause of many accidents. Speeding causes loss of control of vehicles, and claims the lives of others in addition to the speeder. Weaving in and out can surprise other drivers creating accidents and leads to careening. Tailgating is a potential for destruction when a sudden stop brings a disastrous result.

People may not use seat belts because of a macho attitude, negligence or a wish to be free of control. But it clearly results in unnecessary deaths and serious injuries. Every policeman has seen countless injuries and deaths by those not wearing seatbelts and thus they are the biggest supporters of seatbelts.

Those who drive while under medication or when fatigued cause accidents. Some people insist on driving long distances without proper rest. Some people like to save hotel expenses by driving straight through between states. It is also dangerous to rely on coffee, pep pills, No Doze tablets and other stimulants. Prescription drugs can make one sleepy, as can antihistamines and other drugs.

When people asked me what could be done about all the auto carnage, I said that they should be as concerned about this as they are about crime and criminals. A car is much more dangerous than guns and knives and a car makes every driver a potential killer.

To decrease drunken driving accidents, we need D.W.I. units, alcohol enforcement units, specialized training, alcohol testing devices, videotape equipment, and education about the facts. MADD and SADD (Students Against Drunk Driving) are good influences.

To minimize dangerous driving, speed laws need to be observed and enforced. They should be realistic because 55 on some highways promotes lawbreaking by most motorists. Lane changing should be enforced but the police cannot be everywhere. Road rage or the case of "the finger" being displayed can result in fate giving the driver the "finger." Tailgating should be aided by education that there should be one car length of space for every 10 mph of speed to allow for stopping distance, which I call "saving room for your life." The law of inertia tells us that a body in motion will continue in motion unless acted upon by some external force, such as the car ahead. In other words, leave room for your life and don't drive in your "living room."

Those who drive without seat belts may not care about themselves, but they should think of their loved ones who care about them. As to those who drive while fatigued, they should realize the dangers of non-stop driving and the effect of pills and drugs. It is much better to spend a few hours and dollars on a motel than spending eternity somewhere else.

I tried to close my comments by reminding listeners of the three Es. They are: engineering, education and enforcement. Engineers try to build better roads with better signs and better traffic lights and better rates of speeds and better cars to travel on the better roads. Education includes drivers' training, publicity, public service announcements, MADD and SADD campaigns, AARP drivers' training for seniors, and governmental efforts to drive right. Enforcement refers to stricter, fairer, and impartial law enforcement.

But the most important element of all, I always emphasized, was to remove the "nut behind the wheel."

I am so glad that you have always been such a safe driver.

Love, Dad

Our Protectors of Liberty

Dear Betty,

When I read about the senseless shootings of young kids at a Jewish Day Care Center in California, I wonder where did we go amiss. What became of the Golden Rule? If we all could live by it, we would have almost no crime, almost no violence, almost no violent deaths caused by others.

Certainly there is much more that parents can do regarding responsibility for their children. To be there for them. To know where they are. Whom they're with. What they are doing. When they are coming home. Who their friends are. How they are getting along in school and otherwise.

Teachers must also be alert to signs of trouble, unrest or strange behavior. Citizens must be more alert and aware of what is going on and take necessary action and report to the proper authorities. But it is the police who must deal with an erupting situation in or at school.

Teamwork of parents, teachers, students, citizens and police is needed to protect our children and our freedoms. What this country needs is a good measure of individual responsibility and respect for our first line of defense: the police.

I have always thought that "Law Protection Officer" would be a more acceptable description of the daily work of a police officer than "Law Enforcement Officer." Police are our fellow citizens, assigned special responsibilities by their fellow citizens, who are dedicated to the protection of their fellow citizens' rights.

The police officer's primary responsibilities are peacekeeping, crime prevention, and the protection of residents from harm and unlawful infringement of their human rights.

I like to think that the letters P-O-L-I-C-E should stand for *Protector of Liberty* for the *Individual,* for the *Community* and for everyone *Equally.* Indeed the police officer is a protector of liberty. I had "Protectors of Liberty" on our police cars in Detroit. Police protect society from the deeds and threats of persons that might be repressive, threatening or harassing. The individual should think of the police officer as his protector, his friend, and one who watches over him.

We must all help to break down the walls of misunderstanding or non-understanding between people and their police. People must realize police are our friends, not enemies. Our nation and our police do have enemies as we have so shockingly realized on September 11, 2001. Police everywhere must go about doing their jobs professionally to not only prevent crime and reduce community tensions but now to help in America's battle against terrorism.

My hope is that police, parents, children, teachers, school administrators, politicians, media and everyone will pull together. It truly takes a team, your police and you to make peace.

Love, Dad

Apathy Will Bring Anarchy

Dear Betty,

I have enjoyed leading classes for seniors on social issues since I retired. You might be surprised at how liberal and creative some of these thinkers are. We discuss crime, drug abuse and capital punishment to mention a few of my topics at the Rio Institute for Senior Education.

You might be startled to learn that some of my students favor legalization of drugs and discontinuance of the death penalty. One lady, a former teacher and school principal said, "Sometimes society tells us a criminal doesn't deserve to live, but ethically, it's wrong to take another person's life. Perhaps being locked up in prison and losing your freedom is worse punishment than dying."

A retired microbiologist for New York City's health department said he opposed the death penalty because it offered no recourse when there's a miscarriage of justice. He said, "I'm always worried that an innocent person could be executed. But I'd also be upset if someone who committed a heinous crime got away with it. Should that person be annihilated?"

When we discussed the war on drugs, the group thought it was lost. So they said why not legalize marijuana and perhaps hard drugs such as cocaine, eliminating the profit motive and gaining control over supply?

A man who was a former teacher and principal said, "I'd like to see drugs legalized, and even prostitution legalized. Then you tax those activities and control them."

I told them how only a few police officers were assigned to New York's drug squad in 1941 when I began but by the mid-1960s, the number had increased to several hundred. It has exponentially increased since then.

One lady, the mother of five who also worked as an engineer, thought the women's lib movement was partly to blame for the rise in drug abuse. She said, "I'm a feminist who believes in equal pay for men and women, but you need a wife or husband at home to take care of the kids. Everyone has gotten selfish and 'me' oriented. If kids have no one at home, they will look for diversions like drugs."

I shared with them my fear that police are becoming less and less committed to their jobs of safeguarding the public. I left them with that saying you have heard too often, "Citizen apathy plus police apathy will bring anarchy."

Love, Dad

The Need for Proper Police Procedures

Dear Betty,

Sometimes I think "if only." My thoughts often go back to several incidents where if only proper procedures had been followed, there would have been entirely different results.

Today, my thoughts settled on the Jon Benet Ramsey murder. We all have our feelings about it, and about who might have committed such a heinous act. This shocking murder is still unsolved. Someone can either live with their conscience or someday confess.

This dastardly complicated and confused case has thwarted the investigators, law enforcement personnel; those close to JonBenet, all of us indeed, except the killer.

It brought me back to the days I taught at the New York Police Academy. We had a specific, detailed procedure for special cases, "Procedure for Report of Missing Child Under 7." If only the Boulder Police response had followed such a procedure to the letter.

The first part mandated a thorough and diligent search of the entire house, every room, every nook and cranny. Then the father of JonBenet would not allegedly find the child later, carry her upstairs possibly causing disturbance or destruction of evidence. Also, the home and crime scene would have been kept from being contaminated by friends, family and whomever.

Then there was that infamous O. J. Simpson horror story. It kept all of us transfixed for months and months. That long-running scenario should have been nipped in the bud. That white Ford Bronco leading 6 or 7 police cars for more than an hour along the California freeways should have been stopped by the police. If any of you were in that vehicle, it would have been. Two people lie in their graves with no one punished. Did justice triumph here? Another case of someone able to live with his or her conscience.

Then the third incident that came to mind was the Rodney King fiasco. The amateur video recording of that incident should have sparked a different reaction by Los Angeles Police Chief Darryl Gates, in my opinion. The camera showed one officer repeatedly using his club on Rodney King, while five or six other police officers stood around. Frankly, the chief should have fired the officer clubbing Mr. King and given suspensions without pay to the other officers involved (or not involved but watching.)

We would not have had that unfortunate Simi Valley jury verdict, which led to the worst riot in modern history with 50 or more killed. It eclipsed the 43 killed in Detroit's insurrection days.

Speaking of Detroit, if only proper police action had been taken that Sunday morning in the raid on an after-hours joint. If only the tactical mobile unit had been used instead of politicians with bullhorns standing on cars. When I, as a captain in the New York Police Department, was attached to the Brooklyn Morals Squad, we raided such joints. The objective was to remove participants from the scene quickly. Get them into precinct lockups and jails and disperse the onlookers. Not let it fester nor leave it to politicians.

Too late! Too bad! If only....

Love, Dad

Capital Punishment is Ineffective

Dear Betty,

I wrote my opinions about capital punishment in the *Times Herald* in Port Huron, Michigan on December 7, 2000. You probably remember my views.

I described how earlier polls showed that 75% of people in America supported the death penalty for capital crimes but it had gone down to 65%. This was chiefly because DNA testing is causing some people earlier thought guilty to be released from prison.

Capital punishment remains an emotional issue. I oppose it for several reasons. Some say that the criminal justice system is an utter failure so why have capital punishment under such a failed system? I say that the death penalty really has no effect on the rapist, the robber, the burglar, the mugger and the crimes that are the most numerous.

Executing some murderers will do little to lessen the threat and effect of these crimes most feared by citizens. But I think that the clamor for the death penalty diverts attention from the great bulk of crimes threatening us.

Our criminal justice system discriminates. The poor are executed but the rich can pay their way out. There is much manipulation within the justice system and each side quotes experts who reach opposite conclusions (the O. J. Simpson case).

There are problems within the jury system. It takes a unanimous verdict to convict in death penalty cases. Jurors may hold out, be reached, threatened, etc. thus mistrials and hung juries occur. Additionally, executions can become ghastly as when a man's head was set on fire in 1997. There can be errors revealed by DNA testing. The truth may remain buried if people are executed.

We all share the outrage people feel over murders. But what does killing people do to us as a society? Are we no better than those we kill?

You know that I believe the power over life and death belongs up above. There are other roads to justice!

Love, Dad

Mariachi Cops

Dear Betty,

On December 9, 2002, forty men (no women?) brandishing pistols and wearing sombreros trotted on horseback into Mexico City's historic downtown center. Why? To fight crime foremost, but also to serve, protect and amuse tourists!

Known as "Charro" police, the Charros are Mexico's original cowboys. The Charro Police Program is one of a string of unusual measures taken by officials desperate to fight the high level of robberies, kidnappings and assaults in the city of 8 million people.

Earlier, officials from another Mexico City neighborhood had introduced "Robo Cops;" men dressed in their reinforced uniforms with shields, tough Plexiglas masks and clubs.

It reminded me of days in Detroit. Remember, Betty, we won the World Series in 1968. We had mounted police. They had two uniforms. One was regular police dark blue and the other was a Sunday best, sharp-looking uniforms of bright blue, Stetson hat, puttees, scarves, etc. They looked good.

The Detroit police mounted worked the downtown area and the area around Briggs Field, the home, then, of the Detroit Tigers.

I directed them to wear those sharp Sunday best uniforms each day when the ball games were on and every weekend, plus special events downtown. Out of towners and tourists should see them.

While I had trouble at times with some of the Common Council where I requested equipment, supplies, and training, I had no trouble with one of them, Billy Rogell, who had been the Detroit Tiger's shortstop. He loved the mounted.

So did I. In New York, they were very effective at special events and particularly in the Times Square area and the theatrical district and the city parks.

In Mexico City, National television had broadcast footage of the "Robo-cop" crime fighters fleeing from stone and metal pole-throwing vendors who refused to leave city sidewalks.

During 1969, during the Viet Nam protest times, some youthful disturbances began in Detroit. A crowd of protesting youths had smashed windows of a music store. My superintendent, John Nichols, and I got into a serious argument that day. He wanted to dispatch the crowd dispersal police units with shields, facemasks and clubs.

I disagreed and countermanded his orders. I said these young people were venting their feelings about Viet Nam and such police force and pressure would only escalate their actions. This was a job for our scooter cops.

I directed our scooter-cop teams to meet them and talk with them. I myself drove down to talk with them. There were no more incidents. That's another time the scooter cops saved the day, as they did during the "Happy Riot," as I called it, when we won the World Series in 1968.

Did you ever see such a town in a frenzy of glee and exultation, when there was absolutely no movement of cars? Talk about gridlock! We had it frozen.

But the scooter cops could move throughout the stopped downtown. They protected downtown and downtown merchants from window breakers, looters and worse. The *Michigan Chronicle*, a black newspaper, carried front-page pictures and headlines crediting the scooter police for excellent work.

Also in 1969, I believe it was Pittsburgh after the World Series win, there was rioting, looting, and much damage occurred. Incidentally, in 1984, Detroit won the World Series again but an unruly mob overturned police cars and created a lot of damage. There were no scooters then!

So today, the Mariachi Cops are getting a friendly reception. They pose for photos with journalists and tourists. One of them said, "To be a Charro Police officer is a source of pride for us because we know that the tourists are going to feel protected and they are going to like that we represent pure Mexican culture."

Yes. Ole to that!

Love, Dad

The Five Ps: People, Politicians, Press, Police, and Pressure Groups

Dear Betty,

I have summed up the main problems the police administrators have. Please forgive the roughness in a quotation I'm using from Joseph Wambaugh, a really fine writer, but he cleverly illustrated one of the problems.

I have always thought that people must be concerned about their police and the politicians who appoint them. They must get to know their police and their important job functions.

People

In teaching at the New York Police Academy, I used various memory or mnemonic devices to make the subject matter more meaningful. Here are two of these that deal with the functions of a major police department.

The first deals with the 5 major duties of a police department: P.D.PEP

I explained those five in this important priority order:

P. Prevent crime and disturbances. There is less hurt, damage, and trouble if it never happens

D. Detect and arrest the offender (if the above happens)

P Preserve the peace. A police officer is a peace officer who should help control community tension and violations of law

E Enforce all laws and ordinances

P Protect life and property

The other memory device was THE FBI RAN. This dealt with 9 other functions of police:

THE: TRAFFIC-HEALTH-ELECTIONS

FBI: FIRES-BEGGARS-INSPECTIONS

RAN: RIOTS-ASSEMBLIES-NUISANCES

The people police serve should have an awareness of the important things and activities police do for their service and protection.

I believe in the wake of the 9/11 tragedy that New York people are realizing how important the police (and, of course, the firefighters) are to them. The many that consider policing a necessary evil now understand that police represent the first line of defense we have against evil or criminal acts.

Politics/Politicians

Politicians must understand that poor police affect their city, and that police departments should not become political footballs or be used as tinker-toys. Political influences and machinations can affect policing adversely.

Generally the further away a police administrator and his department can stay from political waters, the better for the people.

Unfortunately police administration often must become involved with politicians, particularly on their requests for manpower, money, materials and the wherewithal to buy the tools and provide the training needed.

Teaching and training are absolutely necessary to provide good policing for the people. But most cities rarely provide enough. Many smaller cities in the past gave the new hire a badge and a gun and said, "Go patrol out there."

I was amazed when I became Police Commissioner of the City of Detroit that the police had only several weeks of recruit training. (In 1941, the New York Police Department provided three months of training before men or women went out in the neighborhood.)

Then when things go wrong, the politicians blame the police. They say to study the problems or investigate, and punish the bad cops, instead of supporting the many good cops with the training, tools and techniques necessary today.

It is difficult for most police administrators to get the support needed from political leaders at the time it is needed. In Detroit, much time was wasted because of party politics, such as when the Council disliked the Mayor.

Police

Policing is in peril all across the country. This is in addition to the general problem of crime, organized and white collar, community tensions and such. Further, we now have the war atmosphere with Iraq, North Korea, Iran (the so-called Axis of Evil), which brings on today's terrorists and the recent sniper shootings.

All this in the immediate incident devolves upon local, county, and state police. Additionally, there has to be coordination and cooperation among the federal agencies involved. Now the Cabinet Office of Homeland Security has been established. We all must work together, but will we?

The past picture is dark because of jealousies, rivalries, turf protection, etc. A complaint often heard from local law enforcement is that cooperation with the FBI was often a one-way street. FBI would accept but rarely divulged data and that seemed to be the case even with other federal agencies necessarily involved. In too many cases throughout the nation, police themselves have been part of today's problem of community tension and crime instead of being part of the solution.

Joseph Wambaugh, former Los Angeles Police Department cop and now author said it better than I can in his 2002 book, *Fire Lover*, on p. 87.

> It has always been remarkable that American law enforcement does as decent a job as it does, in spite of the Balkanization of the profession. The U.S. fear of a national police force has resulted in thousands of autonomous police agencies staffed by people who jealously guard their turf, their sources, and every scrap of information both vital and trivial. Many times the networking that takes place is appallingly fragmented and informal.
>
> The vast-government-conspiracy theories floated in hundreds of books and films have never failed to produce howls of laughter when mentioned at law-enforcement gatherings, especially in the aftermath of JFK, when the vast government conspiracy included the FBI, CIA, and all the other three-letter agencies staffed by bureaucrats who are mostly loathed and distrusted by street cops. Those with an alliterative flair call them grandstanding government geeks in penny loafers, or bumbling back-stabbing bureaucrats who would conspire to peek inside a girl-friend's underwear without the approval of a U.S. attorney and a search warrant.
>
> But what really brings down the station house is when, in order to make the JFK conspiracy work, all the revisionists had to include the Dallas Police Department. And *that* does it every time. Cops get to knee slapping and falling out of their chairs over the thought of it. Because everyone who's ever worn a badge knows that the moment a cop gets a *real* secret, the drums start beating and the asphalt jungle wireless starts humming, and the first leggy news chick with tits out to here will be blabbing the *secret* on the news at ten even before the cop wives get to tell it to the gang at the office and the girls at the gym.

Straight from the shoulder, the police can often be a major problem. Police officers that do not measure up to professionalism are police that are biased, bigoted or brutal, including police who do the wrong thing or do improper things. Yes, a few bad apples will infect the whole box, the media will see to that. And that hurts all other police officers nationwide.

Police officers today must combat the feelings or attitudes of cynicism. That's somewhat different because their duties expose them to the many bad experiences of conflict and hostility with people.

Police feel a constant frustration with human imperfection. Police work mostly at night. Who do they see? Who do they have to handle? The bums, the pimps, the prostitutes, the criminals, and the parasitic scum that abounds.

He or she do not often meet the decent people that are home in bed, who get up, go to work in the morning, come home at night, take care of their families and lead a pretty decent moral life.

Police must have more opportunities to meet and interact with some of the decent, caring people.

Press

The news media tend to cater and pay more curious attention to the abnormal than the normal. Just as curiosity killed the cat, such media philosophy helps to kill a city. Extremists get a disproportionate amount of attention in our media, and therefore create a false sense of alienation between those in the mainstream of life. The media often give people a chance to vent their spleen. Good news gets the back page because controversy is what sells.

Advertisements cater to basic appetites, as do news stories. Sexual material sells well and stories about sex sell well also. Big disturbances and loud noises catch the headlines, the camera and the microphones. People who are quiet, reflective, and weigh all the issues acting with moderation are toast in the papers.

The press should be fair, even-handed, giving equal space to all sides of issues and not tending toward the negative. The media newsreaders have special impact on a city's image and therefore a special responsibility. They should balance negatives with positives to keep a city's image in balance. I've often said, why can't the newspapers have one page, at least, called the "Good News Page." It may not sell papers but it can sell the city's favorable image. Improper or erroneous reporting can wreck a police department and it can wreck a city.

Betty, dear, you know how much I believe in Community-Oriented Policing. I was glad to see that my organization, the International Association of Chiefs of Police, gave an award to the Halton, Ontario Regional Police for their work in community-oriented policing last year.

Halton, a suburb of over 250,000, had a rash of crime and two riots in the mid to late 1990s by gangs and youth using drugs and alcohol. The police created a program involving bicycle police, foot patrol and high police visibility. The results were remarkable. Crimes of assaults, stolen autos, thefts, mischief, parking complaints, damages, littering and calls for service decreased by 75%. A public survey in the community showed that citizens had increased their confidence and satisfaction from 88% in 1995 to 94% in 2001.

I know what you're thinking. There is no way that all these problems are going to be solved in our lifetime. But we must keep trying and I, for one, will never give up.

Love, Dad

American Police Dilemma: What Is the Dilemma?

Dear Betty,

Now we come to the crux of this book. What is the dilemma referred to in the title of this book? A dilemma involves two or more assumptions or alternatives sometimes involving a choice between equally unsatisfactory options.

This is what I feel is the police dilemma viewed from my 83 years of life experiences and over 40 years in the practice of law enforcement and policing. In those last words, law enforcement and policing, lies the dilemma. It permeates through the pages of this book as you have seen. Should American police be law enforcers? Yes, they have to. But should law enforcement be the end-all of policing? What should policing be? What should policing include?

Webster defines "police" thusly: "The internal organization or regulation of a political unit through exercise of governmental powers, especially with respect to general comfort, health, morals, safety or prosperity."

Does law enforcement do this? Yes, but mainly in a certain way and that is the *response* way, the *after the fact* way mostly.

The best policing prevents crime! My belief is that the true measure of the effectiveness of policing is not only the absence of crime but also the approval of police methods by the people served. Russia or Germany might have boasted about the absence of crime but the people probably disapproved of authoritarian police methods that scared the population.

What are the main functions of police departments? They are first and foremost to prevent crime, detect and arrest offenders, preserve peace, enforce laws and ordinances, and protect life and property. There are other functions of police departments; e.g. regulate vehicular and pedestrian traffic, guard the public health, preserve order at elections, assist at fires, make inspections of certain places, preserve order at assemblages, suppress riots and remove nuisances and mendicants.

But really does the officer in the automobile do all this? No!

The old-time beat cop, the foot patrol officer did, but foot patrol is a thing of the past since August Vollmer, former chief of the Los Angeles Police Department, declared *with the advent of the automobile patrol that foot patrol was obsolete.*

True, the automobile has many advantages but to me, the worst culprit in the alienation between the police officer and the people is the automobile. Yes, the automobile provides fast response, in most cases, but provides very little of preventive patrol or furtherance of the many other police functions and good community relations.

Professor George Kelling of Harvard University has criticized some of the "Vollmerian" results of emphasis on the automobile. Kelling suggests that we "put the cops back on beats" and restore close contact with the public. Professor Kelling stated that a police officer was "in service" when he was in a car but "out of service" when dealing with citizens.

I agree. The officer in an automobile is in a "cocoon of glass and steel." He has lost the ability to stop, talk, and get to know people.

Yes, the officer in the police car responds quickly but to whom? The criminal, the assailant, the aggressor and those in their clutches. No wonder he becomes cynical, hardened and alienated dealing with such people.

It is my thesis that Vollmer was partly right and partly wrong. He tolled the bell for foot patrol and all of its benefits.

No doubt foot patrol was costly but it was very important. People who went shopping or out for entertainment saw the officer. They felt they could trust someone they knew. That old-time trust is missing with the officer in the car. You can't talk with him with windows closed.

In my opinion, police patrol for a better future should include some form of the old-time beat patrol, which had citizen respect. I suggest an addition to the police radio motor patrol car (New York term), the scout car (Detroit term), that the old-time foot cop rapport be restored in three ways:

1. By bicycle cops (very old-time) Some police departments have realized their benefits in some special areas.
2. By motor scooters (as I have instituted in New York City and Detroit, and assisted with in Washington, D.C. and Flint, Michigan)
3. And for business areas, shopping malls, boardwalks, a real old-time device, the foot scooter, now modernized with gyroscopes in the Segway. Police officers now could literally again be foot patrol officers but greatly aided by the Segway to cover streets containing business and commercial stores or what we used to call in New York, the "glass posts."

All three methods in the city should be used to recover the "sight" of our true police function, which is the reduction of crime and community tensions. We need to take another direction on the road toward combating crime and violence, a road toward the people.

As police became more modernized and motorized crime still increased, community tensions exacerbated, and youth hostility rose. The police officer of today was set apart in his police car, dealing impersonally with the public and less responsive for the enforcement of community standards and neighborhood interactions.

The good, trusted police officer of yesterday, the policeman on post has now given way to the "law enforcement officer" which implies a punitive or repressive role.

The Future of Police Patrol

Let's return to some of the values and respect of yesterday. Granted that today's police officer must gain respect, but let's put him in a position to do so. The bicycle, and now perhaps the Segway, can literally bring back the beat or foot patrol officer. Lastly the motor scooter I feel is the real answer to our police problems, the solution to the *American police dilemma!*

The origins and success of the motor scooters as developed in New York City was astounding, even after much derision. "Macho" cops looked with disdain at this small two-wheeled vehicle. They would prefer motorcycles. They did not get it. The motorcycle, which is good for escorts and chasing speeders, is a two-wheeled "pursuit and punitive" machine. The motor scooter is a "protective patrol vehicle."

Police departments in the United States followed along with August Vollmer's dictum regarding how the automobile made foot patrol obsolete. But let us consider statements from two of the most respected New York City Police Commissioners (Spreen, 1966):

"...the rugged and versatile scooter opens new vistas in crime control. As its use grows it is anticipated that the 'scooter patrol' will provide unprecedented control over crime and criminals in all our far-flung recreational areas." Michael J. Murphy, New York City Police Commissioner in 1964.

"The scooter is the most effective police patrol technique which has been developed in recent years. It preserves the concept of the foot patrolman and yet provides a mobility and responsiveness which the foot patrolman lacks." Vincent L. Broderick, New York City Police Commissioner in 1965.

August Vollmer's statement was far-reaching. These two statements should be also. Commissioner Broderick actually changed his budget, which was almost finalized, to include the purchase of 700 scooters for city street coverage after the wonderful results we had in the parks. Inquiries came from many cities in the United States and foreign countries for information and specific operational techniques. The scooter *could and did extend the range of delivery* of available police personnel at minimum expense.

The history and results of scooters in the City of New York, first for parks and then for city street patrols, is documented in the aforementioned "Journal" of the Northwestern University School of Law.

As a result of the scooter patrol successes in New York City, some police departments are using either the two-wheeled scooters or bicycles to restore the advantages and benefits of the old foot patrol officer system for crime prevention along with neighborhood rapport and respect. Bicycles incorporate many of the advantages of the motorized scooter except for the ability for fast mobilization in team concepts.

Detroit, Washington D.C., Flint and other cities have utilized scooters for various purposes. But the concept of scooter team units with unique unpredictable patterns of patrol coverage remains to be advanced.

Scooter Unit—Team Patrol

A few words about scooter team patrols, which I believe is the way to go into the future, are in order. One of my regrets was that I was promoted by Commissioner Broderick from Deputy Inspector, Liaison with the Department of Parks and the New York World's Fair to Inspector and Command of the Operations Bureau of the New York Police replacing Deputy Chief Thomas Fay who was retiring.

It took me away from further developing the Tactical Scooter Team Unit, which was so successful in the 7th precinct. This I believe is the way scooters should be used in cities in team concept.

The team should have sharp step-in scooters, not quite as big as straddle motorcycles, with sharp officers wearing sharp uniforms with a sharp leader (sergeant or corporal). The leader and his scooter team should be responsible for a neighborhood and knowledgeable about crime trends, community conditions, problems, programs, people, etc.

Scooter patrol officers should operate as partners, each responsible for part of the neighborhood or community or city. Every effort should be made to have minorities and both sexes represented by the scooter teams though each individual works separate streets or areas.

This can result in a sharp tactical team, a flying unit of scooter officers able to act in concert by keeping in constant touch by radio. Such sharp teams will appeal to kids, as well.

New concepts of team patrol can be developed. Various patterns of street patrol can be systematically unsystematic. The scooter team and their leader can improvise and change patterns of street patrol as fast as basketball or football players adopt set plays and then rapidly change them according to conditions.

There were many advantages to scooter patrol. Visionary police leaders can discern even more with scooter team operations.

With my fortunate promotion to command, unfortunately I could not continue to develop the team concept I believed in. But I have some suggestions from the School of Hard Knocks for other visionaries.

1. Police officers selected for scooter team operation should *only* be volunteers. Forcing someone to ride a scooter when he or she wants a car or motorcycle can ruin the program.

2. Careful training must be given with emphasis that the scooter's function is as a slow-moving *protective* patrol device, although speedy response as a team is available.

3. There should be no stunt riding or cowboying with scooters. Scooters do not chase cars. (I removed one officer who pursued a wanted car in Central Park even though he made a good arrest.)

4. Officers for team scooter patrol should be intelligent, educated, sensitive to cultural differences, adept at good community relations since they are selling good police services.
5. Such officers should be considered generalists, knowledgeable in all aspects of good police work, and should be just as important as specialists, investigators or detectives, and should have opportunities for promotion and pay advancement within the patrol division, which is not always so today.
6. Motor scooter teams should not be deployed after 10 p.m. or 11 p.m. and certainly not after midnight. Those hours are for automobile response units when most good people are home in bed. Better hours encourage volunteers for scooters.
7. Scooter patrols, especially in scooter team configurations, have great potential not only for crime reduction and traffic alleviation but can quickly mobilize as a "task force" when necessary.

Most particularly with proper leadership and deployment during hours when the "good people" are around, a resurgence of public confidence will take place. The scooter patrol officer can answer today's plaintive cry: "Where is the former neighborhood cop on the beat? He was always around when we needed him."

With the old-time foot patrol in various new forms (bicycle, scooter, Segway, etc.) all working cooperatively with the automobiles; it will truly be a coordinated team. This will bring back to the people truly Community Oriented Police Services to restore the comfort, health, morals, safety and prosperity to America.

Let us hope for the best.

Love, Dad

Epilogue

So after 44 years in policing, people ask me about my After-Life. They say, "What have you been up to since you retired in 1985?"

I believe in keeping the mind, the body and the spirit active. For the mind, I've gone on for a Ph.D. at Wayne State University and have completed all but the dissertation. I teach memory improvement at several colleges and senior centers. I joined Toastmasters International in 1994 and I am now a Distinguished Toastmaster, having won several speaking awards. I also teach about controversial issues in law enforcement at Arizona State University and Rio Salado Community College in their senior education institute.

For the body, I trained to become a certified "Body Recall" instructor at Body Recall World Headquarters in Berea, Kentucky. I teach exercises for seniors using a system recognized for over 15 years. Additionally I've continued tennis, race-walking, swimming (winning Senior Olympics medals.)

For the spirit, I am now a "thespian" acting in shows like "Off Our Rockers" in Marine City, Michigan and at Macomb Center for the Performing Arts. This gives me great joy and enthusiasm.

Sallie and I travel all over the world. We have visited Germany four times, Austria, Australia, New Zealand, Hawaii, Alaska, England, Switzerland, Italy, Canada, Panama, Mexican Riviera, Caribbean Islands, San Blas Islands, QE2 from England.

I was also thrilled to be a chauffeur for Sallie when she became Ms. Senior Michigan in 1999 and was in the "top ten" for Ms. Senior America.

And I recently became a substitute teacher at Algonac High School and enjoy it immensely. I "guest teach" for any high school subject when teachers are sick. I was very touched by the students' reciprocity of my joy, even having a half page article in the school newspaper headed, "Substitute Shares Unique Past."

They wrote, "When the students see that Mr. Spreen is the substitute, they are more than happy that it is not a 'blow-off day.' They love hearing all the stories and *life lessons* that Spreen has to give them." The school paper ended with "Spreen brings a lot of joy to the halls of Algonac High School." The feeling is mutual.

If I can be a motivator, if I can help young people steer around the shoals of life and keep them in their goals and pursuits, I am joyful.

I've met some interesting people along the road of life including presidents. I met President John F. Kennedy at the groundbreaking for the New York World's Fair shortly before he died. I met Vice President Richard Nixon at the groundbreaking for Shea Stadium. I met President Lyndon B. Johnson at the opening of the World's Fair in 1964. I met President Ronald Reagan when he toured a General Motors plant in Oakland County, Michigan.

There have even been a few assorted other encounters with people like General Douglas MacArthur, Robert Kennedy, Mayor John Lindsay, and seven astronauts at a New York City reception for John Glenn circling the globe.

It's kind of fun to remember that I've met some movie stars like Rosemary and Priscilla Lane, Eva Gabor, Claude Rains, Edward Everett Horton, Red Skelton, Bob Hope, George C. Scott, Curly of the Three Stooges, and Frank Sinatra who sang a special song for Elinor. In fact Elinor often said that Frank Sinatra's song "I Did It My Way," epitomized my life. I'll never forget that she told me, "You are still your own man, aren't you."

I woke up the last two mornings, and at my age I'm thankful that I did. The first morning, around 6:30, was a most beautiful sunrise. The next morning, it was very nice to see the sun, but it was just an ordinary sunrise.

What is it that makes the difference? Clouds! Is that God's plan? I wonder? Are the clouds there so we can appreciate the real beauty of some sunrises and sunsets? They are really beautiful in Arizona most days, but much more beautiful under certain cloud conditions. The old Master Painter at work?

It made me think of the "clouds" but you might call them "pressures" in our lives, some white and fluffy (light pressures) and some heavy and black. I think of them as adding color to our lives, as clouds do to the sunrises and sunsets. Though now past, they have added color to our lives, experiences that have enhanced us.

As the clouds enhance our sunrises and sunsets, so too the clouds or pressures we face from time to time can enhance or color us richly.

I have found that light clouds (slight pressures) can give us an excitement, a spur to action. Handled, or seen properly, they can provide a stimulus for us to get things done. Dark clouds (problems, troubles, heavy pressures) are real challenges for us to ponder, confront and act or else.

Yes, isn't it true, like the clouds at sunrises and sunsets, that later we can remember with fondness, so too with our clouds, the colors, the excitement, the sense of purpose, the added wisdom and the accomplishments that they have brought to us.

The purpose of clouds may be to enhance and color our sunrises and sunsets. Our clouds and our pressures, whether light or heavy, have a purpose, too. They move one to cope. Clouds make a difference in our lives. We have no control over our clouds but we can control how we react.

Properly viewed and handled, they can add brilliance, excitement and fulfillment to our lives. Yes, clouds can make things beautiful, as the old Master Painter shows us. It is up to us to handle our clouds, our pressures with our own master brush strokes.

I have always told people, "You must make your life memorable, exciting, colorful and worthwhile. Use the clouds and the pressures you will face. With the proper strokes, light and heavy at times, make a beautiful canvas of your life, one worth looking at and remembering!"

In that way, each day will be gloriously different and will be greeted with eager expectations.

About the Authors

Johannes Spreen, B.S., M.P.A., and Ph.D. (all but dissertation) was in law enforcement and police service from 1941 through 1984, interrupted by service in the U.S. Army Air Corps from 1943-1945 as Lieutenant Bombardier.

He was a career officer with the New York City Police Department, rising through the ranks to Inspector and Command of Operations.

After he retired from the NYPD, he became Police Commissioner of the City of Detroit. Later he was Sheriff of Oakland County, Michigan, for twelve years as the only Democrat at the County level.

Spreen was also Associate Professor at John Jay College in New York, Professor and Director of the Law Enforcement and Protection Program at Mercy College of Detroit. He was a columnist for the *Detroit News* and the *Port Huron Times Herald.*

Johannes Spreen instituted Scooter Patrols in New York City and Detroit and assisted the Washington, D.C. police with their scooter program.

Diane Holloway, Ph.D., was a Dallas psychologist and was appointed the first Drug "Czar" of Dallas by the Mayor. She also helped the Dallas Police Department develop their first police assessment center for upper ranks in 1987-8, was an associate member of the International Association of Chiefs of Police and is a member of the American Psychological Association.

She wrote *Before You Say 'I Quit'; The Mind of Oswald; American History in Song; Analyzing Leaders, Presidents and Terrorists* and edited *Dallas and the Jack Ruby Trial.* She helped Johannes Spreen compile and organize this work.

Bibliography

Gado, Mark. "The Insanity Defense: Mad Dogs", *The Crime Library,* Internet web site.

McNulty, John. "Squelch Esposito Break at Gates of Death House." *New York Daily News.* May 8, 1941, p. 4.

Spreen, Johannes F. "The Motor Scooter: An Answer to a Police Problem." *The Journal of Criminal Law, Criminology and Police Science,* Northwestern University School of Law, V. 57, No. 3, 1966.

Wambaugh, Joseph. *Fire Lover,* HarperCollins, New York, 2002.

Index

0-595-26982-6

Printed in the United States
48351LVS00003B/37-54

9 780595 269822